Funding Policies and the Nonprofit Sector in Western Canada

Evolving Relationships in a Changing Environment

EDITED BY PETER R. ELSON

IPAC
The Institute of
Public Administration of Canada

IAPC
L'Institut d'administration
publique du Canada

UNIVERSITY OF TORONTO PRESS
Toronto Buffalo London

ISBN 978-1-4426-3700-9

Printed on acid-free, 100% post-consumer recycled paper with
vegetable-based inks.

Library and Archives Canada Cataloguing in Publication

Funding policies and the nonprofit sector in Western Canada : evolving
relationships in a changing environment / edited by Peter R. Elson.

(Institute of Public Administration of Canada series in public management and
governance)
Includes bibliographical references and index.
ISBN 978-1-4426-3700-9 (bound)

1. Human services – Canada, Western – Finance. 2. Nonprofit organizations – Canada,
Western – Finance. 3. Nonprofit organizations – Government policy – Canada,
Western. 4. Charities – Canada, Western – Finance. 5. Charities – Government policy –
Canada, Western. I. Elson, Peter R., 1948–, author, editor II. Series: Institute of
Public Administration of Canada series in public management and governance

HV105.F85 2016   361.2'509712   C2015-907181-X

 Institute for
Community Prosperity

Acknowledgment is gratefully extended to the Institute for Community
Prosperity, Mount Royal University, for funding in support of this publication.

University of Toronto Press acknowledges the financial assistance to its publishing
program of the Canada Council for the Arts and the Ontario Arts Council, an agency
of the Government of Ontario.

 Canada Council **Conseil des Arts**
for the Arts **du Canada**

ONTARIO ARTS COUNCIL
CONSEIL DES ARTS DE L'ONTARIO
an Ontario government agency
un organisme du gouvernement de l'Ontario

Funded by the   Financé par le
Government   gouvernement
of Canada   du Canada | Canadä

Contents

Foreword

Here's a good question to prompt stalled cocktail chatter: When was the first nonprofit created? Readers will undoubtedly think of the Catholic Church – some two thousand years old, approximately. But why not think back further, to the first Jewish temple organizations? Why not even further back, say, and consider my candidate: Noah's Ark Organization?

Noah thumbed his nose at "authority" (it was corrupt, see *Genesis* 6:11) and decided to do good work on his own (let's call it the NAO). His idea was to round up a few friends and family, build something durable, and, well, save the planet. By any modern metric, it turned out to be a success; God said "never again will there be a flood to destroy the earth" (*Genesis* 9:11). It is worth noting that God did not make his deal with governments. One can only guess if informal nonprofit organizations predated government. If government did come first, the voluntary sector likely came soon afterwards to correct the ruler's mistakes and excesses. Another reality is much more plausible: nonprofits long preceded the private sector. Yet, for some reason, they are treated as some sort of poor second cousin of government. This is an error, one the editor and contributors of this fine volume have demonstrated admirably well.

What can possibly be learned from the NAO and its links with nonprofits in Western Canada?

Both can be trusted with very important tasks and relied on to manage risk. Nonprofits know how to stretch a buck (Noah did that too, only he did it literally). They have thrived against near impossible odds, and have more-or-less learned to live with uneven support. Nonprofits are necessary to create a fair, stable society that is welcoming of those in need and are essential to the cultural, spiritual, artistic, and amateur sports worlds. In fact, they are indispensable.

God was easy with Noah, compared to governments today vis-à-vis the nonprofit sector. While the state relies on the third sector to deliver sensitive services to a wide range of citizens, it is also more exacting in its demands for accountability. Nonprofits are forever subject to the whims of the government, and accommodate as best they can their natural missions with the desires of the state. They do so with incessant budget restraints, yet seldom get to choose their customers. They are under tremendous pressure to assume more risk, and governments all too easily assume that these often very small agencies have the capacity to deliver on policies and programs while maintaining a consistent liaison with government departments. The reality, again, is that most do not. Most are very small, operate on shoe-string budgets, are daily challenged in terms of their capacity, and are brutally underpaid for the work they do. Employees of nonprofit enterprises are more than likely working for wages far below those who do the same work in government agencies or in the private sector. Most work with no benefits and have few opportunities for training. Only a slight majority actually work full-time. The provision of living wages and benefits, let alone training opportunities for staff, is elusive.

Through its various chapters, this book documents the many dimensions of the relationship between government departments and the nonprofit sector. Whether it is housing, social and employment services, sport, culture, or even economic development, governments in Western Canada depend on the nonprofit professionals and volunteers. The authors examine the vital contribution the nonprofit sector makes to society and push us to consider how it fits, or should fit, in the governance structure. The nonprofit sector does face unique challenges in our society today. As governments retrench, NGOs try to palliate the needs of a needy clientele. They have to fill voids and programming holes.

There is a governance issue raised in all these chapters that goes beyond funding. If the idea of nonprofits is as old as the Bible, nonprofits themselves are relatively new to governance. The overwhelming majority were created over the past forty years; we only started talking about "nonprofit organizations" in the 1970s. Yet this sector is probably the fastest growing in the country. Their relationship to government has to change and must command the highest reaches of the public service as well as elected officials.

The lessons of the West are those of Canada writ large, but no matter their location, they must be recognized. We need to understand their origins, their impulses, their capacities, and their potential as well as their limitations. The talented contributors to this volume sit with the Noahs of the West, and write as the rain falls endlessly. Hopefully, the doves they send out to governments, looking for support and respect, will return with promising news. As governments continue to rely heavily on contracting out services and depend on charities and non-profits to provide needed services, they must give the many arks of the world a safe place to rest so that society can thrive.

Patrice Dutil, PhD
Editor, IPAC Series in Public Management and Governance
Ryerson University

Acknowledgments

First and foremost, I would like to express my deep appreciation to the authors who have individually and collectively made this book a reality. Their positive response to participate in putting Western Canada and nonprofit funding policies on the map is truly gratifying, as I hope you will find their contributions. The Institute for Community Prosperity at Mount Royal University has been a steadfast supporter of this important project. Acquisition, promotion, and editorial staff at the University of Toronto Press – Daniel Quinlan, Stephen Shapiro, and Wayne Herrington – have been great from the outset, providing all the necessary guidance and support one could expect. Copy editor Barry Norris is a dedicated student of the written word, and in this case the student definitely taught the instructors and has made them look very good indeed. The support of this book by the Institute of Public Administration of Canada, and accepting it as a new publication in their series in Public Management and Governance, is truly appreciated. The relationship between the nonprofit sector and public management in Canada is a long-standing one that is heavily weighted towards interdependence, co-production, and, at times, constructive co-governance. For this, we have hard-working and dedicated public servants and nonprofit leaders to thank.

Peter R. Elson, PhD
January 2016

FUNDING POLICIES AND THE NONPROFIT SECTOR IN WESTERN CANADA

Evolving Relationships in a Changing Environment

Introduction

Funding Regimes: From the Outside Looking In

SUSAN D. PHILLIPS

Accounts of funding for the charitable and nonprofit sector are generally presented in one of two ways. The first is the familiar story of cutbacks. Beginning in the 1990s, propelled by fiscal restraint and by neoliberalism that favoured smaller government, market-based instruments, and stricter accountability, government funding for nonprofits was reduced dramatically and operating grants were replaced by fee-for-service contracts, leading to enormous instability, increased competition, and greatly expanded administrative loads (Scott 2003, 2006). Larger, multiservice organizations were better able to withstand the consequences than were small, advocacy-oriented or government-dependent ones, but the effects were widespread and long lasting across the sector. The second account focuses on the potential of venture philanthropy, entrepreneurship, and new forms of social finance, all of which are expected to spark an explosion in social innovation. A still unfolding story, this one is more aspirational than evidentiary, and it often diminishes the role of government outside the current enthusiasm for "social impact bonds." Both accounts are only partial, leaving major gaps in our understanding of the evolution of government funding policies for this sector, and offering little differentiation of funding practices by subsector.

This volume is a Canadian first to fill in some of these gaps by undertaking much more detailed and nuanced analyses of the history and current state of government funding policies and practices through an interesting set of case studies of different human services. For all the talk about how social entrepreneurship will transform the nonprofit sector, government will remain an important funder, particularly of human services, and will do so using more traditional instruments of grants, contribution agreements, and contracts. The challenge is that these instruments remain too traditional and too standardized, based on the conventional principal-agent contracting model, and so are not equipped to support rapidly changing service delivery models or evolving government-nonprofit relationships. The need, as this volume demonstrates, is to modernize and reinvent these funding arrangements and relationships.

Although provincial governments are the largest source of revenue for Canadian charities (Statistics Canada 2009, 18), mainly because they have primary responsibility for human services, there has been little analysis, until now, of the implications of their funding policies. This collection is by necessity both diverse, covering a broad representation of service subsectors, and focused, concentrating on Western Canada. Each chapter offers a rich assessment of the developments in provincial government funding for a particular service sector and associated relationships with the sector that revolve around such funding. Although centred on the western provinces, the main findings will resonate with scholars in other provinces; those of us east of Winnipeg are simply envious that we do not have comparable assessments.

How the authors approach the study of government funding of the nonprofit sector is as important as their findings. First, they all recognize that government is not a unitary funder and, second, that funding is about more than the money. In Chapter 1, Peter Elson appropriately defines the focus of the volume as funding *regimes*. The concept of a regime implies multiple actors who, through both formal and informal interactions, work collectively towards achieving some shared outcomes, and in the process develop relationships, norms, and expectations that govern their own behaviour and that of others (Mossberger and Stoker 2001; Peters 2011). The degree of coordination and formality of a regime might vary considerably (see Pross and Webb 2003) and, as Elson notes, a regime creates "multiple layers and types of relationships" between government and nonprofits. Although government is part of a broader financing regime that includes foundations, corporations, donors, and earned revenue, the multiplicity of departments that fund human services within any level of government could in itself be considered a regime.

The *amount* of funding that flows to the nonprofit sector or to particular organizations matters, of course. Contrary to the refrain that recent history has been all about funding cuts to nonprofits, Joe Garcea and Gloria DeSantis remind us in Chapter 7 that, given responsibility for human services for which demand is rising, the trend over the past two decades (in Saskatchewan, at least) has been an increase in provincial funding, although once adjusted for inflation and other factors, the increase is not as great as annual budgets suggest. Equally important is *how* the money flows – the instruments used (for example, grants, contracts, loans), the time horizons and timeliness, the conditions attached (such as reporting requirements, expectations of matching funding or collaboration) – and how funding regimes are governed (for example, the degree of coordination among departments and mechanisms for engagement with the sector to understand their perspectives). The main findings of the cases in this volume point to some remarkably consistent themes, despite the diversity of services examined. In particular, they demonstrate that, as governments seek to encourage social innovation while continuing to steer paths of fiscal restraint, they need to address these bigger governance and regime issues, rather than focus on individual funding instruments or specific departments.

Of Patchworks and Laggards

The predominant theme of the analyses of quite diverse regimes in each of the four western provinces is that they are "patchwork" and inconsistent. As Garcea and DeSantis note in the funding of human service organizations in Saskatchewan, and as echoed in several other chapters, the "patchwork system ... runs along a continuum from extreme fragmentation to certain degrees of integration, depending on the particular population being served, the location of the service delivery, and the available resource base, to name but three factors." Such fragmentation not only leads to inefficiencies and to the potentially inequitable delivery of services; it also negatively affects government relationships with the sector, and hinders the coordination of a change agenda. In Chapter 9, Sid Frankel and Karine Levasseur report that, at a 2013 Manitoba summit, nonprofit leaders suggested that the sector perhaps had become little more than a training ground for the public and corporate sectors because government funding was so unstable and short term that it leads to "precarious work arrangements, with low salaries, absence of benefits, few training opportunities, and limited tenures."

The chapters also demonstrate that service delivery is undergoing some fundamental rethinking and re-engineering that extend far beyond achieving efficiencies and cost savings. Service delivery is becoming more integrated, more systems based, and more client centred, as Keith Seel demonstrates in Chapter 5 with Alberta's services for persons with disabilities and as Garcea and DeSantis show with Saskatchewan's human services. In some instances, it is also becoming more place based, as Brendan Reimer, Kirsten Bernas, and Monica Adeler observe in Chapter 10 with community economic development in Manitoba. Such reform is not distinctive to Western Canada – it was recommended by the Commission for the Review of Social Assistance in Ontario (2012), and is evident as part of public services restructuring in the United Kingdom and other countries. The signals and implications for service providers, argues Seel, are clear: "unprecedented change is under way." Although smaller service providers might be vulnerable in this changing environment, he notes that, if they draw on their ability to be nimble and responsive to change, this could play to their advantage.

A challenge as services integration proceeds is that it is occurring quite separately from government funding regimes, as Garcea and DeSantis note. Current funding systems, as an interview respondent notes in Chapter 6 by Liz O'Neil and colleagues with respect to the Alberta Mentoring Partnership, "don't lend themselves particularly well to funding complex initiatives." Funding regimes, including their principles, instruments, and time horizons, have significant catching up to do and little time to do it if they are to keep pace with and support the unfolding transformation in service delivery systems. Aligning funding with system integration and community empowerment is certainly feasible and affordable. For example, in Chapter 8, Lynn Gidluck demonstrates how Saskatchewan's lottery-based funding for the sport, culture, and recreation sector has long empowered people at the community level, involving them in the development of innovative programs. This rests on an alignment of processes and institutional structures that facilitate communication and enable community organizations to help shape public policy and innovate in ways that meet real community needs.

The Shift towards Impact

One already evident change is that funding is increasingly tied to performance – specifically, to outcomes and impacts. Although governments at all levels, as well as foundations and other philanthropic institutions, have for some time presented themselves as "impact funders," requiring evaluation and reporting on outcomes, in reality much of this evaluation is not adequately funded, has time lines that are not long enough to capture actual outcomes, and uses measures that still only reflect activities and outputs, not outcomes (Carman and Fredericks 2010: Hall et al. 2003; Harlock 2013). As a result, funding for impact is comforting rhetoric, at least for funders, but it often creates confusion among funding recipients and falls far short of having any real effect on improving programs and services. It appears, however, that impact funding is entering a new era that could dramatically reconfigure funder-nonprofit relationships. United Way has been on the leading edge of this change in requiring demonstration of impact as the basis for agency funding, which for some has created considerable disruption in relationships. In addition, some Canadian private foundations and philanthropists are beginning to emulate their US counterparts in taking impact seriously. The most recent manifestation is the keen interest of several Canadian governments in following UK and US experiments with social impact bonds, which some see as a major innovation and others regard as the latest substantiation of performance contracting.

Impact funding sounds as though it should be the gold standard, but it requires different approaches and has consequences for relationships with nonprofits that might present difficult adjustments, particularly for governments. It implies not only more sophisticated measurement, but also that funders support fewer organizations with larger amounts for longer periods (Fulton, Kasper, and Kibbe 2010; Phillips and Teplova 2014). When the primary goal of a funder is to achieve systemic change, the funder probably already has its own theory of change, sets priorities on this basis, is prepared to take risks, and either picks winners by funding organizations with existing capacity to perform or invests in building such capacity (Carrington 2009). Principles of equity or distributing funding broadly are likely traded off in favour of picking winners. Risk is mitigated by providing value-added technical assistance (Center for Effective Philanthropy 2010), and performance assessment is routine, but is not treated as an audit or accountability tool; rather, it is infused in the culture of both funder and funded organizations. The scale of impact sought generally requires the funder to collaborate with others, making effective use of networks both with other funders and nonprofits. Preparing nonprofits to work in such an environment is an important part of this transition, and thus the role of nongovernment funders as part of the broader financing regime might become increasingly important; as a leading example, the Community Foundation of

Calgary has an interesting initiative to help nonprofits develop competencies for impact measurement and its use.

From experience to date, a funder clearly cannot suddenly switch to impact funding, as both internal and sector infrastructure need to be built. One concern, as Jill Atkey and Karen Stone note in Chapter 3 with nonprofit housing in British Columbia, mid-course alterations in funding policies and even apparently minor changes can be enormously disruptive for funding recipients. The overall assessment, however, is that provincial governments have a long way to go to develop the capability for genuine impact funding at a systems level. In Chapter 2, Evert Lindquist and Thea Vakil, for instance, are blunt in summing up the situation in British Columbia, which appears to be typical of most provincial governments: "There is no capacity for generating more systematic understanding of the performance of programs sector by sector in British Columbia in terms of services delivery models and where investments might be made to address emerging needs and new approaches." It is also evident, though, that change is afoot in both funding regimes and relationships, although the precise focus and direction of such reform is still uncertain.

More than Money: The Importance of Infrastructure

An important contribution of this volume is its emphasis on infrastructure, in the sense that the structures and relationships that underpin and support financing regimes affect specific funding arrangements and expectations. Collectively, the chapters identify three kinds of infrastructure: (1) within the sector; (2) mechanisms that connect the sector and government, creating a sense of shared purpose; and (3) connective and coordinating mechanisms within government and among funders. In all three areas, there appears to be considerable need for new approaches and capacity building.

The infrastructure of the sector can be conceptualized as having both a vertical dimension (federations, membership organizations, and other mechanisms that connect the provincial, local, and grassroots levels) and a horizontal dimension that links different subsectors and different kinds of civil society organizations (Phillips 2013). A constraint of the nonprofit sector in the western provinces, and undoubtedly elsewhere in Canada, is that both vertical and horizontal connections are generally quite weak (see Elson, and Lindquist and Vakil in this volume). As Lindquist and Vakil observe for British Columbia, the sector lacks a strong cross-sector associational structure, although there is considerable variation by subsector. Moreover, the attempt to strengthen infrastructure in that province through nonprofit knowledge centres dissipated, as these centres, even when three merged into one, could not develop a sustainable funding model to remain viable. The consequence, the authors note, is that there has been "little capacity to help the sector develop new knowledge and skills to adjust to this new funding regime." The cases also point to the sector's need to undertake advocacy to promote more effective funding regimes, rather than be a passive recipient of changing regimes, but this too is hindered by capacity – and by a reluctance to step out in the advocacy sphere.

The field of nonprofit housing (Atkey and Stone) is a good example of where the presence of a strong intermediary organization and advocate – the BC Non-Profit Housing Association – played a constructive role in bringing together a diverse, complex sector and synthesizing information at the sectoral level to ensure nonprofits were "treated consistently and fairly," thereby rebalancing the power dynamic between the funder and nonprofits; see also Chapter 4, where Nilima Sonpal-Valias, Lori Sigurdson, and Peter Elson discuss civic action in addressing homelessness in Alberta. Although the provincial associations of nonprofits might not have played this role at the sectoral level very effectively in the past, in Saskatchewan and Manitoba at least these organizations are positioning themselves to be voices for the aggregate (Garcea and DeSantis; and Frankel and Levasseur).

A second type of infrastructure, sometimes formal and institutionalized and sometimes informal and temporary, aims at fostering shared purpose, providing a forum for addressing cross-sector and policy issues, and promoting relationship building. Elson offers a comprehensive overview of the kinds of initiatives and mechanisms that populate this landscape, many of which are examined in more depth in the following chapters. The verdict on their success seems decidedly mixed, in part because these collaborative mechanisms seem to be particularly vulnerable to changes in government (Sonpal-Valias, Sigurdson, and Elson). Often, they are managed off the "side of the desk" (in both government and the sector), making them at best a secondary priority for a relatively small number of busy individuals, so they do not become institutionalized (Lindquist and Vakil; see also O'Neill et al.), remaining fragile and vulnerable.

Finally, coordinated regimes require the development of cross-government norms and practices and the means to build relationships, both internally and externally. The analysis in this volume indicates that this internal infrastructure is quite weak. For example, departments vary on norms and decision-making structures (Frankel and Levasseur), the work of lottery agencies is not well integrated with the rest of government, sometimes intentionally so (Gidluck), and rarely is a unit designed to represent the nonprofit sector within government. Indeed, in asking whether a government funding regime exists at all, Frankel and Levasseur suggest that it is, at best, a weak one, and there actually might be counter-regimes. Still, there are signs that more attention is being paid to this regime architecture – for instance, the development of a community economic development policy framework in Manitoba (Reimer, Bernas, and Adeler), the emergence of funders' consortiums in communities of various sizes in Saskatchewan (Garcea and DeSantis), and the creation of a Social Innovation Council in British Columbia (Lindquist and Vakil).

Conclusion: Timbits for a New Era

The question that all the contributors have been asked to consider is whether we are entering a new era for nonprofit funding in Canada. Each provides a slightly different assessment, depending on the focus of the analysis. In attempting to amalgamate their assessments across human services in all four western provinces, a good heuristic is useful. Here, I turn to that Canadian icon, the Tim Hortons Timbit. Ultimately, a Timbit is nothing more than a donut hole: the piece left over, which otherwise might be irrelevant, when a donut is made. Necessarily, this implies that there is substance all around to form the frame from which this bit can be removed.

Collectively, this volume suggests that a frame of a new era for the nonprofit sector is emerging. It is formed by four major components: (1) reinvented, more integrated services delivery; (2) pressures to demonstrate impact in both programming and funding; (3) social innovation and venture philanthropy that encourage new business models, risk taking, and scaling up; and (4) new forms of community mobilization and responsibility taking. The piece in the middle, which touches on all of these, is the funding regime. The cases in this volume consistently observe that funding regimes are not keeping pace with the developments and innovations around them, and that they are becoming increasingly irrelevant. The brilliant lesson of the Timbit, however, is that it has become more than a bit of dough – with some reconfiguring (and rebranding), it has become better than the donut itself. Clearly, it is time for nonprofit funding regimes to transform themselves from left-overs of another era to become the Timbits of the emerging one.

REFERENCES

Carman, Joanne G., and Kimberly A. Fredericks. 2010. "Evaluation Capacity and Nonprofit Organizations: Is the Glass Half-Empty or Half-Full?" *American Journal of Evaluation* 31 (1): 84–104. http://dx.doi.org/10.1177/1098214009352361.

Carrington, David. 2009. "Funding Our Future: Challenges and Opportunities in the Next Decade." London: National Council for Voluntary Organisations.

Center for Effective Philanthropy. 2010. *More than Money: Making a Difference with Assistance beyond the Grant*. Cambridge, MA: CEP.

Commission for the Review of Social Assistance in Ontario. 2012. *Brighter Prospects: Transforming Social Assistance in Ontario*. Toronto: Ministry of Community and Social Services.

Fulton, Katherine, Gabriel Kasper, and Barbara Kibbe. 2010. *What's Next for Philanthropy? Acting Bigger, Adapting Better in a Networked World*. New York: Monitor Institute.

Hall, Michael H., Susan D. Phillips, Claudia Meillat, and Donna Pickering. 2003. *Assessing Performance: Evaluation Practices & Perspectives in Canada's Voluntary Sector*. Toronto; Ottawa: Canadian Centre for Philanthropy and Centre for Voluntary Sector Research and Development.

Harlock, Jenny. 2013. "Impact Measurement Practice in the UK Third Sector: A Review of Emerging Evidence." Third Sector Research Centre Working Paper 106. Birmingham: University of Birmingham, Third Sector Research Centre.

Mossberger, Karen, and Gerry Stoker. 2001. "The Evolution of Urban Regime Theory: The Challenge of Conceptualization." *Urban Affairs Review* 36 (6): 810–35. http://dx.doi.org/10.1177/10780870122185109.

Peters, B. Guy. 2011. *Institutional Theory in Political Science: The New Institutionalism*, 3rd ed. London: Continuum International.

Phillips, Susan D. 2013. "Restructuring Civil Society: Muting the Politics of Redistribution." In *The Fading of Redistributive Politics: Policy Change and Policy Drift in Canada*, ed. Keith Banting and John Myles, 116–40. Vancouver: UBC Press.

Phillips, Susan D., and Tatyana Teplova. 2014. "From Control to Learning: Accountability and Performance Assessment in the Voluntary Sector." In

The Management of Nonprofit and Charitable Organizations in Canada, 3rd ed., ed. Keith Seel. Toronto: LexisNexis.

Pross, A. Paul, and Kernaghan R. Webb. 2003. "Embedded Regulation: Advocacy and the Federal Regulation of Public Interest Groups." In *Delicate Dances: Public Policy and the Nonprofit Sector*, ed. Kathy L. Brock, 63–122. Montreal; Kingston, ON: McGill-Queen's University Press.

Scott, Katherine. 2003. *Funding Matters: The Impact of Canada's New Funding Regime on Nonprofit and Voluntary Organizations, Summary Report*. Ottawa: Canadian Council on Social Development.

———. 2006. *Pan-Canadian Funding Practice in Communities: Challenges and Opportunities for the Government of Canada*. Ottawa: Canadian Council on Social Development.

Statistics Canada. 2009. *Satellite Account of Non-profit Institutions and Volunteering, 1997 to 2007*. Cat. no. 13-051-X. Ottawa.

1 Western Canada's Nonprofit Landscape

PETER R. ELSON

Whether it evokes a sense of pride or envy, Western Canada has caught the attention of pundits, politicians, economists, investors, entrepreneurs, and skilled job seekers alike. Not for the first time in Canadian history, natural resource extraction has taken the limelight. Oil and gas extraction has replaced the fish, lumber, beaver pelts, and other raw resources that once filled the holds of ships heading to Europe. Economists consistently predict that the western provinces will lead real growth of gross domestic product (GDP) in Canada over the next decade (Ferley, Hogue, and Cooper 2012; Lovely and Enenajor 2012).

Western Canada is home to 30 per cent of Canadians, is the gateway to Asia, contains vast stocks of natural resources, and has thriving urban areas. Many of Canada's largest corporations are located in the region, and half the nation's National Hockey League franchises are in western cities. Western Canada is home to 45 per cent of Canada's Chinese population; its population is, on average, younger than that of the rest of Canada; and the region continues to grow both in diversity and overall population (Roach 2010, 39, 44).

Two-thirds of Canada's Aboriginal people live in the West. Aboriginal people living in large cities such as Regina, Saskatoon, and Winnipeg continue to experience a significant employment gap, despite overall improvements. An even more sobering statistic is that Aboriginal people comprise a disproportionate percentage (up to 80 per cent, and 50 per cent on average) of the jail population (Canada 2013; Canadian Council on Social Development 2010). If there is a silver lining to this dark cloud, it is that, in tighter labour market conditions, particularly in British Columbia and Alberta, private and public sector organizations actively recruit Aboriginal Canadians (Luffman and Sussman 2007).

Parallel to the cyclical booms and busts that are but one trademark of natural resource dependency is a nonprofit sector that seeks to address inequality and inaccessibility through the provision of services, and to advocate for progressive social and economic policies. For example, although Alberta's economy has the third-highest percentage share of national GDP and the highest provincial per capita GDP, the province also faces ever-widening income inequality. In 2010 provincial income taxes and transfers in British Columbia and Alberta had the dubious distinction of having the least impact on post-tax income inequality of those in any other provinces (Sharpe and Capeluck 2012). The Alberta government's own Social Policy Framework (see Chapter 4), released in March 2013, states that "the gap between rich and poor is growing in Alberta" and that "rising income disparity diminishes social cohesion and challenges the idea that all Albertans have an equal opportunity to be successful" (Alberta 2013, 6).

Conspicuously absent from Alberta's flagship social policy document is any mention of introducing a provincial sales tax (Alberta currently has none) or a progressive provincial income tax (Alberta has a flat tax of 10 per cent). The fiscal and social policy tensions created by this policy paradigm are highlighted in a case study of the neoliberal legacy of the Ralph Klein era by Songpal-Valias, Sigurdson, and Elson in Chapter 4 and in Seel's review of Alberta's Persons with Developmental Disabilities Community Governance Act in Chapter 5. O'Neill and colleagues present an intriguing and contrasting case study of the Alberta Mentoring Partnership in Chapter 6, and Reimer, Bernas, and Adeler offer another case study of community economic development in Manitoba in Chapter 10. These case studies demonstrate that, whether a provincial government is on the right or the left side of the political spectrum, a substantial degree of policy and program collaboration can be achieved between the nonprofit and public sectors.

Western Canada's Nonprofit Statistical Landscape

At the time of the 2011 census, the four western provinces had a population of more than 10.7 million, with a population growth rate of 7.5 per cent since 2006. Their share of Canada's population was 30.7 per cent, for the first time surpassing that of the Atlantic provinces and Quebec combined (30.6 per cent) (Statistics Canada 2012). Between 2006 and 2011, Alberta experienced the fastest growth rate of all the provinces, at 10.8 per cent. A turnaround also occurred in Saskatchewan over the same period, with the population increasing by 6.7 per cent following declines of 1.1 per cent in each of the two previous intercensal periods. Much of Western Canada's growth was urban, with five of the six fastest-growing cities in Canada located there, led by Calgary, Edmonton, Saskatoon, and Kelowna. These are the statistics underlie media editorials and reports about the growth of resource-based industries, the rising cost of housing, and labour shortages.

As elsewhere in Canada, the economy of one western province does not define a whole region, although some regional trends do transcend provincial boundaries. Nonetheless, there are important differences among the western provinces, and the cases profiled in this volume are designed both to profile the specific examples of funding regimes within provinces, while drawing the reader's attention to regional trends. The National Survey of Nonprofit and Voluntary Organizations conducted in 2003 and released in 2005 is an example of where profiled trends previously were camouflaged by anecdotal evidence alone. The survey provided the first comprehensive picture at the national and provincial levels of the scope, composition, and economic size of the nonprofit sector in Canada (Hall et al. 2005b), and was used in conjunction with a qualitative survey to profile the issues and concerns facing the nonprofit sector (Hall et al. 2003). As a result, the four provincial governments and the leading voluntary organizations in those provinces were able to see and appreciate the size and scope of the nonprofit sector in their particular province, many for the first time.

The scope and depth of these surveys enhanced the nonprofit sector's legitimacy, and the research itself established that the results were representative of the sector as a whole, at least in most provinces. The qualitative and quantitative reports arising from these surveys and affiliated Voluntary Sector Initiative (VSI)[1] activities such as Statistics Canada's National Satellite Account of Non-profit Institutions and Volunteering (Statistics Canada 2007) clearly identified funding and contractual relationships that demanded greater attention by provincial governments and nonprofit sector leaders alike (Hall et al. 2003, 2005a, 2005b). This is a substantial relationship that can be measured not only in policy proposals, services rendered, and volunteering efforts, but also in terms of employment and economic growth.

These statistical reports highlight the size of the nonprofit workforce and the importance of nonprofits in the delivery of services. Forty per cent of nonprofits and 75 per cent of the nonprofit workforce provide services, while 59 per cent of nonprofits and 25 per cent of the nonprofit workforce are involved in expressive activities (see Figures 1.1 and 1.2). Most important in this context is the amount of revenue nonprofit organizations receive from different levels of government (Hall et al. 2005a) (see Figure 1.3). A recent report from Johns Hopkins University pegs the percentage of services-focused nonprofit employment in Canada at 85 per cent and that of expressive organizations – that is, faith-based, sport, culture, and other voluntary organizations through which people voluntarily "express" themselves – at 10 per cent, with 5 per cent being "other" (Salamon et al. 2013). This brings to the fore important questions regarding the nature, purpose, funding, and advocacy role of nonprofit organizations, particularly since provincial governments continue to be the largest source of government revenue for nonprofits by a wide margin, due to their jurisdictional responsibility for health, social welfare, and education.

Figure 1.1. Percentage of Total Nonprofit Sector Workforce, by Type of Organization, 2003

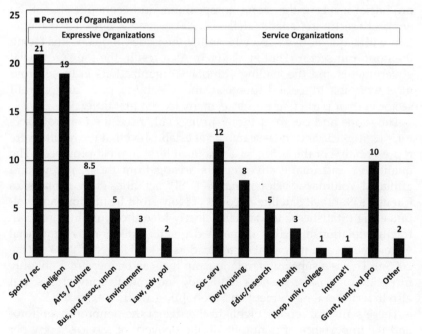

Source: Hall et al. 2005a.

Figure 1.2. Nonprofit Organizations by Type, 2003

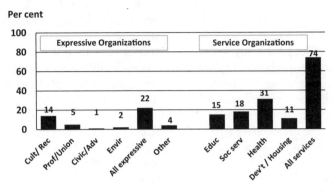

Source: Hall et al. 2005a.

Figure 1.3. Sources of Revenue of Core Nonprofit Organizations (excluding Hospitals, Colleges, and Universities), 2007

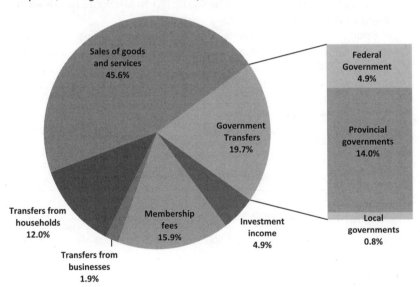

Source: Statistics Canada (2009), "Revenue by source: core non-profit sector, 2007."
Reproduced and distributed on an "as is" basis with the permission of Statistics Canada.

Government funding, as robust as it appears, was also identified as a source of difficulty for nonprofit organizations in the 2003 national survey and continues to be so for many nonprofit organizations dedicated to services delivery (Eakin 2007; Eakin, Kealey, and Van Kooy 2007; Hall et al. 2005b). As Frankel and Levasseur point out in Chapter 9, funding relationships can vary considerably, not only across, but within government departments. Short-term, often inadequate funding, combined with copious reporting requirements, puts a strain on staff recruitment and retention, and has an impact on the capacity to plan for the future. These issues are independent of the challenges associated with recruiting and retaining volunteers, which the majority of nonprofit organizations have also reported (Hall et al. 2005b, 43).

At the macroeconomic level, the 2003 National Survey of Nonprofit and Voluntary Organizations led to the creation of Statistics Canada's Satellite Account of Non-profit Institutions and Volunteering, which shows that the voluntary sector is larger than the accommodation and food services, agriculture, and motor vehicle manufacturing sectors (Statistics Canada 2008). It is no surprise, then, that policymakers and politicians at the provincial level have started to take note of this sleeping giant in their midst.

As Table 1.1 shows, there are at least 56,000 nonprofit organizations in Western Canada. They generate almost $25 billion in revenue, employ more than 325,000 people, and receive a total of $10.2 billion in funding from all levels of government. At the same time, nonprofit organizations consistently report being chronically underfunded, understaffed, and underskilled for the role they are asked to assume in society (Calgary Chamber of Voluntary Organizations 2011; Eakin 2007; Scott 2003).

Table 1.1. Statistical Profile of the Nonprofit Sector in Western Canada

Core Nonprofit Sector*	British Columbia	Alberta	Saskatchewan	Manitoba**
Provincial population (2011)	4,600,000	3,800,000	1,070,000	1,250,000
Nonprofits (number)	20,000	19,000	17,000	
Social services organizations	9%	9%	11%	

Core Nonprofit Sector*	British Columbia	Alberta	Saskatchewan	Manitoba**
Revenue	$9 billion	$9 billion	$6.5 billion	
Revenue from government	$4.1 billion (46%)	$2.7 billion (30%)	$3.4 billion (32%)	
Social services revenue	9%	10%	7%	
Earned income	31%	51%	46%	
Gifts and donations	16%	18%	18%	
Employees (number)	114,000	105,000	113,000	
Volunteer hours	114 million	449 million	301 million	

* Excludes hospitals, colleges, and universities.
** Saskatchewan, Manitoba, the Northwest Territories and Yukon Territory are combined due to sample size.
Sources: Statistics Canada (2012); Hall et al. (2005b).

Western Canada's Nonprofit Policy Landscape

Although the provinces did not participate officially in the VSI, they were kept informed of its developments (Brock 2010), as were provincial and local voluntary associations, either directly through their participation in the initiative or indirectly through national associations. The experience of sitting at joint policy tables with colleagues from across the country and senior government officials was a new experience for many. If nothing else, it was a training camp in which to learn about the thrust and parry of agenda setting, power relations, and policy dialogue.

Athough Manitoba, Saskatchewan, and Alberta initiated some activities during the period of the VSI, within a year of the end of the initiative in 2005, substantive changes started to emerge in most provinces across Canada (see Figure 1.4). Between 2004 and 2010, eight of the ten provinces initiated an agenda to address issues associated with their voluntary sector. In Quebec, community activists, social economy actors, and the relevant provincial government departments had undertaken such policy initiatives in the mid-1990s, independent of the VSI (Ninacs 2000). Whereas the VSI was driven by a desire to improve the relationship between the federal government and the voluntary sector across a number of areas, including funding, governance, and accountability (Panel on Accountability and Governance in the Voluntary Sector 1999), the policy agenda in Quebec aimed to reduce and/or eliminate high levels of unemployment, poverty, and social exclusion (Mendell 2003; Ninacs 2000).

As illustrated in Figure 1.4, six of ten provinces (British Columbia, Manitoba, New Brunswick, Newfoundland and Labrador, Nova Scotia, and Ontario) initiated a voluntary sector-provincial government policy agenda following the completion of the VSI; three provinces, Saskatchewan, Alberta, and Manitoba, initiated their own policy initiative while the VSI was still under way.

In British Columbia, a minister for the voluntary sector was in place between 1999 and 2001, but this position was terminated along with many sector-focused initiatives when the New Democratic Party (NDP) was defeated by the Liberals in the 2001 provincial election. Subsequently, the Government Non-Profit Initiative (GNPI) was launched in 2007 with a focus on building delivery capacity in the human services sector (see Lindquist and Vakil, Chapter 2). The GNPI reached a point of contextual and purpose uncertainty 2012 as the political and policy backdrop against which both initiatives were launched had undergone considerable changes, including a new premier and the rise of a social innovation policy agenda.

In Alberta, a group of voluntary sector leaders initiated a "Leaders Group" in 2004 that was formally established in 2007 as the Alberta Nonprofit/Voluntary Sector Initiative (ANVSI) (van Kooy 2008). Co-chaired by representatives of the provincial government and the voluntary sector, its goals, while broad and well meaning, lacked policy

Figure 1.4. Year of Transition to a Provincial Sector Policy Agenda

Province	1995	2000	2002	2004	2006	2008	2010	2012	2013	2014	2015
British Columbia								→	?	?	?
Alberta				—				→	?	→	→
Saskatchewan			—		●				—		→
Manitoba		—									→
Ontario								—			→
Quebec		—									→
New Brunswick						—					→
Nova Scotia						—					→
Prince Edward Island										n/a	
Newfoundland and Labrador							—				→

Note: The bars mark the years in which a collective nonprofit sector policy agenda has been in place.

substance and direction. The ANVSI is currently in remission, and a small group of nonprofit sector and provincial government representatives is assessing what the future of an intermediary policy forum, if any, would or could look like.

In Saskatchewan, NDP premier Lorne Calvert established a Premier's Voluntary Sector Initiative in 2002, but this was dissolved after the election of the Saskatchewan Party in 2007 (see Garcea and DeSantis, Chapter 7). In 2012, province-wide nonprofit sector consultations culminated in the establishment of the Saskatchewan Nonprofit Partnership, which received a mandate from participants to develop an organizational structure, goals, and operational priorities (Langen 2012).

In Manitoba, the sector-led Manitoba VSI was initiated in 2000 and ran for a three-year period (see Frankel and Levasseur, Chapter 9). The Manitoba Federation of Nonprofit and Voluntary Organizations, currently an active member of the Alliance of Manitoba Sector Councils, was formed in 2003 to build on the momentum established by the Manitoba VSI (Manitoba Federation of Non-Profit Organizations 2013), with a focus on labour force issues.

By 2013, eight provinces (British Columbia, Alberta, Manitoba, Ontario, Quebec, New Brunswick, Nova Scotia, Newfoundland and Labrador) had an affiliated minister or deputy minister responsible for the relationship of the provincial government with the voluntary sector; the other two provinces (Saskatchewan[2] and New Brunswick) had significant bilateral policy forums with the community human service segment of the voluntary sector (Elson 2011a).

There has been a remarkable degree of political stability in Western Canada over the past decade, even with multiple leaders at the helm. The Liberals have been in power in British Columbia since 2001, the Progressive Conservatives in Alberta from 1971 to 2015, the Saskatchewan Party in Saskatchewan since 2007, and the NDP in Manitoba since 1999.

Funding Regimes

Funding regimes for the voluntary sector are characterized by the kinds of funding instruments used, how they are implemented, and the accountability that occurs between government departments, agencies, and programs and the nonprofit organizations they fund (see Frankel and Levasseur, Chapter 9).

It is important to focus on funding regimes for two reasons. First, nonprofit organizations have multiple layers and types of relationships – including statutory, regulatory, policy, contractual, and capacity relationships – with governments at all levels (Elson 2011b). To attempt to dwell on all these layers and types would make the type of patchwork funding relationship that Garcea and DeSantis profile in Chapter 7 and Frankel and Levasseur describe in Chapter 9 seem simplistic in the extreme. It would also be difficult to provide an analysis that lends itself to clear cross-provincial comparisons.

Second, of all the relationships nonprofit organizations have with provincial governments, funding regimes are rich territories to explore, and are revealing not only because of the size and volume of contractual relationships, but also because the size and nature of funding regimes reflect policy priorities and political will. Lindquist and Vakil (in this volume) bring this particular dynamic to light as they chronicle and analyse the evolution of nonprofit funding regimes in British Columbia over the course of the sequential mandates of the Gordon Campbell government. Sonpal-Valias, Sigurdson, and Elson explore an even longer time frame in Chapter 4 as the legacy of the Ralph Klein government continues to influence modern-day Alberta. The implications of policy priorities and political will for funding regimes are also echoed by Garcea and DeSantis in Chapter 7 on Saskatchewan; they also highlight the intended – but more often the unintended consequences – that stem from insufficient coherence among changes in policies and programs, contractual requirements, and the uneven participation of community-based organizations.

Conclusion

This book blends theoretical and practical perspectives to provide a strong contextual overview for each province, in addition to in-depth case studies by the very people who have been instrumental observers, actors, or researchers. Every lead chapter for each province has been written by outstanding scholars in that province who present the historical context and an analysis of core funding regime issues. Nonprofit case studies of the scope and variety presented in this book are rare and much in demand by academics and practitioners alike, but that is neither the only reason nor even the primary justification for the volume. The primary reason is that case studies, presented in a systematic fashion, profile similarities and differences, while providing a rich tapestry of historical, contextual, and contemporary analysis. There is no apology here for the cases selected or for the choice of authors, who, in several cases, have unique "insider" knowledge of events. The cases have been chosen deliberately to provide a meaningful analysis of provincial government funding regimes for the nonprofit sector, and these funding regimes are dominated by human services.

Each author was asked to provide the historical context for the case study, profile a specific funding regime, embed the case analysis with specific examples, and draw out future implications. In doing so, we hope to give academics, students, policymakers, and managers alike a contextual framework that deepens their understanding of funding regimes in a practical and realistic fashion, and that offers ample opportunity to assess the comparative effects of policies and programs. Some of these case studies do not have neat conclusions, as the dynamic of relations between the nonprofit sector and government is ever changing. This is how it should be. Each case study, however, provides important lessons for governance and public administration, nonprofit sector representation, and nonprofit-government relations.

NOTES

1 In 1999 the federal government clearly recognized the need for an active partnership with the voluntary sector, and in June 2000 Ottawa and the voluntary sector announced a joint initiative entitled *Partnering for the Benefit of Canadians: Government of Canada–Voluntary Sector Initiative*. The announcement provided a five-year funding commitment of $94.6 million for the work of the VSI. The work undertaken during the VSI was divided into two phases: Phase I from June 2000 to October 2002, and Phase II from November 2002 to March 2005 (Voluntary Sector Initiative 2008).

2 Saskatchewan also has a significant bilateral relationship with its sport, culture, and recreation community, as these three subsectors collectively manage the provincial lottery scheme (see Chapter 8).

REFERENCES

Alberta. 2013. *Alberta's Social Policy Framework*. Edmonton: Government of Alberta.
Brock, K.L. 2010. "A Comprehensive Canadian Approach to the Third Sector: Creative Tensions and Unexpected Outcomes." In *Policy Initiatives Towards*

the Third Sector in International Perspective, ed. B. Gidron and M. Bar, 21–44. New York: Springer. http://dx.doi.org/10.1007/978-1-4419-1259-6_2.

Calgary Chamber of Voluntary Organizations. 2011. *Points of Light: The State of the Alberta Nonprofit Sector*. Calgary: Calgary Chamber of Voluntary Organizations.

Canada. 2013. Office of the Correctional Investigator. "Backgrounder: Aboriginal Offenders - A Critical Situation." Available online at http://www.oci-bec.gc.ca/cnt/rpt/oth-aut/oth-aut20121022info-eng.aspx; accessed 5 April 2013.

Canadian Council on Social Development. 2010. "Social Challenges: The Well-being of Aboriginal People." Kanata, ON: CCSD. Available online at http://www.ccsd.ca/resources/CrimePrevention/c_ab.htm; accessed 5 April 2013.

Eakin, L. 2007. *We Can't Afford to Do Business This Way: A Study of the Administrative Burden Resulting from Funder Accountability and Compliance Practices*. Toronto: Wellesley Institute.

Eakin, L., M. Kealey, and K. Van Kooy. 2007. *Taking Stock: Examining the Financing of Nonprofit Community Organizations in Calgary*. Calgary: Calgary Chamber of Voluntary Organizations.

Elson, P. 2011a. "The Emergence of Structured Sub-national Voluntary Sector-Government Relations in Canada: A Historical Institutional Analysis." *Voluntary Sector Review* 2 (2): 135–55.

———. 2011b. *High Ideals and Noble Intentions: Voluntary Sector-Government Relations in Canada*. Toronto: University of Toronto Press.

Ferley, P., R. Hogue, and L. Cooper. 2012. *Provincial Outlook*. Toronto: Royal Bank of Canada.

Hall, M., A. Andrukow, C. Barr, K. Brock, M. de Wit, D. Embuldeniya, L. Jolin, et al. 2003. *The Capacity to Serve: A Qualitative Study of the Challenges Facing Canada's Nonprofit and Voluntary Organizations*. Toronto: Canadian Centre for Philanthropy.

Hall, M.H., C.W. Barr, M. Easwaramoorthy, S.W. Sokolowski, and L.M. Salamon. 2005a. *The Canadian Nonprofit and Voluntary Sector in Comparative Perspective*. Toronto: Imagine Canada.

Hall, M.H., M.L. de Wit, D. Lasby, D. McIver, T. Evers, C. Johnston, J. McAuley, et al. 2005b. *Cornerstones of Community: Highlights of the National Survey of Nonprofit and Voluntary Organizations (2003 revised)*. Cat. no. 61-533-XPE. Ottawa: Statistics Canada.

Langen, S. 2012. *Saskatchewan Network of Nonprofit Organizations: Feasibility Study & Organizational Options*. Regina: McNair Business Development.

Lovely, W., and E. Enenajor. 2012. "Assessing Long-Term Growth in Canada's Provinces: Surmounting the Fiscal Challenge." *Economic Insights* (CIBC World Markets), 31 October.

Luffman, J., and D. Sussman. 2007. "The Aboriginal Labour Force in Western Canada." *Perspectives on Labour and Income* 8 (1): 13–27.

Manitoba Federation of Non-Profit Organizations. 2013. "About Us." Available online at http://www.mfnpo.org/about-us/; accessed 18 March 2013.

Mendell, M. 2003. *The Social Economy in Quebec*. Montreal: Concordia University.

Ninacs, W.A. 2000. "Social Economy: A Practitioner's Viewpoint." In *Social Economy: International Debates and Perspectives*, ed. E. Shragge and J.M. Fontan, 130–58. Montreal: Black Rose Books.

Panel on Accountability and Governance in the Voluntary Sector. 1999. *Building on Strength: Improving Governance and Accountability in Canada's Voluntary Sector*. Ottawa: Voluntary Sector Roundtable.

Pierson, P. 2000. "Increasing Returns, Path Dependence, and the Study of Politics." *American Political Science Review* 94 (2): 251–67. http://dx.doi.org/10.2307/2586011.

Roach, R. 2010. *State of the West: 2010 Western Canadian Demographic and Economic Trends*. Calgary: Canada West Foundation.

Salamon, L.M., S.W. Sokolowski, M.A. Haddock, and H.A. Tice. 2013. "The State of Global Civil Society and Volunteering: Latest Findings from the Implementation of the UN Nonprofit Handbook." Working Paper 49. Baltimore: Johns Hopkins University Centre for Civil Society Studies.

Scott, K. 2003. *Funding Matters: The Impact of Canada's New Funding Regime on Nonprofit and Voluntary Organizations*. Ottawa: Canadian Council on Social Development.

Sharpe, A., and E. Capeluck. 2012. *The Impact of Redistribution on Income Inequality in Canada and the Provinces, 1981–2010*. Ottawa: Centre for the Study of Living Standards.

Statistics Canada. 2007. *Satellite Account of Non-profit Institutions and Volunteering*. Cat. no 13-015-X. Ottawa: Statistics Canada.

———. 2008. *Satellite Account of Non-profit Institutions and Volunteering: 1997 to 2005*. Ottawa: Cat. no. 13-015-X. Statistics Canada.

———. 2012. *The Canadian Population in 2011: Population Counts and Growth*. Cat. no. 98-310-X2011001. Ottawa: Statistics Canada.

van Kooy, K. 2008. *Counterparts Gathering of the Nonprofit/Voluntary Sector and the Provinces and Territories*. Calgary: Counterparts Gathering.

Voluntary Sector Initiative. 2008. "History of the VSI." Available online at http://www.vsi-isbc.org/eng/about/history.cfm; accessed 4 April 2013.

2 Adapting to British Columbia's New Era and Moving Beyond: Relationship Building, Funding, and the Nonprofit Sector

EVERT LINDQUIST WITH THEA VAKIL

Nearly fifteen years have passed since the election of the first Gordon Campbell Liberal government in British Columbia in 2001. With Campbell's departure as premier in early 2011, observers are now in a position to take stock of the various reforms implemented during his three terms in office. For British Columbia's nonprofit sector, the New Era reforms of the Campbell government's first mandate (2001–05) – with the restructuring of ministries and the removal of community sector voices from the cabinet table, soon followed by significant cutbacks in all program areas – brought instant upheaval. Although most policy and administrative changes of the first mandate did not target the nonprofit and voluntary sector directly, they nevertheless had significant effects across the sector, particularly with respect to the nature and stability of funding, as well as reporting and accountability. British Columbia's nonprofit and voluntary sector spent the mid- to late 2000s recovering and adjusting to a tsunami of new funding realities, while nonprofit sector and government leaders sought to engage in policy dialogue and address outstanding funding-regime issues.

In this chapter, we explore how the governance and funding environment of British Columbia's nonprofit and voluntary sector has evolved since 2001. This sector is so broad and diverse that we can provide only an overview of developments, particularly since it is difficult to separate out nonprofit-specific funding initiatives from broader governance and policy decisions. Understanding the provincial government's effect on nonprofit and voluntary sector organizations requires having a good sense of the Campbell government's more general philosophical approach to governance and administration, and other significant priorities that emerged during its first and second mandates. We suggest that the Campbell government's primary goals were, first, to reshape how government works in British Columbia and, second, to deal with significant issues such as eliminating the government's structural deficit, making the province more competitive, making government operations more business-like, taking leadership on climate change, and creatively addressing the Aboriginal relationship. Indeed, even though the Liberals were, in principle, supportive of nonprofit and voluntary organizations, the Campbell government did not have specific or coherent views and plans for the sector despite the profound implications of the government's New Era agenda.

This chapter is organized into four sections. The first provides an overview of the main features and key developments associated with the Campbell government's New Era initiative, which dramatically reprofiled the structure and operations of programs, the public service, and relationships with external stakeholders, including the nonprofit sector. The second section takes a closer but high-level look at the evolving relationship between the nonprofit and voluntary sector and successive BC governments, reaching back just before the election of the Campbell government in 2001 and on to the Government Non-Profit Initiative (GNPI) that followed in 2007 in the wake of the implementation of New Era restructuring across every domain of government. The third section examines developments in funding flowing from the BC Labour Market Agreement, 2010 Legacies Now, Community Gaming Grants, and the Social Innovation initiative. The concluding section considers the progress that has been made since 2001, particularly the recent momentum with the GNPI and the Social Innovation agenda, and, despite suggesting they might be precarious, considers the potential, requirements, and some additional ideas for institutionalization.

Nonprofit and voluntary organizations and associations have had to find ways to respond to dramatic changes in specific policy and services delivery domains, and to extend a hand to government to engage on policy, administrative, and funding issues, and in forums leading to and then proceeding under the GNPI. Through this and other initiatives, the Campbell government's response was interesting but generally uneven. This has continued under the Liberal government of Christy Clark with the Social Innovation initiative (now called Partners for Social Impact), which is consistent with a small-government and self- or community-reliance approach. We suggest that reprofiling the GNPI might be a way to fill critical gaps, to ensure a more integrated, coherent approach for government-nonprofit relations, and to better institutionalize the relationship beyond a few dedicated personalities inside and outside government.

The New Era: Government Restructuring in British Columbia in the 2000s

On 16 May 2001, Gordon Campbell's Liberal Party achieved a stunning victory in the provincial election, having narrowly lost to the New Democratic Party (NDP) in 1996. The Liberal Party's electoral platform of a "New Era for British Columbia" (BC Liberal Party 2001) identified how it would govern and the key initiatives it would enact if it won the election. It envisioned a leaner, innovative, and results-oriented government, and set out an impressive series of commitments. Driving this paradigm shift was the fiscal reality of declining provincial tax revenues due to the worldwide economic downturn, a softwood lumber dispute with the United States, sharply rising health care costs, and the short-term impact of a campaign-promised income tax cut. In this context, fiscal duress was interpreted to mean that traditional services delivery models were unsustainable, requiring more innovative and cost-effective ways to deliver services. From the community sector perspective, however, the initial announcement of a new Liberal cabinet was a portent of a dramatic shift and things to come: the Ministry of Community Development, Cooperatives and Volunteers was immediately eliminated and its programs either dispersed among other ministries and soon to be phased out or eliminated in the restructuring to come.

After the election, the new government announced several initiatives to review programs and restructure the BC public service: mergers and ministry downsizing; alternative services delivery arrangements inspired by previous New Zealand, Alberta, and Ontario initiatives; and private sector approaches to managing services. The government was committed to create the "most open, accountable and democratic government in Canada" (British Columbia 2001b). Many of the proposed reforms focused on political governance, and included making the operations of cabinet more transparent, enhancing the role of Members of the Legislative Assembly, improving the electoral system, and introducing recall and initiative legislation. Crown corporations were to be directly accountable to the Select Standing Committee on Crown Corporations. Within ninety days of taking office, the Campbell Liberals promised to introduce legislation to ensure a merit-based, professional public service and to eliminate waste. The government increased funding to the provincial auditor general's office by 20 per cent, and announced pay incentives for ministers and deputy ministers designed to encourage them to meet the government's fiscal and expenditure targets.

A Core Services Review was then undertaken, with the goals of eliminating nonessential programs and units, removing duplication and overlap with other levels of government, and redirecting spending to the highest-priority areas. This process, reminiscent of Ralph Klein's actions in Alberta (see Chapter 4) and similar efforts in Ontario and at the federal level, was designed to force individual ministers and ministries to review the mandate, affordability, public interest, and efficiency of all programs, activities, and business units, as well as those of their agencies, boards, and commissions. The Campbell government aggressively pursued the outsourcing of revenue collection, corporate services, and services delivery to for-profit providers. In September 2001, the minister of finance requested that all ministries, except Health and Education, prepare budget planning scenarios with 20, 35, and 50 per cent reductions over three years for Treasury Board review (British Columbia 2001a,b, 2002). In November of the same year, the government announced a three-year plan to reduce the BC public service by one-third (Dobell 2002), including a Workforce Adjustment Strategy with incentives for voluntary departures.[1]

A new governance model quickly took shape in British Columbia. In almost every policy and services delivery domain, the Campbell government encouraged ministries to consider steering delivery, rather than providing it directly. Although this paradigm shift suggested that greater reliance would be placed on the nonprofit sector, the government never articulated a clear vision for the sector. The changes cascading down on the nonprofit sector were largely by-products and spillovers from other decisions, but often amounted to tectonic shifts. In short, the Core Service Review and ministry cutbacks had a significant impact on the nonprofit sector. Decreases in ministry budgets directly affected both project and grant funding. The government relinquished some responsibilities, and increased its reliance on a mix of for-profit and nonprofit services delivery and financing solutions. The effects of these changes were neither assessed nor coordinated across ministries, and they varied across ministries and their respective policy and services delivery domains.[2]

Some nonprofits were able to adjust by securing funding through contracts for specific "deliverables." Others competed for services delivery contracts through the BC Bid procurement system, which became the government's preferred vehicle for awarding contracts and fee-for-services funding (as distinct from grants and contributions). To compete, nonprofits had to have the knowledge and skill to operate in this new funding regime. This meant developing a results-based orientation and making improvements to their reporting and cost-analysis capacity. Performance agreements and explicit deliverables dominated this new funding regime.

For several months senior management teams of multiple ministries were occupied with meeting financial and full-time equivalent-position downsizing targets. Consequently senior officials had relatively little time to cultivate relationships with nonprofit sector leaders. For organizations with federal government contracts, this wave of change was magnified by Ottawa's own growing risk-averse environment (Phillips and Levasseur 2004).

The Campbell government won a second mandate on 17 May 2005, and the drive for change continued. This mandate will be remembered for the Climate Action Plan, the New Relationship with BC First Nations, preparations for the 2010 Winter Olympics, and efforts to transform the BC public service. This latter transformation was executed by corporate rebranding, aggressive recruitment, employee engagement, and a data-driven human resource strategy (Lindquist, Langford, and Vakil 2010). Yet this was also a time when the nonprofit and voluntary sector experimented with different ways to organize within the sector and to re-engage government, and it is on these change strategies that we now focus.

Aftermath: Reconnecting Government and the Nonprofit Sector

For the community sector, the breadth, scale, and pace of change induced by the New Era government mandate was breathtaking. The initial focus in the nonprofit sector was on survival and coping with funding cuts in the face of ongoing demands for services. Although many nonprofit and community organizations sought to reach out to government funders, the dramatic changes to ministries, programs, and the provincial workforce attenuated communications. British Columbia's nonprofit and voluntary sector did not have a strong cross-sector associational structure, although some subsectors – such as children and family services and nonprofit housing – did. There was little capacity to help the sector develop new knowledge and skills to adjust to this new funding regime. As a result, there soon emerged a shared sense that new capacities and a cross-sector dialogue would be needed if the nonprofit sector was to regain its footing.

Several independent initiatives sought to address, in different ways, the challenge of building capacity in the sector. The Voluntary Organizations Consortium of British Columbia (VOCBC) was created in 2002. In Vancouver the Vancouver Foundation sponsored the start-up of the Centre for Sustainable Development, and on Vancouver Island the Centre for Non Profit Management (CNPM) was created to engage nonprofit organizations about how to take a more entrepreneurial approach to their activities. In 2003, the Ministry of Public Safety and the BC solicitor general funded a Centre for Nonprofit Development (CNPD) at the University College of the Fraser Valley to develop and deliver courses for nonprofit and voluntary organizations in BC community colleges.

In July 2004 the CNPM released a discussion paper, "Building Bridges" (CNPM 2004), calling for more dialogue between government and the nonprofit sector. In October 2005 VOCBC invited leaders of several organizations to discuss an approach to galvanizing the sector (VOCBC 2005). In early 2007, with funding support from several ministries, the CNPM and the University of Victoria's School of Public Administration published a discussion paper entitled "Strengthening the Relationship" (CNPM 2007a). In late May 2007 the centre and the university hosted a roundtable discussion with leaders from the government and nonprofit sectors. British Columbia's deputy minister of public safety and solicitor general and the chief executive officer of the Vancouver Foundation served as roundtable co-chairs (CNPM 2007b). Both government and nonprofit sector representatives identified their challenges and perspectives about funding, accountability, capacity, and procurement.

In late 2007 three task forces and a steering committee were established, each co-chaired by government and nonprofit sector leaders and supported by coordinating staff and contract researchers. Each task force was to gather information, explore issues, and make recommendations to feed into a larger roundtable or summit event. The process, which came to be known as the Government Non-Profit Initiative, took longer than planned, as the task forces had to organize, commission background work, and have sufficient dialogue. Nonprofit sector representatives were realistic and cautious, aware of how the national Voluntary Sector Initiative had petered out, and took time to survey models and legislation from other jurisdictions. Participants sought a process without political engagement, focused on making a practical, direct difference to those who deliver, manage, and oversee services. It was hoped that this new GNPI policy forum would result in some quick wins and cultivate a relationship that could withstand changes in government.

It was recognized that relationship building would be a multiyear process that could proceed at four levels in this complex domain: program, policy sector, horizontal initiatives, and sector-to-sector. A distinctive feature of the GNPI that emerged was the involvement of First Nations: although nonprofits were used extensively by off-reserve organizations such as the Aboriginal Friendship Centres, they were relied on less by First Nations communities. With the "new relationship" and treaty settlements in progress, it was agreed that promoting capability building and the use of nonprofits would be a priority. A joint governance structure was adapted to further the GNPI, set up a website, and host future roundtables or summits. The first annual GNPI Summit took place in November 2008, followed by three more November day-long summits in 2009, 2010, and 2011.

The GNPI activities were coordinated by an interim steering committee led by the co-chairs (later to become the Leadership Council, with several standing committees). Working groups included those on contractual reporting requirements, working with intercultural communities, mentoring, and training programs. Significant partnerships were also established with the BC Association of Native Friendship Centres to promote nonprofit organizing and capacity building. The GNPI hosted regional consultations designed to elicit a better sense of how the initiative and the BC government could assist collaboration on the ground in various regions of the province. Perhaps the most significant initiative involved leveraging the Labour Market Development Agreement with the federal government, which led to the development of a Non Profit Sector Labour Market Partnership Agreement for British Columbia, much as it has for other western provinces (see Chapter 9).

Other efforts to build capacity and engage the sector

The GNPI process was not the only initiative set in motion in British Columbia to address challenges confronting the nonprofit sector, to build capacity, and to foster engagement. Some were ultimately more successful than others, but collectively they reveal a sector seeking to

rise above a weak capacity to mobilize and to develop more cooperative, comprehensive approaches.

The collaborative success of the May 2007 roundtable was offset
by considerable confusion about apparent duplication and overlap
among the CNPM, the CNPD, and Centre for Nonprofit Sustainability (CFS), each dedicated to building nonprofit capacity. Indeed, they
were often confused with one another, and each had challenges securing additional funding, in part because of the existence of the other
organizations. In fact, each was tackling the capacity challenge with
very different, but complementary, approaches and programs. Reflecting the tight funding environment, potential funders indicated that a
merger of the organizations would be optimal, but would not provide
any financial inducements to merging. By early 2010 the three had in
fact merged, but sustained funding remained difficult to secure, and
the consolidated entity dissolved in 2012. Looking back, it now appears
that an important opportunity was missed at a crucial time, and a lot
of scarce volunteer energy and resources were wasted. Even so, resilience and a fragile new momentum towards representation and capacity building started to emerge during the mid- to late 2000s.

Representation and capacity, fits and starts

British Columbia's nonprofit sector was knocked on its heels in the
early 2000s, but by the mid-2000s ideas about how to build capability
and resilience had taken root, and the groundwork was laid for moving
forward. The GNPI, Vantage Point, the Federation of Community Social
Services of BC, Board Voice, the Vancouver Foundation, and Vancity –
to mention only a few – began to take leadership roles in identifying
an agenda, building needed capabilities, and fostering dialogue, as the
following examples illustrate.

- *Vantage Point*: Led by the dynamic Colleen Kelly, Volunteer Vancouver and its board set out to rebrand its activities informed by
  a vision of excellence in volunteering, thought leadership, and
  the need to engage the next generation of volunteers. This led
  to creation of Vantage Point, a dynamic physical and e-presence
  operating out of Vancouver, levering its extensive contacts in the
  Vancouver area and elsewhere in the province.[3] Since 2009 Vantage
  Point has had a multiyear plan for rebranding, and has steadily
  expanded its professional development offerings, speakers' events,

conferences, in Vancouver and beyond, relying on diverse partner-ships with voluntary organizations and associations.

- *The Federation of Community Social Services of BC*: The federation, which began its life in 1982 as the Federation of Child and Family Services of BC, was buffeted by New Era cuts to its member orga-nizations. Led by Jennifer Charlesworth, the federation proactively and concertedly worked with the Ministry of Children and Family Development to develop better funding and reporting regimes, to become a knowledge partner,[4] and to support member organiza-tions. The federation works both independently and in collabora-tion with other organizations to improve practice through access to research and dialogue.[5] Indeed, the federation was instrumental in establishing the Board Voice initiative, and has been represented on both the GNPI Leadership Council and the more recent BC Social Entrepreneurship initiative.
- *Board Voice*: This initiative grew out of a meeting of board members and executive directors in mid-2008 called by the Federation of Community Social Services of BC to discuss challenges confront-ing the sector. This led to a founding conference of the Board Voice Society in November 2009.[6] The idea driving Board Voice is to stim-ulate dialogue and representation from community-based mem-bers, as opposed to executive directors, on initiatives and challenges confronting the sector (see Figure 2.1). It has since held several events, and provided input into the BC Gaming Grants Review and the BC Social Entrepreneurship initiative. Board Voice held its third annual conference on 23–24 November 2012.

In what could be called an ongoing pattern of ambiguous forward momentum, several underlying challenges continued to challenge the nonprofit sector and its efforts to secure better governance and funding. First, the vertical and horizontal associational structure of the sector remained relatively weak, with strengths in some services sectors and weaknesses in others. Second, much of the GNPI focus was not on the nonprofit sector in general, but, by design, on social and human services organizations. Third, despite the myriad of named organizations, only a relatively few, very busy, and usually older individuals were involved in leading and supporting these initiatives. Consequently organizing was led from the corner of a score of desks, and the capacity issue remained. Finally, the key premises underpinning the GNPI did not include going after threshold increases in funding from government or

Figure 2.1. Relational Aspects of the Community Social Services System

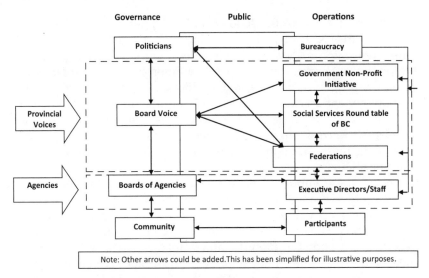

Source: Adopted from Board Voice (2011).

eschewing direct political engagement, although it appears Board Voice has since started to bridge the latter gap.

Recent Developments: From Cuts to Investments in Social Innovation

The late 2000s and early 2010s coincided with the Campbell government's third term in office, the aftermath of the global financial crisis, and the arrival of Christy Clark as the new Liberal premier in March 2011. In this period four important initiatives affected the governance and funding of nonprofit organizations in British Columbia: (1) the evolution of 2010 Legacies Now funding; (2) cuts to community grants from the BC Lottery Corporation; (3) the implementation of the Canada-British Columbia Labour Market Development Agreement; and (4) political interest in the possibilities associated with social entrepreneurship. These developments, which galvanized support of government relationships with the nonprofit and community sector, also reflected a new approach to multistakeholder investment in social innovation in British Columbia.

The Non Profit Sector Labour Market Partnership Agreement

On 28 February 2008, the federal and BC governments signed the Canada-British Columbia Labour Market Development Agreement, which delegated responsibility for federal employment programs to the province. Ottawa transferred $300 million in federal employment insurance programs, 250 staff, and 32 offices, along with programs such as employment assistance services for the unemployed, skills development, wage subsidies, and job creation for employment insurance recipients.[7] Since signing the agreement, the BC government has been combining these programs with existing programs for income assistance recipients.

Beyond these important programs, however, key officials saw the opportunity to channel some Labour Market Development Agreement funds to develop a labour market strategy for the nonprofit sector and to strengthen the sector. Consequently, in 2009, $5 million over three years was set aside for nonprofit and voluntary labour force development under the Non Profit Sector Labour Market Partnership Agreement (Vancouver Foundation 2009). This was particularly important, given the need to address British Columbia's aging demographic profile, to which the nonprofit sector is not immune. The funds were to be administered on behalf of the sector by the Vancouver Foundation, but allocated under the auspices of the GNPI and various committees created for this purpose.

Planning and groundwork activity was guided by secretariat staff, a committee of the GNPI Leadership Council, and the GNPI's Human Resources (HR) Advisory Committee.[8] The key tasks involved the hiring of consultants to gather labour market data and assess trends in British Columbia's labour market, develop a strategic human resources strategy for the sector informed by labour market information, and identify priorities for pilot projects on a partnership basis in different parts of the province. The ultimate goal was to appoint an Employers' Council and to develop a sustainability plan. Consultation events in 2009 included a Social Service Sector Human Resource Summit (with the Federation of Community Social Services of BC) and a BC Regional Forum (with the Vancouver Foundation and the GNPI's HR Council) focusing on the rest of the nonprofit and voluntary sector. Six "action areas" for building capacity were identified: shared services, sufficient compensation, funding, leadership development, workforce diversity, and sector branding. It was agreed that progress on all fronts would require collaboration, building on existing capabilities and accomplishments, and good data. An Indigenous HR Summit (November 2010) was held in collaboration with the BC Association of Native Friendship Centres, part of developing an Aboriginal nonprofit HR development strategy.

At the time of writing, several projects have been completed under the Non Profit Sector Labour Market Partnership Agreement. Pilot projects were commissioned to explore promising practices and concepts in various regions of British Columbia, as well as for the province as a whole, and framework documents and reports have been completed. An overall strategy has been articulated, along with the recruitment for, and the establishment in July 2011 of, a Nonprofit Sector Employers' Council.[9] Although most projects were completed by 2014, without an infusion of funding from multiple sources, it is hard to imagine how such a comprehensive and focused set of activities would have proceeded.

Legacies Now: From bid to venture philanthropy

Legacies Now was created in 2000 as part of the early package assembled in support of the bid to host the 2010 Olympic and Paralympic Winter Games in greater Vancouver and Whistler. Established jointly by the BC government and the BC Vancouver 2010 Bid Corporation, Legacies Now was envisioned as a way to prepare and engage youth and communities across the province in support of the Olympics and to promote both sport and recreational activity and development.[10]

The ambition for Legacies Now soon broadened from sports and recreational development to include funding for the arts and culture, literacy, and volunteerism, as well as engagement with communities and First Nations across the province. These themes, which connected with marketing and preparations for the Olympic spectacle, also resonated with broader themes championed by the premier (such as Act Now, Literacy BC, and the New Relationship). During the 2004/05 fiscal year year, Legacies Now received $74 million in revenue (some came from the BC Lottery Corporation), which, it started to draw down[11] with program outlays of over $17 million in 2005 and close to $25 million in 2006. These funds were dispersed to an impressive array of nonprofit and community voluntary organizations.

After the Winter Games were over, Legacies Now had to consider what its future might be. Nonsalary and operating program disbursements amounted to $31 million in 2009 and $21 million in 2010, but even though far less revenue was coming in, by 2011 Legacies Now had a surplus of funds in the millions of dollars. The decision was made to wind up Legacies Now, based on the understanding that it needed to focus its efforts and "rebrand the organization with a new name and logo in order to effectively deliver on its evolved function in Canadian society, while continuing to carry on its work as an important social legacy of the Games" (Weiler 2011, 4). This involved, for example, spinning off key programs, such as website management, to capable organizations. But the most interesting decision was to transform Legacies Now into a "venture philanthropy" organization to help promising nonprofits in British Columbia and elsewhere in Canada "scale up" their services delivery by providing business expertise over a sustained period. LIFT Philanthropy Partners was announced as the ultimate legacy of Legacies Now in February 2011.[12]

BC Lottery Corporation and community gaming grants: Restoring cuts

Community gaming grants have been an important source of funds for many nonprofit and community organizations in British Columbia. In 1988, when the BC Lottery Corporation was permitted to operate casinos, the provincial government agreed to provide funding from its new source of revenues to charitable groups that had previously managed casinos (Triplett 2011). However, these grants were soon made available to all eligible community organizations across the province, usually nonprofit, voluntary, community-oriented programs governed by elected boards of directors.

About six thousand organizations in British Columbia receive community gaming grants, with a limit of $100,000 for individual local organizations and $250,000 for province-wide organizations. The key categories include arts and culture, sports for youth and people with disabilities, human and social services, public safety, and parent advisory councils. More than $1 billion is generated from gaming each year, with about $82 million going to local organizations running casinos or gaming centres, $147 million to a health fund, $687 million to general revenues, and $135 million to charities and nonprofit organizations that meet certain criteria.[13] This is significantly higher than the net lottery funds generated in Saskatchewan, although in that province the dedicated contribution of funds to sport, recreation, and culture is a key asset (see Chapter 8).

On 27 August 2009, in response to the global financial crisis and economic downturn and to a rapidly increasing provincial deficit, the BC government reduced the funds available to other charities and nonprofit community organizations by $15 million to $120 million, and announced that environmental, adult sports, alumni, and some arts and culture groups would be ineligible for further funding. The government also announced that two- or three-year funding would cease, and that eligible recipients would have to reapply for ongoing funding.

There was a sharp, negative public response to these announcements, and shockwaves were felt among smaller nonprofit and community organizations across the province. Concerns were raised about whether the cuts would fall proportionately on the administration of gaming and other recipients of funds, and the message cut across the grain of signals from the GNPI. In March 2011, after announcing her new cabinet, Premier Clark commissioned Skip Triplett, an independent consultant and former university president, to review the program, undertake consultations with stakeholders, review submissions, and develop options for the government to consider regarding the eligibility, funding, and administration of gaming grants. Responsibility for the granting program (as opposed to gaming licensing and enforcement) was transferred to the Ministry of Community, Sport and Cultural Development, and Triplett proceeded with his consultations.

In his final report, submitted on 31 October 2011 (Triplett 2011), Triplett recommended reinstating the $15 million in funding that had been cut, eventually raising it to $156 million, and broadening the range of eligible organizations. He also suggested that essential services provided by community organizations should be funded directly out of ministry budgets. Triplett called for more specificity in criteria and the purpose of grants, and suggested that the government consider streamlined reporting and multiyear funding (no longer than three years), similar to ideas discussed in forums of the GNPI.

Triplett went on to suggest that the provincial government and public service view grants as "community investments," to be administered by a foundation or trust, and that some funds should be set aside for innovative projects, which resonated with larger "social innovation" themes that were beginning to emerge. On 11 January 2012, Premier Clark announced that she accepted Triplett's main recommendations, including restoring funding, broadening eligibility, streamlining the application process, and considering how to introduce multiyear funding (British Columbia 2012).

From social entrepreneurship to Hubcap

Perhaps the most interesting development concerns the establishment of what is now called the Social Innovation Council and the articulation of a proposed action plan to encourage ideas and investment in social enterprise in British Columbia, some of which are in progress. The initiative began to take shape during the Campbell government's third mandate with the formation of a Government Caucus Committee on Social Innovation and Volunteerism and the appointment on 25 October 2010 of Gordon Hogg as parliamentary secretary for social entrepreneurship to the minister of finance.

Just a few weeks later, in January 2011, the BC government announced the draft terms of reference for an Advisory Council on Social Entrepreneurship, with a mix of nongovernment representatives from the social enterprise, nonprofit, community, foundation, and university sectors. This was complemented by an assistant deputy minister's Committee on Social Entrepreneurship, with representation from several relevant ministries.[14] This work was also seen as building on the GNPI.

Meanwhile Premier Campbell announced his resignation and the Liberal Party appointed Christy Clark its new leader. In April 2011 the Advisory Council, very much still in an organizing phase, seized the opportunity to release a discussion paper and seek the new premier's support of the initiative, explaining that its role was to "to make recommendations that maximize social innovation in British Columbia, with an emphasis on social finance and social enterprise" (BC Social Innovation Council 2012, 3). It also appealed the premier to continue encouraging ministers and senior officials to create a more receptive environment for the promotion of social enterprise and innovation.

With the affirmation of its mandate, the Advisory Council continued its consultations, information gathering, and events with international experts. This led to the release of a background paper (Tansey 2011) and a substantial interim discussion paper (see BC Social Innovation Council 2012) setting out a comprehensive reform agenda that included creating "change labs"; looking for and supporting scalable innovations; establishing competition for new ideas; finding new ways to finance social enterprise through bonds, capital funds, equity, tax credit, innovation bonds, and so on; changing procurement models to support community enterprise; and moving the impetus for change to the federal level of government. As well, the Advisory Council, convinced that "social innovation" was a more inclusive term, recommended that its name be changed to the BC Social Innovation Council, which the government accepted. There was also some effort to coordinate the Social Entrepreneurship and Innovation initiative with the GNPI. For example, the largest forum for the latter was held on 25 November 2011, the day after the 4th Annual GNPI Summit, with overt support from Premier Clark.[15]

In March 2012 the Social Innovation Council released its final report, *Action Plan Recommendations to Maximize Social Innovation in British Columbia* (BC Social Innovation Council 2012). Virtually all of the recommendations were the same as in the November 2011 discussion paper (BC Advisory Council on Social Entrepreneurship 2011), but greater emphasis was put on engaging youth and Aboriginal communities, supporting different kinds of partnerships with universities, improving ministry recognition of social innovation in services plans, and, interestingly, broadening the Social Innovation Council to include a wider circle of participants. The action plan was announced jointly on 27 April by the council and the minister of social development and social innovation, again showing considerable political engagement.

Some ideas in the action plan have been put into effect. For example, the Sauder School of Business at the University of British Columbia is hosting, with foundation and other support, BC Ideas, a competition for ideas bolstered by a strong website presence;[16] the BC government and Vancity have funded the Resilient Capital initiative; and the BC government has passed legislation allowing for the creation of community contribution companies.[17] The Social Innovation Council has expanded its composition and been renamed Hubcap, BC's Social Innovation Hub.[18]

Social entrepreneurship, innovation, and investment in perspective

The recent momentum under the social entrepreneurship/innovation banner stands in sharp contrast to the New Era cuts of the early 2000s, and the inability of capacity-building entities to secure support from the provincial government and foundations during the mid- to late 2000s. There has been a positive shift in the balance. The GNPI, the BC Social Innovation Council, Legacies Now, and gaming funding are all important for the sector, and together indicate a better dialogue between government and leaders from the nonprofit sector. Although considerable public sector funding uncertainty continues, these initiatives have moved forward, often relying on considerable imagination.

Underlying the rhetorical shift reflected in the language of social entrepreneurship and innovation is agreement that government is only part of the solution for supporting innovation in the community sector, ranging from incubating new ideas and scaling them up if successful to establishing the necessary conditions and legislative and policy frameworks to attract private financing and investment. There is also recognition that government will continue to contribute funding and investment for many initiatives, but also that this might, and perhaps should, be leveraged by other forms of financing.

The recent progress on social innovation is also noteworthy because, unlike the GNPI, it has relied on an explicit strategy of political engagement. This carries opportunities insofar as securing political support for legislation, brokering higher-level investments with selected nongovernment partners, and securing media coverage are concerned. However, political attention and support can evaporate with a change in party leader and government. Indeed, this raises an additional consideration: although these recent developments in social innovation in British Columbia are exciting and promising, what is the real potential for institutionalization, not only in policy terms but also with respect to the community sector more generally? How widely and deeply will these changes affect the community sector across the province (not just in the Vancouver area), and can this agenda proceed and be institutionalized without a high level of government commitment?

Beyond the New Era?

The GNPI could be seen as a forum for identifying administrative and related issues and improvements, and the BC Partners for Social Impact as a place to incubate and test ideas. To this we could add the Legacies Now and BC Lottery Corporation funding, and Board Voice. Characteristically, these initiatives and energy have yet to be effectively joined up with each other, and there is relatively little staff capacity.[19] More important, there are several capacity gaps:

• There is no capacity for generating more systematic understanding of the performance of programs sector by sector in British Columbia in terms of services delivery models and where investments might be made to address emerging needs and new approaches.

- There is no comprehensive picture of how government funding supports the sector, let alone how it connects to other sources of funding. There is also no forum for debating these findings or for thinking about how newer initiatives fit into this large infusion of resources.
- There is no forum similar to the Union of BC Municipalities, where elected leaders can meet regularly with boards and directors from the nonprofit and voluntary sector.
- There is relatively little evidence of widespread engagement beyond a few institutional leaders, reflecting the relatively poor associational structure across the community sector.

Looking forward, Figure 2.2 sets out our vision for better integrating and introducing complementary forums to address these gaps. We suggest reserving the GNPI brand as a more encompassing term that builds on the progress made with the initiative as currently focused and BC Partners for Social Impact; as well, the GNPI might be more aptly renamed the Government Non-Profit Executives Dialogue. We also propose the creation of two new forums under the broader GNPI rubric.

Figure 2.2. Rethinking the Government-Nonprofit Relationship: Embracing Related Initiatives and Filling Critical Gaps

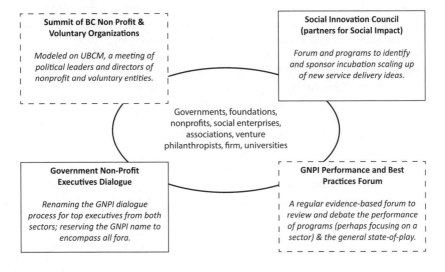

One would bring together elected government officials (both provincial and local) from around British Columbia to meet with the directors of nonprofit and voluntary organizations. The other new forum would comprise officials, services delivery organizations, and advocates and would review publicly available reports and evidence on how well programs in selected policy or services delivery sectors (chosen on a rolling basis) are working and examples of practice in other jurisdictions. The goal of the forum would be to foster perspective, learning, and debate, and to provide a better sense of where investments in new initiatives could be made.

Together, these forums would extend the reach and coherence of the government-nonprofit relationship in British Columbia, build on progress to date, and improve understanding of how funding works in different policy and services delivery sectors and where innovation is most likely to add public and community value.

Conclusion

British Columbia's nonprofit and voluntary sector has experienced significant upheaval since the early 2000s. The transition from an NDP to a Liberal government in 2001 and the Campbell government's implementation of the New Era reforms and restructuring fundamentally affected every corner of government and its programs during the early 2000s. As well, the 2007–09 global financial crisis continues to have a lingering effect on provincial budgets and charitable giving. Although the nonprofit and voluntary sector in British Columbia lacks a strong, vertically and horizontally integrated associational structure to represent it, the leaders of this sector have not remained passive in the face of cuts and restructuring. Leaders and organizations have scrambled to adjust to significantly tighter funding and mounting demands, learned how to adapt to new procurement and reporting regimes, reorganized their operations and internal capacities, and grown accustomed to competing for and then effectively managing contracts.

With fewer grants and contributions and greater reliance on a procurement approach, many organizations fell by the wayside, while others merged and became stronger. Significant efforts were made to mobilize interests across the sector and to engage the provincial government: several new organizations joined established ones in the early 2000s to build capacity; various informal and formal dialogues led to the GNPI and its specific initiatives; and the social entrepreneurship initiative led in 2011 to the creation of British Columbia's "first ever" parliamentary secretary for social entrepreneurship, the BC Social Innovation Council (now Partners for Social Impact), and an ADM committee focusing on the agenda for social entrepreneurship and innovation. As well, the Non Profit Sector Labour Market Partnership project was temporarily rebranded in early February 2013 as the "tHRive Project."

These initiatives led to some excitement, confusion, and perplexity, all leavened with the normal holding of breath before what promised to be a transformational provincial election on 14 May 2013, regardless of which party won. Premier Christy Clark's Liberals won a surprising and substantial victory. As part of her new cabinet and ministry structure, the premier designated a minister of social development and social innovation and established a small Government, Non-Profit and Volunteer Secretariat that reported to the deputy minister. In November 2013 the tHRive Project announced a StepUp BC web portal as part of its rebranding presence. The Next Steps collaboration (VOCBC, the Vancity Community Foundation, and SPARC BC) have undertaken research for an initiative called "Next Step for BC's Not-for-Profits"[20] on the diverse values and networks constituting the sector and are holding dialogue sessions on the results. As well, the BC government is in the midst of a new Core Services Review that is considering alternative delivery of government services. All of this, if drawn together in a coherent way, could put the nonprofit sector and relations between the sector and government on a new footing. Making it all work well in the future, however, will require the sector to get better organized, horizontally and vertically, which remains a big challenge.

NOTES

1 The goal was to reduce the 35,000-strong public service by between 8,050 and 11,550 full-time equivalents over three years starting in April 2002, with 2,500 expected voluntary departures. A strong take-up of voluntary and early retirement programs and the use of existing vacancies meant that only 869 bargaining unit employees and 168 excluded (management) employees were terminated. A second "window" was announced for late 2002: 1,900 more employees left voluntarily and only 200 more were terminated by 31 March 2003. A third extension occurred in the final phase before the end of fiscal year 2003/04. These figures were taken from BC Public Service Agency (n.d., 2002a,b, 2003).

2 In rare instances, funding increased — for example, in the area of immigration settlement, which was funded largely by the federal government, although the service providers had to make huge adjustments to the new contracting and bidding systems introduced by the Campbell government (see Dickson et al. 2013).

3 For more detail on Vantage Point's programs, activities, and aspirations, see http://www.thevantagepoint.ca/. Interestingly, like CNPM, CFS, and CNPD it works with a very modest budget of about $300,000 per year.

4 The federation's 2012 Annual Report, for example, reports on discussions with the Ministry of Children and Family Development regarding a residential review, balanced contract management and reporting, and an organizational learning and research initiative. It also reports on discussions with the Ministry of Social Development on the implementation of a new employment program, the Healthcare Benefit Trust, and communications with Community Living BC.

5 This led to the establishment of a Research to Practice Network and, more recently, CoreBC: Centre for Dialogue and Learning on Community Practice.

6 For details, see http://www.boardvoice.ca/.

7 The agreement can be accessed at http://www.esdc.gc.ca/eng/jobs/training_agreements/lma/index.shtml. For more details on British Columbia's annual plans and reporting, see http://www.esdc.gc.ca/eng/jobs/training_agreements/lmda/bc_agreement.shtml.

8 One of the authors, Evert Lindquist, served on this latter committee.

9 For founding members, see https://www.vancouverfoundation.ca/sites/default/files/documents/NPSLMPAStrategyandSustainabiiltyPlan.Final.pdf.

10 See 2010 Legacies Now Society. 2006. Annual Report, June, p. 47.

11 See http://www.2010legaciesnow.com/fileadmin/user_upload/About_Us/Annual_Reports/2010LegaciesNowSocietyFS_June_30_2006.pdf.

12 See http://www.liftpartners.ca/news/2010-winter-games-continue-to-inspire-new-legacies.

13 See British Columbia, Ministry of Finance, Gaming Policy and Enforcement Branch, "About Community Gaming Grants," available online at http://www.communitygaminggrantreview.gov.bc.ca/about_community_gaming_grants/.

14 Ministries of Social Development, Finance, Health, Aboriginal Relations and Reconciliation, Children and Family Development, Labour, Citizens' Services and Open Government, and Education. See BC Social Innovation Council, http://socialinnovationbc.ca/, for all the documents pertaining to this initiative.

15 See http://www.newsroom.gov.bc.ca/2012/04/recommendations-chart-
the-course-for-social-innovation.html; and http://www.sauder.ubc.ca/
Faculty/Research_Centres/ISIS/Media/~/media/6BB321A37C814E8A95
2A185AC4DEA9B6.ashx.

16 See http://www.liftpartners.ca.

17 On the origins, advantages, and limitations of community contribution
companies, see Amyot (2012).

18 See http://www.hubcapbc.ca/.

19 When the social entrepreneurship initiative was announced, it was not
clear how it would connect with the existing GNPI. Several members of
the Social Innovation Council have served as nonprofit/voluntary sector
representatives in the GNPI process, but it remains confusing to many
outsiders. The number of staff attached to these initiatives is quite small.
What has changed is the engagement of selected private, foundation, and
university sector representatives, but, interestingly, some well-established
programs and entities across British Columbia were not engaged.

20 See http://vocbc.org/2012/09/next-steps-for-bcs-not-for-profits/.

REFERENCES

Amyot, Sarah. 2012. "Province introduces a new business form – the
Community Contribution Company." 22 March.

BC Advisory Council on Social Entrepreneurship. 2011. "Together: Respecting
our Future." Discussion paper. N.p., November. Available online at http://
tamarackcci.ca/files/discussion-document-bcac-together_-_respecting_our_
future.pdf.

BC Liberal Party. 2001. "A New Era for British Columbia: A Vision for Hope
and Prosperity for the Next Decade and Beyond. " Vancouver: BC Liberal
Party. Available online at https://www.poltext.org/sites/poltext.org/files/
plateformes/bc2001lib_plt._27122008_141728.pdf.

BC Public Service Agency. 2002a. "Workforce Adjustment Bulletin." Victoria,
BC, 23 May.

———. 2002b. "Workforce Adjustment Bulletin." Victoria. BC, 1 August.

———. 2003. "Workforce Adjustment Bulletin." Victoria, BC, 8 May.

———. n.d. "Workforce Adjustment Information Bulletin." Victoria, BC.

BC Social Innovation Council. 2012. "Action Plan Recommendations to
Maximize Social Innovation in British Columbia." N.p., March. Available
online at http://tamarackcci.ca/files/social-innovationbc_action_plan.pdf.

Board Voice. 2011. "Relational Aspects of the Community Social Services
System." May. Victoria, British Columbia.

British Columbia. 2001a. Office of the Premier. "Five deputy ministers hired."
  News release. Victoria, BC, 26 October.
———. 2001b. Office of the Premier. "Deputy minister hired." News release.
  Victoria, BC, 8 November.
———. 2002. Office of the Premier. "Government begins three year
  restructuring." News release. Victoria, BC, 17 January.
———. 2012. Office of the Premier. "B.C. acting on commitment to support
  community groups." News release. Victoria, BC, 11 January. Available
  online at https://www.gaming.gov.bc.ca/grants/index.htm.
CNPM (Centre for Non Profit Management). 2004. "Building Bridges:
  Strengthening Provincial Government and Community Voluntary Sector
  Relationships in British Columbia." Victoria, BC: University of Victoria,
  Centre for Non Profit Management and School of Public Administration.
———. 2007a. "Strengthening the Relationship: Round Table on Government
  and Nonprofit Relations in British Columbia." Discussion paper. Victoria,
  BC: University of Victoria, Centre for Non Profit Management and School
  of Public Administration. May.
———. 2007b, *Strengthening the Relationship: Round Table on Government and
  Nonprofit Relations in British Columbia*, Proceedings, 30 May 2007. Victoria,
  BC: University of Victoria, Centre for Non Profit Management and School
  of Public Administration.
Dickson, Heather, Evert Lindquist, Ben Pollard, and Miu Chung Yan.
  2013. "Devolving Settlement Funding from the Government of Canada:
  The British Columbia Experience, 1998–2013." Paper prepared for the
  Western Canadian Consortium on Integration, Citizenship and Cohesion.
  Available online at http://umanitoba.ca/faculties/arts/media/BC_
  DevolvingSettlementFunding_1998_2013.pdf.
Dobell, Ken. 2002. "The View from the Top." Speech to the Public Service of
  Tomorrow conference, Victoria, BC, 19 February.
Lindquist, Evert, John Langford, and Thea Vakil. 2010. "Government
  Restructuring and the BC Public Service: Turmoil, Innovation, and
  Continuity in the 2000s." In *British Columbia Politics and Government*, ed.
  Michael Howlett, Dennis Pilon, and Tracy Summerville, 217–43. Toronto:
  Emond Montgomery.
Phillips, Susan, and Karine Levasseur. 2004. "The Snakes and Ladders of
  Accountability: Contradictions between Contracting and Collaboration for
  Canada's Voluntary Sector." *Canadian Public Administration* 47 (4): 451–74.
  http://dx.doi.org/10.1111/j.1754-7121.2004.tb01188.x.
Tansey, James. 2011. "A Social Innovation Primer." Vancouver: University of
  British Columbia, Sauder School of Business. November.

Triplett, Leslie. 2011. "Community Gaming Grant Review Report: Options for Improving the Program and for Predictability to Grant Recipients." N.p. Available online at https://www.gaming.gov.bc.ca/reports/docs/rpt-gaming-grant-review.pdf.

Vancouver Foundation. 2009. "Nonprofit Sector Labour Market Partnership (LMP)." Presentation notes for the GNPI 2nd Annual Summit, 27 November.

VOCBC (Voluntary Organizations Consortium of British Columbia). 2005. "What We Know: A Roundtable for Leaders in BC's Voluntary/Nonprofit Sectors." 15 October.

Weiler, Joeseph. 2011. "The Evolution of 2010 Legacies Now: A Continuing Legacy of the 2010 Winter Games through Venture Philanthropy." N.p.

3 The Power of Collective Voice in Influencing Funding Policy for the Nonprofit Housing Sector in British Columbia

JILL ATKEY AND KAREN STONE

In British Columbia today roughly seven hundred nonprofit housing providers operate about two thousand buildings comprising more than sixty thousand units of short- and long-term nonmarket housing for British Columbians in need (BCNPHA 2012).[1] These units house a broad range of people, including families, independent seniors, those requiring support because of mental illness or addiction, people with developmental disabilities, and homeless youth, to name just a few. Nonprofit housing providers are equally diverse, both in their mandates and in their capacity to respond to emerging issues within the nonprofit housing sector. Although a handful of large providers operate hundreds or even thousands of units, nearly two-thirds of nonprofit housing providers in British Columbia are small and provide fewer than fifty units of housing in just one building (BCNPHA 2012). BC Non-Profit Housing Association (BCNPHA), formed in 1993, gives these diverse nonprofits a collective voice and supports its members in the delivery of high-quality, affordable housing. The association advocates to all levels of government on behalf of British Columbia's nonprofit housing providers and negotiates with funders on their behalf. BCNPHA has grown considerably since its beginning, and now offers an array of services, from education to advocacy, research, energy management, capital planning capacity development, and member supports, with about twenty full-time employees.

This chapter offers a British Columbia case study of funding policy in the nonprofit housing sector, and details BCNPHA's role as intermediary and advocate for this diverse and complex sector. Following a short overview of nonprofit housing policy at the federal and provincial levels, we describe the emergence of BCNPHA and its work today, outlining the creation of a shared-purpose statement between BCNPHA and BC Housing, the Crown corporation responsible for administering funding agreements in the province. Three recent examples of BCN-PHA's work demonstrate how the association tailors advocacy strategies to specific contexts along the funding continuum, and uses both anticipatory and responsive strategies, depending on the nature of the issue. We conclude by noting the power and challenges of providing both a collective voice and, when appropriate, evidence-based action to ensuring that all British Columbians have access to safe, secure, and affordable housing.

Federal Funding Policy for Nonprofit Housing in Canada

Housing policy in Canada has been the victim of significant jurisdictional wrangling, as have other areas of social policy, given the country's flexible federal framework and its associated fluctuations in federalism (Fallis 1990; Leone and Carroll 2010). The provinces have constitutional responsibility for housing, but historically the federal government has played a strong role in housing policy and funding for social housing. Indeed, at both levels of government, political will has played a greater role in the development of strong housing policy than has constitutional jurisdiction itself (Hulchanski 2003). Generally speaking, in the past fifty years, the political will to support social housing has ebbed and flowed. When it was high, in the 1970s, tens of thousands of units were developed across the country; when it has been low, there has been a nearly complete withdrawal of government funding for social housing. Housing policy at senior levels of government has focused primarily on home ownership. In most cases, early investment in affordable housing was driven by the need for economic stimulus, with strong periods of development after each of the world wars to ensure sufficient housing supply for returning soldiers. The creation of the National Housing Act and associated programs in 1938 contributed to a supply of public housing across the country (Findlay and Stobie 2005). This housing was funded, developed, and owned by the federal government prior to 1964, and owned and operated thereafter by provincial governments.

The growth of a third sector – the social economy, or nonprofit sector – in the 1960s fuelled a number of housing policy shifts in subsequent decades as governments increasingly saw nonprofits as an effective vehicle to deliver high-quality, community-based, affordable housing (Colderley 1999; Hulchanski 2003). Housing is just one of a range of government-financed services delivered through the nonprofit sector, but it relies more heavily on public investment than do other services because it requires significant operational and capital revenues to be sustained in the long term, while financing, construction, and the land required for its development add significant costs. In the absence of public investment, the ability of nonprofits to develop and deliver housing for the most vulnerable is unlikely (Colderley 1999).

Funding negotiations between the nonprofit sector and various levels of government historically have followed an individual agency contract model, with nonprofits contracted to develop and operate specific housing projects. In the 1970s, federal policy contributed to the creation of a considerable number of nonprofits by offering start-up and capacity-building funds to create a sector that had the professional expertise to develop and operate housing (Pomeroy 2007). Indeed, most social housing advocates consider the early 1970s to be the heyday of support and funding for the development of nonprofit housing. Amendments to the National Housing Act in 1973 created, for the first time, funding mechanisms specifically for nonprofits and cooperatives (Carter 1997). This boost to nonprofits meant a move away from the government-operated public housing that had dominated public investment programs in previous decades (Pomeroy 2007). Through its nonprofit programs, the federal government provided loans that covered 100 per cent of capital project costs, with an additional grant built in to ensure that rents were affordable. Importantly, the programs did not require matching funds from other levels of government (Colderley 1999). What might have fuelled the nonprofit sector's development the most, however, was the 1973 amendment to the National Housing Act that created the Community Resource Organizations Program to support the development of expertise and capacity in the community sector (Pomeroy 2007). A unique element of financing under this amendment allowed for households with incomes significantly higher than their rent to pay a surcharge that was used to create a subsidy fund for lower-income households. This was the first time that income mixing was seen in affordable housing developments in the country (Carter 1997), as previous public housing investments had been targeted at those in core need (Fallis 1990).[2]

These elements reduced the need for interjurisdictional negotiation, and helped to develop the sector's capacity to deliver housing. In the five-year period ending in 1978, nearly seventy thousand housing units were built across the country (Colderley 1999). Then, in 1978, several additional amendments to the National Housing Act were introduced. These restricted the nonprofit program and emphasized guaranteed loans made through the private sector, rather than direct lending from government. Provincial authorities became the program administrators, with the loans insured by Canada Mortgage and Housing Corporation (CMHC) (Carter 1997).

These changes did not appear to dampen enthusiasm for the non-profit program, however, as even more units were developed across the country in subsequent years (Colderley 1999). Federal funding of the nonprofit sector reached an all-time high in 1980 with the development of more than thirty-one thousand units in that year alone (Dreier and Hulchanski 1993). The income mixing that was characteristic of developments during this period came to an end in 1985 with further changes that restricted qualifying households once again to those in core housing need (Carter 1997).

The nonprofit programs created federally in the 1970s were designed to ensure affordability for residents. Depending on the period in which their housing was developed, between 25 and 100 per cent of residents pay rent based on their income, with most residents paying between 25 and 30 per cent of their income on rent. The land and housing are removed from the open market, and nonprofits enter into agreements with government to ensure affordability for tenants during the life of the mortgages (Dreier and Hulchanski, 1993). The low rents collected by nonprofits would not be sustainable on the open market given the costs associated with operating housing. Government operating subsidies linked to the mortgage payments are a key feature of the nonprofit programs, allowing housing providers (theoretically) to break even each year. Most of the subsidy goes towards what is typically the operator's largest payment: its mortgage debt. Thus, the operating agreement between government and nonprofit typically is tied to the life of the mortgage, with amortizations generally ranging from thirty-five to fifty years. The inherent assumption is that, once the mortgage is paid off, a development can continue to operate affordable housing with no subsidy (Pomeroy 2011).

The latter half of the 1980s and early 1990s saw spending restraints at the federal level that culminated in the virtual elimination of new dollars for affordable housing in the 1993 budget (Carter 1997; Colderley 1999; Shapcott 2004). Post-1986 programs were cost shared with the provinces, so the elimination of new federal funding meant a reduction in most provincial spending, with British Columbia being one of three exceptions at the time. The federal government would continue to subsidize projects to which it was already committed, but would not create new funding agreements (Carter 1997), meaning that dollars spent on social housing would be reduced from $1.7 billion in 1998 to zero in 2040 (Shapcott 2004). The 1996 federal budget announced a commitment to devolve responsibility for the administration of federally funded programs to the provinces and territories (Prince 1998; Wolfe 1998). In 2006, CMHC and BC Housing signed a Social Housing Agreement covering more than fifty-one thousand housing units (BC Housing 2006); critics argued that the deal, by being structured around the phase-out of federal spending, virtually locked in annual reductions in spending in British Columbia (Shapcott 2004).

Funding Policy for Nonprofit Housing in British Columbia

The provision of nonprofit housing in British Columbia reflects the political swings that have characterized much of the province's history. Given the flexible federal framework referenced earlier, British Columbia's history of nonprofit funding is tightly interwoven with the national history. Federally and provincially, housing policy historically has meant a heavy reliance on the market for housing provision and an emphasis on home ownership, while housing programs – the funding mechanisms through which policies are realized – often are short term in nature. Given the traditional lack of coordination between policies and programs, British Columbia has not had an established long-term housing policy framework in which to operate (Grieve 1985). This policy and funding dynamic is consistent with the provincial government-nonprofit sector analysis presented by Lindquist and Vakil in this volume.

The province's first commitment to social housing stemmed from concerns about poor housing conditions that were evident across the country after the Second World War. In 1949 British Columbia entered into a federal-provincial-municipal partnership agreement to develop low-cost rental housing. Vancouver's Little Mountain was the first project developed under the agreement, providing 224 government-operated units for families in 1954 (Peter Oberlander, cited in Findlay and Stobie 2005). The following year saw the introduction of the Elderly Citizens Housing Aid Act, which was combined with a section of the National Housing Act to assist the development, construction, and management of housing for seniors by nonprofit organizations.

Through the program, the provincial government provided one-third of the total cost of land and buildings in the form of a grant, while a long-term loan and preferred interest rates for the remainder of the capital costs were provided through CMHC, then known as Central Mortgage and Housing Corporation. Indeed, the bulk of public investment for affordable housing during the 1950s and 1960s was directed to meeting the housing needs of seniors (Grieve 1985).

In 1967 the province created the BC Housing Management Commission (now corporately branded as BC Housing) to centralize the operation of directly managed housing stock. Several years later, roughly coinciding with the 1973 amendments to the National Housing Act, a new government was elected in British Columbia with a focus on housing strong enough that it created the country's first Department of Housing. One of the department's first actions was the purchase of a private development company to produce public housing (Findlay and Stobie 2005). The focus during this period was largely on developing public and cooperative housing, and resulted in the development of thousands of new units.

The province also made significant contributions of land in the 1970s. As nonprofits were accessing newly developed federal programs, the BC government purchased sites suitable for housing, titles to which it transferred to nonprofit organizations upon their mortgage approval. The rise in capital costs in British Columbia during this period nearly jeopardized the program, however, before the province reached an agreement with the federal government to make shelter subsidies available and to share equally in their costs (Grieve 1985). Given that post-1986 federal agreements were cost shared with the federal government, British Columbia made more substantive investments in affordable housing than it had in the past, investing one-third of the program costs for projects in the province and administering those projects through BC Housing (Findlay and Stobie 2005).

With the federal withdrawal of new funding for social housing in 1993, British Columbia's role in funding social housing began to diverge from that of most other provinces. British Columbia's then-New Democratic Party government went from a funding partner with the federal government to committing to fund social housing unilaterally, spending the same funds annually as it would have had the federal programs continued (Findlay and Stobie 2005). To do so, it created the HOMES BC program, which saw a return to income mixing in nonprofit developments, with a focus on families, independent seniors, and people with disabilities. Additional elements of the program were targeted at homeless or at-risk individuals, low-income urban singles, and seniors requiring support to live independently (BC Housing n.d.).

HOMES BC was designed to produce new units, but to do so it depended on contributions from nonprofit sponsors. The program began strongly, however, with nearly four thousand new units constructed in the first four years alone, exceeding the number of units previously provided under federal programs. By the late 1990s, HOMES BC was one of only two provincial funding initiatives for social housing in Canada (Carter 1997), indicating British Columbia's unique commitment to social housing. (The other initiative, in Quebec, focused almost exclusively on revitalization and renovation.)

With the election of a Liberal government in 2001, the province shifted its social housing priority, indicated by the renaming of HOMES BC as the Provincial Housing Program. New funding dollars were allocated to develop nonprofit units for those in deep core need, including people with disabilities, those at risk of homelessness, frail seniors, and low-income women leaving violent relationships (Findlay and Stobie 2005). Not long after being elected, the new government also created a housing initiative called Independent Living BC that focused on housing for low-income seniors and adults with disabilities delivered through a public-private partnership between the provincial government, health authorities, the private sector, and nonprofits. Under this initiative, 4,300 new and converted units were created for these target populations between 2006 and 2014 (Housing Matters BC 2014).

Over the past decade, however, the province's role in funding social housing development has become more restricted and targeted more specifically at those in deepest need: frail seniors, Aboriginal people, the homeless, and people with physical and developmental disabilities. The funding programs associated with these specific population groups have helped create several thousand new units and beds in the province (BC Housing 2012), although the loss of existing stock means that the net increase in stock is lower (Copas and Klein 2010). However, BC Housing's service plan for fiscal years 2012/13 to 2014/15 indicates diminishing targets for the development of new units and beds in priority areas over that period. Collaboration with nonprofit housing partners is the plan's first strategic priority, indicating a desire on the part of government to ensure the sustainability of existing stock (BC Housing 2012).

That government has a role in providing social housing is clear given the considerable costs of developing housing, but the diminishing commitment of senior levels of government and a robust nonprofit sector's wish for an advocacy voice underscored the need to develop a mechanism by which the sector could engage with government. Just such a mechanism, BC Non-Profit Housing Association, emerged.

The Emergence of BCNPHA

The flurry of nonprofit housing development enabled through federal and provincial programs in the 1970s and 1980s led to the creation of numerous nonprofit housing societies. As provinces began to develop their own social housing programs, the nonprofit sector needed representation by a unified voice to provide some mechanism for input into those programs. Until the 1990s, however, the sector as a whole had no such voice. A motion to develop provincial branches was passed at an annual congress of the Canadian Housing and Renewal Association (CHRA) in the late 1980s, but the branches failed to materialize. In Ontario in the 1980s, "[t]he evolution of the sector was largely ad hoc, unguided and top down. There was no preconceived notion of what a non-profit sector should be – it was simply a funding system that facilitated development of individual projects with expectations of less bureaucracy and possibly some cost savings via voluntary involvement of professionals on boards" (Pomeroy 2007, 4). These factors, coupled with federal withdrawal from new funding for social housing, were the catalyst for the formation of the Ontario Non-Profit Housing Association in 1988.[3] According to a number of BCNPHA founders, the same factors acted as a catalyst for its formation in British Columbia.

Collective voice was important to the nonprofit housing sector to ensure equitable and transparent treatment across the sector. As is the case today, the funding model for social housing in British Columbia was an individual agency contract model, with the bulk of the sector comprising small nonprofits. The largest nonprofits "held a lot of weight" with government,[4] in that they could negotiate project budgets in a way that smaller nonprofits could not. Not only did some smaller nonprofits feel they had little voice with which to negotiate, but budget reductions could affect small nonprofits more profoundly. As a BCNPHA founder frames it, the political impact of cutting a million dollars from a large organization's budget is more significant than cutting $10,000 each from the budgets of a hundred small nonprofits.[5] Moreover, their lack of collective voice reduced their political impact, feeding the perception that smaller nonprofits were disadvantaged by their size.

This power imbalance was recognized by nonprofit representatives[6] and development consultants who worked with a broad range of groups and noted a lack of consistency in how nonprofits were supported.[7] Because large nonprofits had direct access to senior executives at BC Housing, their opinions on emerging issues within the sector were often solicited, but these nonprofits were increasingly uncomfortable speaking for such a diverse sector.[8] At about the same time, others were taking note of the co-op housing sector's ability to advocate for itself and to speak with one voice since the Cooperative Housing Federation of BC was formed in the early 1980s.[9] From these lessons learned and from the formation of the Ontario Non-Profit Housing Association (ONPHA), consensus began to emerge in British Columbia that a unified voice was critical to the sector's sustainability, not unlike a similar realization by the Federation of Community Social Services of BC (see Lindquist and Vakil, in this volume). Although not necessarily an articulated benefit of forming an association, the growing advocacy freeze felt throughout much of the nonprofit sector in the 1990s also meant that individual nonprofits were increasingly reticent to speak out about government housing policy and programs for fear of the effect on their funding. The development of a collective voice, they believed, would afford some measure of protection.

With the emerging consensus that there was high value in the development of an association of housing nonprofits, a handful of large nonprofits came together to determine how to ensure that all nonprofits had a representative voice. One of the largest housing providers took on the administrative responsibility to survey all nonprofit housing providers in the province, using lists provided by BC Housing and CMHC,[10] to gauge their interest in establishing an independent association in the province. The response was overwhelmingly positive, and a working group was established to develop the concept, chaired by the Capital Region Housing Corporation in Victoria, and with representation from nonprofits in other areas of the province.[11]

The working group was still laying the groundwork for the formation of an association when a new provincial government was elected in 1991. One of its new officials was a deputy minister with responsibility for housing who had recently come from Ontario – where the value of a nonprofit housing association had already been demonstrated – and who supported the development of such an association in British Columbia.[12] This support contrasted with the views of ministers in the previous government, who had seen little value in an independent organization that spoke with a unified voice.[13] Another recent arrival from Ontario was the former executive director of the ONPHA. She had led the establishment of the ONPHA, and was contacted by the working group in British Columbia for advice on how to set up a similar association.[14] She assisted considerably in developing the association's bylaws, goals, and regional representation.[15]

The working group also worked closely with the provincial government to secure funding to establish the association and to organize the first provincial nonprofit housing conference. The conference was held in November 1993, with 360 delegates in attendance, alongside the first annual general meeting of the new association, BCNPHA, and the election of its first board of directors. Roughly two hundred organizations and individuals became members immediately,[16] indicating the strong desire for such an association. By this time both the provincial government and BC Housing saw the broader benefits of the nonprofit sector's driving its own education and capacity development initiatives.[17] After considerable discussion, BC Housing agreed to include membership fees in the operating budgets of nonprofits to ensure that the association's benefits could be equitably accessed.[18]

Education and professional development were strong points of emphasis in BCNPHA's early years[19] and they remain so today. Early documents also reveal, however, a focus on advocacy for a sector at the cusp of experiencing profound changes to its primary funding structures. One of the first letters the association wrote was to the newly elected prime minister, Jean Chrétien, articulating that, although eliminating new funding for social housing would have short-term savings for government, it would do so at significant cost over the long term.[20] When the BC government was crafting the HOMES BC program after Ottawa stepped away from new social housing provision, the minister of housing invited the newly formed BCNPHA to consult on the program. The BCNPHA board worked with BC Housing to negotiate the first operating agreements under the HOMES BC program.[21] For the first time, the nonprofit housing sector in British Columbia could influence funding frameworks and program development as a unified voice with elected representatives. A key outcome of BCNPHA's formation was the ability to think and act as a sector, rather than as a group of individual agents.[22]

The Work of BCNPHA Today

About 700 nonprofit housing providers, one-third of which are large and the rest small ones providing fewer than 50 housing units, operate more than 60,000 units of short- and long-term nonmarket housing in British Columbia today (BCNPHA 2012). These units house a broad range of people. Their nonprofit providers are equally diverse. To support and lead such a diverse sector, BCNPHA has developed a range of services, from education and member support to research and energy management. The organization's annual conference offers more than sixty-five workshops, which are accompanied by many other workshops and web-based seminars throughout the year. Member support programs include the bulk purchasing of insurance, benefits plans, and aggregated goods and services. BCNPHA's work is sustained through many sources, but the association receives no year-to-year core funding. Instead the bulk of its operating dollars come from membership fees and member programs operated in partnership with the private sector.

In 2007 BCNPHA's advocacy efforts focused on developing a strong evidence base for the value of the sector through the creation of a research department to collect and analyse sector-related data. Advocating with a strong data set earned BCNPHA two funded positions through the province's utility companies as a way to bring energy savings to nonprofit housing providers; discussions with BC Housing are ongoing to ensure that nonprofits are able to retain these savings. In 2013 BCNPHA received funding from BC Housing to develop the capacity of housing providers to undertake capital planning, a partnership that underscores one of the association's fundamental roles as the sector's capacity developer.

Given the sector's diversity and complexity, it is not possible or desirable for BCNPHA to advocate to government on behalf of a particular member. Rather, it advocates within funding policy frameworks at the sectoral level only on issues that have an immediate impact on the sector as a whole or that impact a group of nonprofits with potentially broader implications.

Developing a Shared-Purpose Statement

A dynamic and often productive tension exists in all relationships between funders and recipients, and that between BC Housing and the province's nonprofit housing sector is no exception. As the sector's voice, BCNPHA advocates on behalf of the sector to all levels of government, but the bulk of its engagement is with the province through BC Housing. In 2007 BCNPHA was involved in negotiations with BC Housing to reform operating agreements, the primary mechanism through which the province funds nonprofit housing societies. After a year of consultations, members of the agreement reform committee concluded that creating strong, representative funding agreements would require redefining the relationship between BC Housing and nonprofit housing providers to make the sector a true partner in housing delivery.

To better understand how to improve the relationship between BC Housing and the province's nonprofit housing sector, BCNPHA set out to identify the opportunities and barriers in existing relationships. Focus groups were held with nonprofit housing providers across the province, with findings developed into a report for BC Housing. Eight themes were articulated in the report, ranging from the recognition of a common purpose, to a lack of mutual understanding between funder and fundee. From these themes, five recommendations with associated actions emerged. Upon receiving the report, BC Housing generated a report from its own internal processes. The two reports agreed on many issues for improvement and reflections of what was working positively, enabling the organizations to reach consensus on where to focus action.

BCNPHA's first recommendation was to create an understanding of a shared purpose between BC Housing and nonprofit housing providers. Extensive engagement between executives at BC Housing and BCNPHA resulted in the creation of a shared-purpose statement that articulates key characteristics of a successful and constructive relationship in four areas: solution-focused engagement; accountability and transparency; communication; and sustainability for the nonprofit housing sector. It was only through the framework of the shared-purpose statement that ongoing negotiations could be productive (BCNHPA and BC Housing n.d.). The three examples outlined below of negotiations since the creation of the shared-purpose statement illustrate three different approaches to advocacy, each occurring at a different point in the funding cycle.

Case 1: The Vancouver city sites

In late 2007 the provincial government and the city of Vancouver signed a memorandum of understanding to build fourteen new social and supportive housing units on city-owned land (BC Housing and

Vancouver 2007). Twelve nonprofit housing providers were selected through a competitive bid process to operate the buildings. As the nonprofits received and reviewed the operating agreements for these sites, they grew increasingly concerned about their lack of involvement in the tenant selection process, their assumption of risk, which was beyond what had been included in previous agreements, and the perceived inadequacy of the funding envelope. A group of operators came together to discuss their options, and contacted BCNPHA, which agreed to facilitate their engagement with funders.

Given that similar sites were being developed in other areas of the province, BCNPHA determined that the issue had sector-wide significance. It met with the housing providers to establish the terms of reference for the working group, the roles and responsibilities of providers and of BCNPHA, and the guiding principles through which they would operate. Key to these principles was a commitment that nonprofits maintain their involvement in the process until resolution was seen by all participants to be achieved. In addition, nonprofits would not undertake separate negotiations with the funders on the issues for the duration of the process, as this could undermine the process and weaken the outcome for the collective.

Despite the presence in the process of a number of funders, BCNPHA primarily engaged with BC Housing on funding negotiations because the latter was the main provider of capital and operational funds. BC Housing acknowledged BCNPHA's involvement in the process, having engaged with the association on numerous issues and having the shared-purpose statement as a framework. In a number of areas, the BC government made significant attempts to meet providers' requirements, and these issues were removed from the negotiations. A series of meetings between BC Housing and the providers over the course of a year, facilitated by BCNPHA, allowed all parties to express their perspectives and find common purpose where possible. Key to these discussions were the preparatory meetings with the providers to ensure commonality of understanding so that engagement with funders came from a unified voice. The government's willingness to engage from a solution-focused perspective, as articulated in the shared-purpose statement, contributed to a strong outcome for all parties.

Ultimately, a number of key elements of the operating agreements were rewritten. The language in the agreements became more reflective of a partnership model, and the assumption of risk inherent in operating supportive housing was shared more equally. Although project-specific budgets would still be negotiated independently, the operating agreements followed a new performance-based funding model whereby providers were given flexibility to meet certain objectives within an allocated budget. For nonprofits, this was a welcome departure from the original agreements that contained more detailed requirements and oversight than nonprofits were accustomed to.

City sites similar to the fourteen in Vancouver were also being funded in other areas of the province. BCNPHA kept nonprofits throughout the province informed of the changes in funding frameworks in the new operating agreements, and BC Housing committed to ensuring consistency in agreements across the province. Participants commended BCNPHA for the leadership it demonstrated and its ability to synthesize the information at a sectoral level to ensure that nonprofits were treated consistently and fairly. Given the power dynamic between funder and fundee, nonprofits' ability to engage with funders without fear of consequences is a strength the association provides, and this example brings that strength to light.

Case 2: Manageable/nonmanageable costs

Just as BCNPHA engages with funders during the development of agreements, it also engages in funding advocacy once projects are operational. The majority of buildings in the nonprofit housing sector are operated through government subsidies attached to federal and provincial programs, as outlined earlier in the chapter. These project-level contracts, known as "operating agreements," outline the terms of the agreements, including the use of subsidy payments (Pomeroy 2012). In each contract is a budget envelope for manageable and nonmanageable costs. Manageable costs refer to those budget expenditures over which a nonprofit housing provider arguably can exert some control, such as administration, maintenance, and staff wages. For each project, a baseline is determined by portfolio size, funding program, and tenant demographic that the project serves. Once a nonprofit submits its annual budget request, the budget is determined through negotiation with BC Housing. Within that negotiation, known manageable costs are allocated by BC Housing (BCNPHA 2009). Nonmanageable costs refer to those items that generally have a fixed price through the year and are outside of the control of a nonprofit housing provider. They include such things as insurance, property taxes, utility costs, and the cost of an audit. The funder budgets for these fixed costs outright.

In late 2010 several nonprofit housing providers notified BCNPHA that they had received letters from BC Housing advising that increases in nonmanageable expenses would have to be covered by reducing manageable expenses in that fiscal year. What might appear to be a slight policy shift such as this, however, can have profound implications for the sector's ability to deliver high-quality, affordable housing. It was BCNPHA's opinion that this policy shift was undertaken without consultation, and that the consequences for housing providers across the province were potentially severe. In response, BCNPHA devised an advocacy strategy to address these financing changes. The association operates on an evidence-based model of advocacy and has focused on developing in-house research capacity in recent years. On that basis, BCNPHA collected data, through a survey of all nonprofit housing providers with a BC Housing funding relationship, to demonstrate the impact of the policy shift on housing providers, so that its advocacy would be informed by evidence, thereby making it less difficult to dismiss. On issues that arise unexpectedly, as this one did, tension exists between members pressing for immediate action and BCNPHA's need to proceed strategically. There is a delicate balance in managing this tension.

BCNPHA's survey results clearly demonstrated that covering nonmanageable costs by reducing manageable costs would have a negative impact on the nonprofits' ability to operate, particularly in an era of stagnating budgets and increasing costs. Many municipalities and regional districts were projecting increases in waste removal, property taxes, and water and sewage fees, while the provincial hydro utility had projected 50 per cent rate increases in the coming five years. These were all considered nonmanageable costs, which previously would have been covered by the funder. With the policy shift, nonprofits would have to absorb these increases through savings in manageable costs, such as staff wages. The BCNPHA survey also found that more than half (55 per cent) of respondents had exceeded their nonmanageable cost budget in the previous fiscal year.

Looking at the manageable cost component of the policy shift revealed similar issues for nonprofits. More than two-thirds (70 per cent) of respondents had experienced increases in their manageable costs over the previous fiscal year, with a median reported increase of 9 per cent. Over half (55 per cent) had exceeded their manageable cost budget in the previous fiscal year, and even those that were able to realize manageable cost decreases still exceeded their budget. Beyond looking at the implications of the policy shift itself, BCNPHA also gathered data on general budgetary pressures faced by nonprofit housing societies, and found that budget increases had not kept pace with rising costs and that the gap between costs and funding was having a significant impact on operations. Given the restrictions of operating agreements and the mandates of nonprofit housing providers, raising rents to increase revenues was not a viable option, as it might be for private landlords.

Only after it had gathered sufficient evidence was BCNPHA able to develop a process for engaging with the funder to articulate the consequences of the policy shift. The process was based on a series of meetings between officials of escalating importance until resolution was achieved, beginning with BC Housing's vice-president of operations. If unresolved there, a meeting would be scheduled between the chief executive officer (CEO) and chair of the board of directors of BC Housing and BCNPHA senior staff and the chair of BCNPHA's board. If still unresolved, a meeting with the minister of social development and housing would be requested, followed by escalation to the media if the issue still lacked resolution.

The focus of communication with BC Housing was on the shared-purpose statement crafted jointly by the two organizations the previous year. BCNPHA emphasized that the lack of transparency in the process behind the policy shift was contrary to the commitments made in the statement. BCNPHA also outlined in written communication and in meetings with members of the BC Housing executive the following impacts of the policy shift on nonprofit housing providers:

- reductions in maintenance and repairs would gain short-term savings with long-term price tags;
- deterioration in housing stock (including in its appearance) ultimately would lead to health and safety issues for tenants;
- nonprofits would be unable to meet performance standards to ensure that social housing is well managed, maintained, and protected over the long term, as prescribed by BC Housing's service plan for fiscal year 2011/12;
- staff would be laid off or wages reduced, leading to higher staff turnover and increased recruitment issues in a sector that already struggles with retention and recruitment;
- staff capacity to cope with growing tenant needs would be compromised;
- tenants would be adversely affected by decreased services;

- insufficient funds would be available to cover capital repairs if replacement reserves were used to pay for operational costs;
- the sector's sustainability would be compromised by the expiration of operating agreements; and
- some operators and their boards of directors might determine that their only option would be to terminate operating agreements with BC Housing.

Engagement reached as high as a meeting between the elected BCN-PHA board chair and the CEO and board chair of BC Housing, demonstrating the importance of the issue at the sectoral level, before the issue was resolved through a reversal of the policy shift. Key to the resolution was respectful engagement and dialogue on the part of both the sector and BC Housing, which gave practical consideration to the evidence BCNPHA presented.

The manageable/nonmanageable cost issue is an example of what can be achieved through sectoral aggregation. Importantly, however, it also speaks to the power of empirical data in advocating on behalf of a diverse sector.

Case 3: Sustaining the supply of nonprofit housing

A third case demonstrates BCNPHA's advocacy work as agreements between government and nonprofit providers come to a close. Through the various federal and provincial funding programs outlined previously, nonprofits have been funded since the early 1970s through operating agreements that originally had a fixed period of forty to fifty years. These agreements have ongoing subsidies that are linked to the project's mortgage amortization period and that allow nonprofit housing providers to pay off the mortgage, typically a provider's largest expense. The agreements were developed on the premise that, once the mortgage was paid off, subsidies no longer would be required and the nonprofit would continue to operate and provide affordable rents without requiring an ongoing government subsidy. More recent research indicates that, for buildings operated under certain programs, these assumptions will prove true. For targeted programs with a high ratio of rent-geared-to-income households that require deep subsidies, the outcome might not be as certain (Pomeroy 2006). By 2030 subsidies for two-thirds of all units in British Columbia's nonprofit housing sector will have expired (BCNPHA and BC Housing 2012). Many of these projects will be viable and will continue offering affordable rents to low-income individuals and families; others will not. The options available to those nonprofits with unviable projects generally include increasing revenues (rents) in some fashion (Pomeroy 2012). The consequences for affordable housing in British Columbia could be significant.

In 2011 BCNPHA and BC Housing formed a joint work plan to look more closely at what is known about expiring agreements and to devise strategies and resources for sustaining the province's nonprofit housing sector. BCNPHA collected information about the potential effects of these expirations and the sector's preparedness for them. It identified small nonprofits as most at risk, because of capacity issues and their inability to cross-subsidize between buildings within their portfolios as larger providers can do. The partnership between BCNPHA and BC Housing, however, makes it possible to develop strategies and resources that providers can use in planning for the expiration of operating agreements, and to ensure the sector's long-term sustainability.

Capital planning and ensuring that housing assets are in good condition will be an important aspect of preparing for the expiration of operating agreements, particularly since many nonprofits are concerned that their replacement reserves have been underfunded, jeopardizing their ability to undertake necessary repairs and upgrades. BCNPHA negotiated with BC Housing for more than five years, finally reaching agreement in fall 2012, to fund a province-wide capital planning initiative, including capital assessments of all nonprofit housing stock (including that not currently funded by government). This will help develop the capacity of small and mid-sized providers to use and understand capital planning software and to make strategic decisions to ensure the sustainability of their assets.

BC Housing is mandated to ensure that public and social housing stock is in good repair, and it collects data on capital planning through its operational review cycle of government-funded nonprofits. A key element of the process for BCNPHA and the sector as a whole is to ensure that, when agreements expire, nonprofits have the knowledge they need to continue capital planning once government no longer has an interest in their assets. Building capacity in the sector is thus a critical element, not only of this process, but also for the sustainability of the sector. To that end, BC Housing has committed to fully fund a full-time staff position at BCNPHA to provide capacity development support to nonprofits across the province. The agreement also includes provisions for data sharing and joint ownership of the asset-management information technology system licence to ensure that nonprofits continue to have software access through BCNPHA after their operating agreements have expired.

Conclusion

The three cases studies illustrate BCNPHA's advocacy on behalf of British Columbia's nonprofit housing sector along all points of the funding cycle, from the development of operating agreements with the funder, BC Housing, through to their expiry. The examples also demonstrate the importance of advocacy as both anticipatory of the sector's future trends and needs and responsive to emerging issues and requests from membership. The approach taken depends on the nature of the issue. Certainly, anticipating issues facing the sector allows the association to plan an advocacy approach that meets the sector's needs through respectful engagement. Where funding issues arise that are perceived to be surprising shifts from previous policy and practice, however, the association is prepared to respond assertively to protect the sector from the inherent power imbalances between funder and fundee. In an individual agency contract model of funding, the importance of protection from negative consequences (whether real or perceived) that might result from voicing concerns is invaluable. A unified voice provides this level of security for individual agencies, while numbers strengthen the voice – indeed, the need for such a unified voice in the nonprofit housing sector was a catalyst for the formation of BCNPHA. Through operational engagement with the nonprofit housing sector and a broad range of other stakeholders, BCNPHA identifies issues of concern to the sector and develops appropriate advocacy strategies. Its board of directors sets the strategic direction for the association and can engage with the funder's board should issues escalate to that level.

Developing a unified voice has not been without its challenges, however, given the sector's broad range of capacities and perspectives and the diversity of British Columbians the sector serves. Finding common ground within the sector is an ongoing project for BCNPHA, and it is an important component of every process. When BCNPHA works with a core group of housing providers, its approach is to develop terms of reference to ensure that each nonprofit is working within the same set of parameters and from the same understanding. For other processes

BCNPHA organizes meetings with a cross-section of nonprofits prior to engaging the funder to ensure that issues are similarly impacting providers and that the issues brought forward to the funder are sectoral in nature.

Establishing a shared-purpose statement between BC Housing and the nonprofit housing sector was a significant achievement because it provides a useful reference point for all parties during advocacy engagements. The terms of new funding agreements, such as the capital planning initiative described above, explicitly reference the shared-purpose statement as a principle of engagement. Equally important was the process behind the statement's creation, as it brought together key stakeholders with historical divisions and power imbalances and focused their engagement on articulating commonalities rather than differences.

This chapter has highlighted BCNPHA's role as intermediary and advocate for a diverse and complex sector. A fundamental component of the association's vision is that the public, private, and nonprofit sectors should work together to develop and maintain safe, secure, and affordable housing for British Columbians. To achieve this goal, particularly within the individual agency contract funding environment that exists in British Columbia and Canada, all parties to the engagement must be respectful and willing to compromise wherever possible. Governments should be willing to engage in solution-focused dialogue, while nonprofits should be willing to "think as a sector" – and encouraging them to do so is a key goal of the association that represents them. Solidarity and clarity of purpose are critical components of BCNPHA's work, and, where empirical evidence clearly demonstrates the need for action, the association acts to ensure that housing providers are protected through a unified voice. Through a collective voice and actions, the BC nonprofit housing sector can ensure that all British Columbians have access to safe, secure, and affordable housing.

NOTES

1 Not included in these figures are housing co-ops, directly managed government units, and rent supplements used in the private market. These exclusions are estimated to account for an additional thirty-five thousand units.

2 In the 1980s Canada Mortgage and Housing Corporation defined core housing need as a measure of the need for social or affordable housing. Households that fail to meet one of the affordability, suitability, or adequacy standards are considered to be in core housing need if they cannot afford the average market rent in their area. Affordability is defined as paying 30 per cent or less of gross household income on shelter costs (CMHC 2012).

3 Deborah Kraus, personal communication, 14 December 2012.

4 Perry Staniscia, personal communication, 5 December 2012.

5 Ibid.

6 Ibid.; Lorne Epp, personal communication, 10 December 2012.

7 Alice Sundberg, personal communication, 3 December 2012.

8 Staniscia, personal communication, 5 December 2012.

9 Sundberg, personal communication, 3 December 2012.

10 Ibid.; Staniscia, personal communication, 5 December 2012.

11 Epp, personal communication, 10 December 2012; Kraus, personal communication, 14 December 2012.

12 Kaye Melliship, personal communication, 7 December 2012; Kraus, personal communication, 14 December 2012.

13 Sundberg, personal communication, 3 December 2012.

14 Kraus, personal communication, 14 December 2012.

15 Melliship, personal communication, 7 December 2012; Kraus, personal communication, 14 December 2012.

16 Epp, personal communication, 10 December 2012.

17 Staniscia, personal communication, 5 December 2012; Epp, personal communication, 10 December 2012; Melliship, personal communication, 7 December 2012; Kraus, personal communication, 14 December 2012.

18 Epp, personal communication, 10 December 2012; Kraus, personal communication, 14 December 2012.

19 Melliship, personal communication, 7 December 2012; Kraus, personal communication, 14 December 2012.

20 Epp, personal communication, 10 December 2012.

21 Ibid.

22 Sundberg, personal communication, 3 December 2012.

REFERENCES

BC Housing. 2006. "Canada-B.C. Social Housing Agreement Signed." Press release. 20 June. Burnaby, BC. Available online at http://www.bchousing.org/ Media/NR/2006/06/20/1192_0606201327-933.

———. 2012. "Service Plan: Housing Matters 2012/13–2014/15." Burnaby, BC. Available online at http://www.bchousing.org/resources/About%20 BC%20Housing/Service_Plans/2015-18_Service_Plan.pdf.

———. n.d. "Housing Provider Kit: Operations, Resident Relations." Burnaby, BC. Available online at http://www.bchousing.org/aboutus/ publications/HPK.

BC Housing and Vancouver. 2007. "Memorandum of Understanding between BC Housing Management Commission and the City of Vancouver Regarding the Development of City-owned Sites for Social and Supportive Housing." Burnaby, BC. Available online at http://www.bchousing.org/ resources/Housing_Initiatives/MOU/MOU_Vancouver.pdf.

BCNPHA (BC Non-Profit Housing Association). 2009. "Frequently Asked Questions from BC's Non-profit Housing Sector on the Impacts of Funding Constraints through BC Housing." Vancouver. Available online at http:// www.bcnpha.ca/.

———. 2012. "Unpublished Data from Asset Analysis Database." Vancouver.

BCNPHA (BC Non-Profit Housing Association) and BC Housing. 2012. "Preparing for the Expiry of Operating Agreements: BCNPHA and BC Housing Work Plan, November 2012 Update." Vancouver: BC Non-Profit Housing Association.

———. n.d. "Shared Purpose Statement between BC Housing and Non-profit Housing Providers." Vancouver: BC Non-Profit Housing Association.

CMHC (Canada Mortgage and Housing Corporation). 2012. Canadian Housing Observer 2012. Ottawa. Available online at http://www.cmhc-schl.gc.ca/odpub/pdf/67708.pdf?fr=1429899044817.

Carter, T. 1997. "Current Practices for Procuring Affordable Housing: The Canadian Context." *Housing Policy Debate* 8 (3): 593–631. http://dx.doi.org/ 10.1080/10511482.1997.9521268.

Colderley, C.A. 1999. "Welfare State Retrenchment and the Non-profit Sector: The Problems, Policies and Politics of Canadian Housing." *Journal of Policy History* 11 (3): 283–312. http://dx.doi.org/10.1353/jph.1999.0003.

Copas, L., and S. Klein. 2010. "Unpacking the Housing Numbers: How Much New Social Housing Is BC Building?" Ottawa: Canadian Centre for Policy Alternatives. Available online at http://www.policyalternatives. ca/sites/default/files/uploads/publications/2010/09/CCPA-BC-SPARC-Unpacking-Housing-Numbers.pdf.

Dreier, P., and J.D. Hulchanski. 1993. "The Role of Non-profit Housing in Canada and the United States: Some Comparisons." *Housing Policy Debate* 4 (1): 43–80. http://dx.doi.org/10.1080/10511482.1993.9521124.

Fallis, G. 1990. "Housing Finance and Housing Subsidies in Canada." *Urban Studies* 27 (6): 877–903. http://dx.doi.org/10.1080/00420989020080891.

Findlay, K.M., and P. Stobie. 2005. *Social and Affordable Housing in BC: From Crisis Response to Preventative Maintenance.* Vancouver: Langara College, Continuing Studies.

Grieve, B.J. 1985. "Continuity and Change: Provincial Housing Policy in British Columbia 1945–1985." Master's thesis, University of British Columbia.

Housing Matters BC. 2014. "Housing Strategy for British Columbia: A Foundation for Strong Communities." N.p. Available online at http://www.bchousing.org/resources/About%20BC%20Housing/Housing_Matters_BC/Housing-Matters-BC.pdf.

Hulchanski, J.D. 2003. "What Factors Shape Canadian Housing Policy? The Intergovernmental Role in Canada's Housing System." Paper presented at the Conference on Municipal-Federal-Provincial Relations: New Structures, New Connections, Kingston, ON, 9–10 May. Available online at http://www.urbancentre.utoronto.ca/pdfs/elibrary/FedMun.pdf.

Leone, R., and B.W. Carroll. 2010. "Decentralization and Devolution in Canadian Social Housing Policy." *Environment and Planning. C, Government & Policy* 28 (3): 389–404. http://dx.doi.org/10.1068/c09153.

Pomeroy, S. 2006. *Was Chicken Little Right? Case Studies on the Impact of Expiring Social Housing Operating Agreements.* Toronto: Canadian Housing and Renewal Association.

———. 2007. "Sound the Alarm Bells: Critical Need for Recruitment and Succession in the Ontario Non-profit Housing Sector." Discussion paper. Toronto: Ontario Non-Profit Housing Association.

———. 2011. "Is Emperor Nero Fiddling as Rome Burns? Assessing Risk when Federal Subsidies End." Available online at http://housing4all.ca/sites/default/files/documents/reports/2_emperor_nero_-_english_only.pdf.

———. 2012. "Addressing the Expiring Subsidy Challenge: Options and Remedies." Available online at http://www.chra-achru.ca/media/content/Addressing%20the%20Expiring%20Subsidy%20Challenge%20GUIDE%20-%20EN.pdf.

Prince, M.J. 1998. "Holes in the Safety Net, Leaks in the Roof: Changes in Canadian Welfare Policy and Their Implications for Social Housing Programs." *Housing Policy Debate* 9 (4): 825–48. http://dx.doi.org/10.1080/10511482.1998.9521320.

Shapcott, M. 2004. "Where Are We Going? Recent Federal and Provincial Housing Policy." In *Finding Room: Policy Options for a Canadian Rental Housing Strategy*, ed. J.D. Hulchanski and M. Shapcott, 195–212. Toronto: CUCS Press.

Wolfe, J.M. 1998. "Canadian Housing Policy in the Nineties." *Housing Studies* 13 (1): 121–34. http://dx.doi.org/10.1080/02673039883524.

4 Alberta's Social Policy: The Neoliberal Legacy of the Klein Reforms

NILIMA SONPAL-VALIAS, LORI SIGURDSON, AND PETER R. ELSON

In December 1992 Ralph Klein won the leadership of the Progressive Conservative (PC) Party of Alberta and became the province's twelfth premier. His leadership win and the subsequent election of the PC Party in June 1993 set the stage for a dramatic shift in Alberta's fiscal and social policy, the structure and role of its government, and its relationship with civil society. Underpinned by principles of free market capitalism and individual entrepreneurism, the "Klein Revolution" is considered the "poster child" of neoliberalism (Albo 2002; Clark 2002; Finkel 2006);[1] and a role model for other provincial governments, including Ontario's under Mike Harris and British Columbia's led by Gordon Campbell (see Lindquist and Vakil, in this volume). The breadth, depth, and speed of the Klein reforms have had a significant impact on the realities of Alberta's nonprofit sector and its funding regime for at least two decades.

Neoliberalism may be best conceptualized as an ideology, a mode of governance, and a policy package (Steger and Roy 2010). As an *ideology*, neoliberalism has saturated the public discourse and imagination with an idealized image of a consumerist, free market world, portraying global markets and interdependence as necessary tools for a better world, "to the point where it has become incorporated into the common-sense way many of us interpret, live in, and understand the world" (Harvey 2005, 3). As a *mode of governance*, neoliberalism is rooted in the values and techniques of the business world: efficiency calculations, quantitative targets and outcomes, and market-oriented behaviour, to improve success defined in monetary terms. Operationalized within government as "new public management" (NPM), its objective is to increase administrative efficiency, effectiveness, and accountability, more so than to maximize the pursuit of public good (see also the reference to NPM by Frankel and Levasseur, in this volume). As a *policy package*, neoliberalism promotes deregulation of the economy, liberalization of trade and industry, and privatization of state-owned agencies. Policy measures include massive tax cuts to businesses, anti-unionization, removal of controls on the global movement of capital, reduction of social services and welfare programs, and government downsizing (Steger and Roy 2010).

Although neoliberalism has been described as a hegemonic discourse (Harvey 2005), differing institutional legacies and socio-political considerations of politicians and policymakers (Pierson 1996) mean that neoliberalism's manifestations are dynamic and heterogeneous, with multiple contours and internal complexity (Bode 2006; Kus 2006; Steger and Roy 2010). Understanding Alberta's funding regime and its social impact means investigating the role of neoliberalism as part of the historical context shaping the provincial government's policies and practices, and also recognizing – as we do in our discussion of Alberta's initiatives to end homelessness, reduce poverty, and develop a social policy framework (see also O'Neill et al., in this volume) – that such an investigation might uncover processes or characteristics that are neither consistent nor homogeneous.

Historical Context: Alberta from 1992 to 2014

In mid-1992, when Ralph Klein ran for the leadership of the PC Party, the Alberta government had been running a budget deficit for the previous six years, had accumulated a net debt of $2.5 billion, and its cumulative debt had increased to more than $15 billion from zero in fiscal year 1985/86 (Alberta 2003).[2] Key factors contributing to the deficit included high expenditures, largely due to spending commitments made during the boom years of the 1970s and early 1980s; a sharp decline in resource revenues following the collapse of world oil prices in 1986;[3] costly losses from government loans, equities, and guarantees provided to encourage industrial development and diversification in the 1980s (Mansell 1997);[4] and gradual decreases in federal transfer payments, essentially downloading the costs for provincially administered social programs (Finkel 2006).

Socio-politically, at the federal level, the Reform Party of Canada and its ideology of small government and lower taxes were garnering increasing support and causing a fundamental reconsideration among the province's business and political elites of government's role in society (Lisac 1995). Demographically, Alberta's historical heritage of a primarily agricultural and petroleum-based economy had created and attracted a skilled and adaptable population that valued entrepreneurship and self-reliance, rather than government intervention. In the late 1980s, the workforce had undergone massive downsizing due to dramatic corporate restructuring in the face of globalization's competitive pressures (Mansell 1997). It was no surprise that, in this environment, Klein's PC Party won the June 1993 provincial election on a platform to eliminate the deficit by slashing spending and restructuring the public sector, in much the same way as had occurred in the corporate world.

The Klein reforms, part I: First wave, 1993–96

Within a year of gaining office, Klein had turned the broad outline of his election promises into a fairly complete program of change. Key elements of the program included (Mansell 1997):

- *improving financial management and controls* by changing the provincial government's accounting, reporting, and budgeting processes, including giving a strong role to Alberta Treasury with respect to budget allocation and to standing policy committees to review departmental business plans (Boothe 1997);
- *redefining the role of government* by mandating all ministries to determine which programs were essential and appropriately provided by government and which ones could be targeted for elimination or privatization, using a review framework developed by Treasury (Kneebone and McKenzie 1997);
- *downsizing government* by decreasing the number of ministries and civil servants, and implementing rapid, deep, and broad-based cuts affecting all ministries, albeit to different degrees (Kneebone and McKenzie 1997);
- *improving program accountability* by introducing strategies such as three-year business plans, performance measures, and spending targets, and expanding the role of standing policy committees to provide closer political oversight (Boothe 1997);
- *decentralizing some aspects of decision making* by restructuring school boards and health authorities, and pushing the actual implementation of budget cuts onto local authorities;

- *expanding public input processes* through mechanisms such as province-wide consultations; and,
- *enacting legislation* to guide fiscal decision making now and in the future (Boothe 1997).[5]

Although these reforms affected all areas of government, their implementation and implications differed across ministries. In Advanced Education, delegation on how to implement a budget cut of 15.5 per cent was accompanied by numerous controls (such as limits on tuition fee increases and minimum enrolment requirements) and strong pressures to implement certain measures (such as a 5 per cent compensation cut and targeted closures of certain programs) (Kneebone and McKenzie 1997). The creation of an Access Fund, through which an advisory board would competitively allocate resources to programs based on labour market needs, was seen by postsecondary administrators as giving the government more direct control over programming, and making universities and colleges more market oriented (Emery 1997). The Fund was also perceived as creating a competitive environment at the same time that institutions were being pressured to cooperate with one another through program consolidation and creation of "centres of specialization" (Kneebone and McKenzie 1997).

Compared to those Advanced Education had to deal with, the measures Basic Education faced were more intrusive and centralized. The discretionary authority of school boards was significantly reduced as a result of highly detailed funding formulas specifying how much money each school district would receive and how expenditures should be allocated. Curriculum development was centralized, and collection of property taxes for school revenues was shifted from local authorities to the provincial government. At the same time, parents and teachers were ostensibly more empowered by implementing school-based management, increasing the role of parent councils, and allowing for the creation of charter schools (Kneebone and McKenzie 1997).

At Family and Social Services, the ministry for which most nonprofit human services provide contracted services, the bulk of its 19.3 per cent funding cuts were achieved in welfare programs by tightening eligibility, reducing benefit amounts, and transferring clients to Advanced Education and Career Development. Disincentives were removed by requiring all able-bodied recipients to find employment or retrain – in other words, by moving clients off welfare into workfare (Kneebone and McKenzie 1997). Targeted supports would go only to "deserving" applicants – that is, those unable to work due to disability or age. The strategies implemented in social services played a particularly significant role in the overall success of Alberta's deficit-reduction goals (Shedd 1997).

Plans for some of these policy reforms had already been under discussion since the mid-1980s (Kneebone and McKenzie 1997), but sufficient galvanization of forces to shake the current arrangements out of their preferred state of inertia (Pierson 2000) had yet to be achieved. As such, although some changes to fiscal policy were implemented prior to 1993 by the PC government of Don Getty, these had little impact in the long run on either the province's fiscal position or its social policies (Mansell 1997). In 1993 the perception of a fiscal crisis and the urgent imperative to resolve the fiscal situation provided the critical push to justify the implementation of rapid, deep, and across-the-board cuts that, in turn, made possible the structural changes needed for large-scale institutional and policy reform.

Wilsford (1994) identifies some common elements, or conjunctural forces, required for lasting and significant social policy reform: (1) the perception of a crisis (typically fiscal); (2) a relatively centralized, hierarchical political system able to move quickly; (3) strong and determined political leadership (typically by the first minister and particularly the finance minister); (4) basic elements of a reform plan already thought out; (5) an electorate ready for change; and (6) fragmented opposition. All of these elements pre-existed or were put in place by the Klein PCs in 1993, enabling them to move quickly and broadly to create the structures and processes for reform and to set the expectations for the provincial government's role and relationships in civil society. Alberta's political and ideological environment in the early 1990s strengthened the climate in which government downsizing, restructuring, and implementation of greater accountability and individual responsibilities would be broadly accepted (or at least tolerated as necessary) by the majority of the population.

The Klein reforms, part II: Second wave, 1996–2006

In 1996, three short years after implementing its reforms, the Klein government announced its first budget surplus in a decade, a trend that was to remain until 2008, due in large part to rising energy prices. By 1997 Alberta's fiscal position had turned around dramatically from having the worst ratio of deficit to gross domestic product (GDP) among the provinces in 1993 to having the best ratio of surplus to GDP in Canada. Low inflation, low interest rates, rapid export growth under the North American Free Trade Agreement, a healthy energy sector investing increasing amounts in exploration and development, expanding forestry and other industries, and accelerated population growth all constituted the context for the economic turnaround (Alberta 1997).

Unlike the earlier period, however, when the fiscal crisis provided the basis for radical reforms, the "revolution lost its momentum" once the deficit was eliminated (Harrison 2005, 10). In response to increasing public pressure and resentment (Gazso and Krahn 2008; Harrison 2005), the second wave of the Klein reforms consisted of reinvesting in targeted areas such as health, education, and career development. Per capita funding (in constant dollars) returned to fiscal year 1992/93 levels by 2000/01 for health and education, but not until 2010/11 for social services. Also at this point the province started to invest in greater horizontal or cross-ministerial strategies. For example, the Children and Youth Initiative Partnering Ministries initiative led, in part, to a group of community organizations coming together to address their common issue of youth mentoring (see O'Neill et al., in this volume).

By 2005 the provincial debt had been eliminated (Alberta 2005). From fiscal year 1992/93, just before the cuts were implemented, to 2005/06, after the debt was eliminated, funding for health increased by $5.4 billion, a per capita increase of 77 per cent, and for education by $3 billion, a per capita change of 40 per cent. In contrast, funding for social services increased by $832 million, a per capita change of only 14 per cent (Alberta 2006a).[6] The reason for this disparity, in part, was due to the replacement of the Canada Assistance Plan in 1995 by the Canada Health and Social Transfer, which allowed provinces to reconfigure social funding allocations, and did not obligate them to recognize citizens' rights to social assistance to the same extent as had the Canada Assistance Plan (Gazso and Krahn 2008).

During the second wave of the Klein revolution, the reforms that were institutionalized during the first wave became the operational norms of a government that had been in power for thirteen years. The changes were manifested in the centralization of authority in the premier's office, Treasury's stronger role over budget allocations, and the concentration of policy and budgetary review powers in the standing policy committees (Brownsey 2005). The information the public was provided about government policies and directions was highly controlled (Sampert 2005). Reflecting NPM practices, greater accountability processes were developed through the use of three-year business plans and performance measures. The decentralization of operational decision making coupled with more centralized mechanisms for overall control and insight were the "new normal" across all ministries.

Social policy, meanwhile, continued to adhere to neoliberal principles privileging marketization and individual entrepreneurship. Even when funding was increased to social programs, services delivery was forced to be more competitive. Organizations were pressured to cooperate and collaborate in order to access resources for programs that fit the government's priorities, and responsibility was shifted increasingly towards individual citizens for their own welfare and that of their families (Shedd 1997). In health care, the Mazankowski and Graydon reports argued that public health care was unsustainable and that innovative solutions were needed, thereby framing the push towards increasing user fees, private payment options, and for-profit delivery of selected medical procedures (Horne 2005). The public school system, similarly, saw greater interest on the part of the provincial government to pursue public-private partnerships, establish structures to encourage the involvement of private business in educational policy development, and significantly increase parents' purchase of private tutorial services (Taylor, Shultz, and Leard 2005).

Beyond Klein: From 2007 to 2014

By 2006 Ralph Klein's charisma had started to wane. With the deficit and debt elimination agenda achieved, the public had grown discontented with his lack of policy direction and focus (*CBC News* 2006). In December 2006, amid declining popularity and pressure from the PC Party membership, Klein resigned as party leader and was replaced by Ed Stelmach. Both Stelmach, who was Alberta's premier from December 2006 to January 2011, and his successor, Alison Redford, who governed from October 2011 to March 2014, were forced to increase expenditures in response to the pressures of rapid population growth, while also dealing with declining revenues resulting from the 2008 global economic crisis.

THE STELMACH YEARS: 2007–11
In fiscal year 2006/07 the Alberta economy grew by an extraordinary 6.8 per cent, the population grew by 3 per cent, and unemployment stood at 3.4 per cent, the lowest recorded in Canada in thirty years.

The government reported a record surplus of $8.9 billion as a result of strong economic growth, high energy prices, and strong investment revenues (Alberta 2007b). The following year saw similar conditions: the economy grew at a more sustainable pace of 3.3 per cent while population growth and unemployment were close to the previous year's levels; the government posted yet another surplus, this time of $4.6 billion (Alberta 2008a). This trend, however, was not to continue.

In fiscal year 2008/09, the government declared Alberta's first budget deficit since 1993/94, due to lower-than-budgeted revenues as a result of the start of the global recession and weakening in world equity markets (Alberta 2009a). This economic situation remained during Stelmach's tenure as premier, with fiscal deficits ranging from $852 million in 2008/09 to $3.4 billion in 2010/11 as revenues maintained a new low of close to $35 billion from 2008/09 to 2010/11 (compared with $38 billion in 2007/08), while program expenditures rose from $33.6 billion in 2007/08 to $36.6 billion in 2008/9 and $38.3 billion in 2010/11 (Alberta 2011). During these years, the deficits were offset by the savings accumulated in the Alberta Sustainability Fund.[7]

To address significant growth and infrastructure needs, Stelmach increased operational expenditures for health, education, and targeted social programs such as child care, children's services, the environment, homelessness, income support for the severely handicapped, justice and law enforcement, and services to persons with developmental disabilities. Capital expenditures rose for the first two fiscal years, but declined significantly from a high of $7.6 billion in 2008/09 to $6.5 billion in 2009/10 and to $5.9 billion in 2010/11 (Alberta 2007b, 2008a, 2009a, 2010b, 2011). Despite this drop, in March 2009, Stelmach publicly stated that he supported borrowing funds for infrastructure projects to capitalize on low construction costs and low interest rates, a position in complete opposition to Klein's anti-debt philosophy (Terry 2009).

Stelmach's approach to funding allocation was to identify efficiencies through program reviews and to impose tight limits on in-year operating expenses, while finding money for priorities such as addressing growth pressures and social programs for vulnerable Albertans. The fiscal year 2010/11 budget, for example, forecast a $4.7 billion deficit. To prepare for this shortfall, the government found $1.3 billion in savings through program reviews and funding reductions, freezing public sector hiring and management salaries, reducing discretionary spending, and streamlining administrative and other noncore functions (Alberta 2010c). The actual deficit was $3.4 billion, due in part to higher-than-forecast revenues from Crown lease sales, higher natural resource royalties and investment income, and lower expenditures. Alberta's economy grew by 3.8 per cent following the severe contraction of 4.5 per cent in 2009, unemployment dropped to 5.5 per cent, and oil prices continued to be strong (Alberta 2011).

Stelmach maintained Klein's taxation policy so that Albertans and Alberta businesses continued to pay the lowest overall taxes in Canada (see Figure 4.1). In fiscal year 2006/07 personal income tax credits were increased and the general corporate income tax was reduced to 10 per cent (Alberta 2007b). In 2009 provincial health care insurance premiums were eliminated (Alberta 2009a), and in 2010 the small business threshold (the amount up to which small businesses pay only 14 per cent tax) was raised to $500,000 (Alberta 2010b). The only significant attempt to increase revenues was the New Royalty Framework, announced in October 2007 and scheduled to start in January 2009, which was expected to increase royalty revenues by about 20 per cent (Alberta 2007c). Widespread negative reaction from the energy industry and declining investment in the sector due to global economic uncertainty

Figure 4.1. Upper and Lower Provincial and Territorial Tax Brackets, 2012

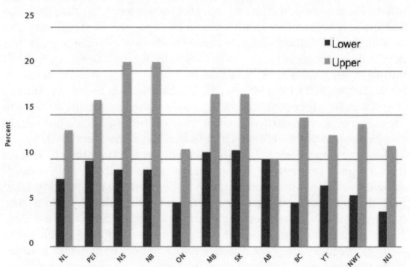

Source: Canada, Canada Revenue Agency; available online at http://www.cra-arc.gc.ca/formspubs/prioryear/t1/2012/menu-eng.html.

led to announcements in March 2009 and May 2010 of a variety of new incentives (such as lower royalty rates and royalty credits for new drilling) to encourage investment (Alberta 2009b, 2010a).

Structurally the Stelmach government made few major changes to the public sector compared to the magnitude of the Klein reforms. Major initiatives included creating a new Treasury Board ministry to oversee "more disciplined government spending" and to undertake program reviews "to identify efficiencies" (Alberta 2007a, 14). Standing policy committees were replaced with four new policy field committees that included representation from the opposition (Pratt 2007). Six ministries were eliminated, leaving a total of eighteen, and each minister was issued a "Mandate Letter" outlining portfolio priorities (Alberta 2006b). The nine regional health authorities were consolidated into one Alberta Health Services Board (Alberta 2009a), and a Minister's Advisory Committee on Health was established (Alberta 2010b).

The consecutive years of deficit budgets, meanwhile, took a political toll on the PC Party. In 2009 the party began losing ground in public opinion polls to the increasingly popular right-wing Wildrose Alliance Party, which had recently won its first seat in the legislature in a by-election in Calgary (Fong 2009). In 2010 a number of PC Members of the Legislative Assembly (MLAs) left the party to join others, including Raj Sherman, who crossed the floor to become leader of the Alberta Liberal Party and led the attack against the government on health care. There was growing negative press about the environmental impact of the oil sands, and the Wildrose Alliance Party and its leader, Danielle Smith, continued to rise in popularity (Thomson 2010). On 25 January 2011 Stelmach suddenly announced his resignation, a move apparently prompted by conflict with Finance Minister Ted Morton, who was not prepared to sign another deficit budget (Wingrove, D'Aliesio, and Vanderklippe 2011).

REDFORD: 2011–14

On 2 October 2011 Alison Redford was declared the new leader of the PC Party, becoming the province's first female premier on 7 October and leading the party to another majority government in April 2012 (Fong 2012). Key elements in the fiscal framework for the party's platform included delivering balanced budgets with no new taxes or service cuts, implementing three-year spending cycles with a results-based budgeting approach (requiring all ministries to build their budgets from zero every three years following a comprehensive review of all programs and services led by the Treasury Board), and establishing three-year predictable funding arrangements for municipalities, postsecondary institutions, and school boards. Of particular note for Alberta's nonprofit human services sector were promises in the election platform to articulate a new social policy framework and a new aging population policy framework. The platform also promised to increase funding to contracted service providers to help them maintain a sustainable workforce, and to implement a ten-year poverty reduction plan (PC Party of Alberta 2012).

In fiscal year 2011/12 the government came close to achieving a balanced budget, posting a deficit of only $23 million – a vast improvement over the forecast deficit of $3.4 billion. The economy grew by 5.2 per cent, unemployment decreased to 4.9 per cent, and oil prices remained strong (Alberta 2012a). The 2012/13 budget, which forecast a $886 million deficit, was based on the key principle that "Alberta's budget is about more than just money or the bottom line. It's about ensuring that this government is supporting the outcomes Albertans want" (Alberta 2012d, 7) – a clear departure from Klein's priority to eliminate the deficit at all costs. The budget increased investment in health, education, and social services, based on expected economic growth of 3.8 per cent and expected revenues of about $40 billion with no tax increases.

During fiscal year 2012/13, although provincial economic indicators remained strong, the decline in global oil prices and deeply discounted prices for Alberta's heavy oil (the so-called bitumen bubble) contributed to an actual deficit of $2.8 billion – close to $2 billion higher than budgeted (Alberta 2013d). Taking into consideration these new realities, the 2013/14 budget maintained operational expenditures at 2012/13 levels even though population growth plus inflation were estimated to increase over 4 per cent – resulting in a de facto cut to services. Notwithstanding the belt tightening, a $451 million deficit was forecast. Borrowing would be allowed for capital projects, but not for rising operational costs (Alberta 2013b). Alberta's largest unions, whose support had helped Redford win the PC Party leadership and the 2012 election, felt betrayed by a premier who had frozen the salaries of public sector managers, was locked in bitter contract battles with doctors and nurses (Wingrove 2013), and had reneged on campaign promises such as a publicly funded full-day kindergarten program and annual 2 per cent funding increases for education.

At the end of fiscal year 2013/14, despite the budget's pessimistic outlook, continuing global economic uncertainty, and southern Alberta's disastrous floods in June 2013, the province realized an operational surplus of $2.5 billion largely due to higher-than-expected oil prices and investment returns, a lower Canadian dollar, and sustained economic growth (Alberta 2014a). Unfortunately, the year did not go as well for Premier Redford as it did for the provincial treasury. Dogged by controversy over a series of travel expenditures and questions about her leadership, Redford resigned as Alberta's premier on 23 March 2014, less than three years after assuming the position and within three months of receiving 77 per cent support in a PC Party leadership review (*CBC News* 2014b). At the end of her tenure, she had limited support from the left (which was angered by her austerity measures and rocky labour relations), the right (which had no appetite for debt or deficit budgets), and even her own caucus (who apparently had their own grievances about her leadership style). Redford was subsequently replaced by Dave Hancock, who played the role of interim premier and PC Party leader, until Jim Prentice assumed the party leadership and became the province's premier in September 2014 (*CBC News* 2014a).

Like Stelmach, Redford continued the PC tradition of maintaining the lowest tax regime of any of the provinces, even as 77 per cent of Albertans polled in early 2013 favoured higher taxes for corporations and high-income earners, and 72 per cent favoured the reintroduction of a progressive income tax and an increase in oil royalties (Wingrove 2013). In the policy arena, Redford's significant contributions were to develop the social policy framework (Alberta 2013d), create legislation to enhance policies affecting children and youth, and raise the minimum wage to $9.95 an hour (Alberta 2014a). Structural and administrative changes included creating the Ministry of Human Services to consolidate a number of social program and services, expanding the authority and independence of the Health Quality Council and the Child and Youth Advocate, establishing the Council of Quality Assurance to advise on the child intervention system (Alberta 2012b), implementing a results-based budgeting process (Alberta 2013d), integrating the government's strategic planning and reporting frameworks with this initiative, and developing an outcomes and measurement framework to guide health care planning and funding decisions (Alberta 2014a).

Alberta's sustained population growth and aging infrastructure, coupled with the province's dependence on a volatile revenue source, have created, on the one hand, a need for greater investment in social programs and infrastructure, and, on the other hand, a need for prudent fiscal management. The Klein reforms were ideologically focused on the latter, with an agenda to reduce the size and scope of government, and keep in check what was framed as gross overspending on social programs; any reinvestments that subsequently occurred were in reaction to public pressure, rather than guided by a clear social policy vision. Both Stelmach and Redford departed from Klein's "no debt, no deficit" fiscal policy in their attempts to address the province's growth demands. Both also undertook important initiatives, which we discuss towards the end of the chapter, that attempted to move the province forward on a lagging social agenda. However, the conjuncture of forces, such as the perception of a crisis, determined political leadership, and a fragmented opposition, that enabled the Klein reforms to have pervasive impact, simply were not present during Stelmach's and Redford's reigns.

The Social Legacy of the Klein Reforms

Alberta's neoliberal approach has profoundly transformed social and political practices in Alberta; more critically, it has dramatically reduced the provincial government's role in income distribution and widened the disparity gap – that is, "the social and economic distance between the richest and poorest households" (ACSW 2010, 16).[8] Social disparities include quality-of-life and well-being measures such as sense of belonging, satisfaction with life, freedom from violence, work versus leisure time, and participation in democratic processes. Income disparity, or income inequality, is the way income is distributed across households, and is the key driver of social exclusion.

Alberta's growing disparity gap

Alberta's economic growth has been extraordinary, but it has been paralleled by rampant social and economic inequality. Alberta's vast natural resources put it in the particularly fortunate position of not having to create wealth but only to manage it. Alberta's GDP more than tripled between 1985 and 2011 from $66.8 billion to $286.6 billion (Alberta 2012f). The most dramatic increase occurred over the first decade of the twenty-first century, with an increase in GDP of almost $174 billion.

Alberta's rapid economic growth between 1999 and 2009 meant that, in 2009, Alberta had both the highest median and highest mean income in Canada. As well, absolute poverty in the province had been reduced, with many who were unemployed before the boom becoming better off during it. Top-income earners, however, benefited more than other Albertans from the boom. Not only did incomes increase dramatically at the top, but those families worked fewer hours, while the opposite was true for middle-income families (Yalnizyan 2007). For many of those who gained employment during the boom, working was not enough to break out of poverty or ensure an adequate quality of life. Food bank usage, for example, rose 45 per cent between 1997 and 2009. The recession of 2008 also left its mark, as the number of Albertans who could afford only one meal or less per day increased by 90 per cent in 2008 over the previous year (Gibson 2007).

THE SOCIETAL IMPACTS OF DISPARITY IN ALBERTA

Social and income disparity jeopardizes the fabric of social relationships that make our communities good places to live, work, raise children, and grow old. Some measures of disparity – rates of violence, lack of trust and absence of community life, and addiction – affect individuals directly in their homes and communities; others – rates of obesity and incarceration and poor education and health outcomes – are expensive and result in higher costs across society (Wilkinson and Pickett 2010). Poverty alone has been estimated to cost Alberta between $7.1 and $9.5 billion per year (Briggs and Lee 2012).

Disparity also has a racist and sexist face: the average income of Indigenous men is two-thirds that of non-Indigenous men, while the average income of Indigenous women is just half that of non-Indigenous women; moreover, levels of unemployment among Indigenous peoples are double and even triple the non-Indigenous average. Indigenous children are significantly overrepresented in children in care, and Indigenous people are disproportionately represented at all stages of the justice system, as both victims and offenders. As well, Indigenous people's levels of educational attainment are much lower, their health outcomes are much poorer, their housing quality is lower, and they have less food security (Statistics Canada 2008). Gender disparity among Indigenous people can be seen in the persistent gap between women's and men's wages. Indigenous women also face greater barriers to employment than do Indigenous men, due to the lack of quality child care and access to training and skills development programs, and discriminatory wage ceilings (Parkland Institute 2012).

The level of disparity in Alberta has serious implications for the province's social fabric, as is evident in the following indicators (ACSW 2010):

- Family violence: Alberta has the highest rates of family violence in Canada, and leads the country in domestic assault, homicide-suicide, and stalking.
- Political exclusion: In the 2008 provincial election, only 41 per cent of eligible voters actually voted, the lowest turnout of any Canadian provincial election in fifty years; in 2012 voter turnout increased to just over 50 per cent. Political exclusion includes growing elitism, cynicism, and distancing of the majority from political processes and participation.
- Sense of belonging to the community: Only 63 per cent of Albertans surveyed, the smallest proportion in the country, reported having a sense of belonging to their community they described as somewhat strong, compared with the national average of 70 per cent and up to 80 per cent in some other provinces.
- University participation: Only 17 per cent of Albertans attend post-secondary education institutions, compared with a national average of 23 per cent; the proportion in other provinces ranges from 21 to 28 per cent.
- Leisure time: Albertans average 5.0 hours of leisure a day, compared with the national average of 5.55 hours; the average in other provinces ranges up to 5.9 hours. In other words, the average Albertan has 200 fewer hours of leisure a year than does the average Canadian.
- Satisfaction with life: Albertans are second from the bottom in Canada in measures of satisfaction with life. This dissatisfaction is evident in Alberta's decreasing social cohesion. Signs of lower social cohesion include rising crime rates, increased social violence, greater class insulation, deepening exclusion for those at the bottom, and a culture of excess among the richest group (Ray and Schmitt 2007). Absolute poverty has long been linked to crime rates, but studies show that relative poverty is also linked and even causally linked, especially to violent crime (Kolkman and Edmonton Social Planning Council 2007).
- Homelessness: The numbers of homeless have risen dramatically in both large and small urban centres in Alberta. In 1992, when

Calgary began its biennial homeless count, 447 people were without permanent shelter; by 2008 there were 4,060 homeless (Calgary Homeless Foundation 2009).

The state of social assistance

Nowhere is economic and social exclusion felt more powerfully than by those who depend on income support programs. Alberta's income support services include various programs, benefits, and subsidies, delivered in a variety of ways through complex systems, each with a different set of requirements and eligibility criteria. These programs fall under numerous administrations. Beyond raising rates for the Assured Income for the Severely Handicapped program and indexing benefits to inflation in 2003, the Klein and Redford governments showed no indication, or political will, to restore benefit levels and community-based support to pre-1994 levels, when Klein slashed public services by 21 per cent. Alberta has the lowest social assistance rates for lone-parent families and single employable adults in Canada (National Council of Welfare 2006).

The 2008 recession left its mark in increased income support cases. Although the caseload has fluctuated from post-war highs in the 1980s to the lowest in Alberta's history in the early to mid-1990s, it has increased again in recent years. This suggests that a segment of the population has not been able to insulate itself sufficiently with secure employment and savings even during boom years to carry it through recessionary times. The increase in caseload numbers also points to the weakened employment insurance program, with less than 30 per cent of the workforce now eligible in many areas.

Public spending in Alberta is closely tied to oil and gas prices, which are highly volatile, making funding for social programs extremely unstable. Moreover, spending on social programs has failed to keep pace with Alberta's growing population and diverse needs. As a result, social infrastructure is inadequate. Waiting lists for social housing can be more than eight years in length. Affordable, quality child care spaces have not kept pace with demand, and the cost of public leisure and culture facilities has left many on the sidelines (Public Interest Alberta and Edmonton Social Planning Council 2009).

The Stelmach and Redford governments attempted to address the needs of a rapidly growing economy by increasing spending on health, education, and social services. However, neoliberal ideals of free markets and individual self-reliance, modes of governance rooted in corporate techniques and the search for monetary efficiencies, and a policy focus on privatization, liberalization, and government downsizing (Steger and Roy 2010) that were institutionalized through the structural and procedural reforms of the Klein Revolution persist, albeit with some modifications over time.

The Impact of the Klein Reforms on Alberta's Nonprofit Sector

Policy shifts rooted in neoliberal principles have rewritten the relations between government and nonprofit human services and significantly affected the political economy of the nonprofit sector and its role in society (Evans and Shields 1998, 2000). These neoliberal policies, in the form of New Public Management, have shaped the autonomy and focus of nonprofit organizations (Scott 2003), changed whom they serve and how (Jenson and Phillips 2000), and affected how work is resourced, organized, and accounted for (Dart and Zimmerman 2000; Evans, Richmond, and Shields 2005). Neoliberal policy shifts have also affected workers' autonomy and creativity (Baines 2004) and diminished advocacy and citizen education capacity (Evans and Shields 2000; Hall et al. 2005; Scott 2003).

In Alberta, the breadth, depth, and speed of the Klein reforms in the early 1990s have had a significant and lasting impact on nonprofit service providers in multiple ways. Meinhard and Foster's (2001) survey of voluntary organizations shows that the impact felt most strongly was an increased demand for services, due, in large part, to more people needing support as a result of tighter welfare eligibility and lower benefit levels, and also perhaps because of a decline in the number of services delivery organizations. The surviving organizations have had to cope with an increased need to demonstrate their accountability, and are subject to greater scrutiny and monitoring activities. As well, reduced funding has forced many to cut their workforce, make better use of the skills of remaining staff, and deploy them to underresourced program areas. Organizations have also been pressured to find new ways to meet funding shortfalls; compared to those in other provinces, nonprofits in Alberta engage in more funding diversification and commercial venture activities.

Although the experience of Alberta's nonprofit organizations has been similar in many ways to that of nonprofits in other provinces, such as Ontario and Nova Scotia, where funding cuts have also been dramatic, Meinhard and Foster (2001) find that the intensity of the effects of cuts has been mitigated by each province's unique political, economic, and socio-cultural contexts. Even though the funding cuts in Alberta were steeper than in other provinces, its nonprofits did not express greater dissatisfaction than their peers in most other provinces to the policy shifts. Alberta is also one of only three provinces to approve of a shift of responsibility for social services from government to the community. These findings do not seem unreasonable given Alberta's culture of self-reliance and entrepreneurship (Mansell 1997).

Even though funding was restored to targeted areas such as health and education once the deficit was eliminated in 1996, adaptations that nonprofit organizations made in response to the Klein reforms have become permanent changes (Meinhard and Foster 2001). Seel's analysis of the review of the Persons with Developmental Disabilities Act (in this volume) supports the assertion that neoliberal principles of greater financial efficiency, accountability, and individual responsibility are firmly entrenched in Alberta's nonprofit organizations, more than two decades after the Klein reforms.

In addition to the challenges created by the Klein legacy, in more recent times Alberta's nonprofit organizations have faced pressures caused by rapid population growth. Surveys of Alberta's nonprofit sector by the Calgary Chamber of Voluntary Organizations reveal that, since 2010 at least, more than 60 per cent of responding nonprofit organizations reported population-growth-driven demands for services; in 2013, 76 per cent of 402 respondents cited increased services demands (CCVO 2013). Combined with rising operating costs (reported by 67 per cent of respondents in 2013) and no change in government contract revenue (reported by 52 per cent) or declining government contract revenue (reported by 21 per cent), it is no surprise – but nonetheless alarming – that 41 per cent of respondents had less than a month's equivalent of operating costs in their cash reserves (CCVO 2013). This supply-and-demand equation has created a great sense of vulnerability among Alberta's nonprofits. These findings paint a somewhat pessimistic picture of Alberta's nonprofit sector. Yet, having experienced the vagaries of a boom-and-bust economy, Albertans are nothing if not resilient: testament to their entrepreneurial capacity is that the proportion of nonprofit organizations reporting an increase in earned income grew almost threefold from 14 per cent in 2009 to 39 per cent in 2013 (CCVO 2013).

The neoliberal underpinnings of the Klein reforms shaped Alberta's political economy and the characteristics of its nonprofit sector in lasting and challenging ways. At the same time the provincial context has continued to evolve in dynamic and multifaceted ways. These shifting contours have created spaces where socially progressive developments could take root in government policy.

A New Legacy?

Three important developments took place during the post-Klein period from 2007 to 2014 that exemplify the beginning of a potential shift in Alberta's policy landscape: the plan to end homelessness, the initiative to reduce poverty, and the development of a social policy framework.

Plan to end homelessness

In 2008 the Alberta Secretariat for Action on Homelessness was given a mandate by the Stelmach government to develop a ten-year strategic plan outlining "a comprehensive, co-ordinated and sustainable approach" to ending homelessness in the province – including goals, timelines, and financial requirements (Alberta 2008b). The plan the Secretariat developed supports community-led action, coordinates province-wide efforts on homelessness, and sets out a series of actions aimed at shifting the work of agencies, communities, and governments that service the homeless away from simply managing homelessness and towards ending it through a "Housing First" philosophy. Under Housing First, investments are to focus on moving homeless Albertans from streets and shelters into permanent housing; helping rehoused clients obtain the assistance they need to restore their stability and maintain their housing; and preventing homelessness through emergency assistance and by providing adequate and accessible government programs and services to Albertans.

The total cost of the plan was an estimated $315 million over fiscal years 2009/10 to 2011/12, including $123 million for outreach support services under the Housing First program. The Ministry of Human Services subsequently provided over $192 million to support the construction of 1,964 housing units for the homeless. The strategy is complemented by a research consortium that supports the gathering and analysis of evidence of the effects of the program and the nature of homelessness among vulnerable subpopulations.

According to the three-year progress report released in January 2013 (Alberta 2013e), 5,926 homeless Albertans had been housed and given the supports they needed to remain housed by nearly 70 community human services agencies in 7 communities throughout the province. The 2013 progress report also stated that 80 per cent of Housing First clients had remained housed for at least twelve months, and that 1,455 people had "graduated" from Housing First programs and achieved housing stability. This is a significant statistic given that 44 per cent of all Housing First clients are considered to be chronically homeless – that is, they have been continually homeless for a year or more or have been homeless at least four times in the past three years. Even more revealing is that interactions with Emergency Medical Services by Housing First clients were reduced by 72 per cent, emergency room visits by 69 per cent, and days in hospital by 72 per cent. In addition, interactions with police were reduced by 66 per cent, days in jail by 88 per cent, and court appearances by 69 per cent (Alberta 2013e).

In February 2013 the provincial government established the Alberta Interagency Council on Homelessness to identify barriers to the success of the ten-year plan, develop solutions, provide strategic advice to the government based on community input and participation, and report annually on progress made. The Council is accountable to the Minister of Human Services (Alberta 2015). In fiscal year 2013/14, $111 million was allocated to eliminating homelessness; by then, approximately 8,800 people had been provided with housing and other supports since 2009 (Alberta 2014a).

Poverty-reduction strategy

A complementary development to the Housing First initiative is the strategy to reduce poverty in Alberta. In February 2011 a nonprofit initiative, Action to End Poverty in Alberta (AEPA), was created with funding from the Inter-City Forum on Social Policy to develop and implement a comprehensive poverty-reduction strategy and action plan in the province by working collaboratively with governments, communities, and people experiencing poverty. In August 2012 AEPA became part of Momentum, one of Canada's most successful community economic development organizations (Action to End Poverty in Alberta n.d.), and in March 2015 the poverty-reduction networks of AEPA, Vibrant Communities Calgary, and the Family and Community Support Services Association of Alberta joined to create the Alberta

Poverty Reduction Network, with goals including championing poverty reduction locally, provincially, and nationally, sharing information and activities across the province, and supporting the provincial government in the development of a provincial strategy (Brown 2015).

In February 2012 AEPA and Vibrant Communities Calgary co-published *Poverty Costs*, a report that posits that poverty costs Albertans as much as $9.5 billion per year in public services such as health care, crime, lost economic opportunities for persons living in poverty, and unrealized tax revenue (Briggs and Lee 2012). The report was positively received by the Redford government: poverty reduction was one of eight priority transformational initiatives (in addition to developing the ten-year plan to end homelessness) identified in the province's Social Policy Framework (Alberta 2013a). A follow-up report, *Poverty Costs 2.0* (Hudson 2013), provides specific recommendations to improve existing policies and legislation in ten "poverty policy" areas, and identifies systems for implementing, monitoring and evaluating a comprehensive provincial poverty reduction strategy. Once again, the report was favourably received by the provincial government. An update to the report, *Poverty Costs 2.5* (Hudson 2015), revises the most recent statistics, and refines policy recommendations to reflect the new data and provincial realities such as the implementation of regional Family and Community Engagement Councils to identify and develop solutions for regional social issues.

Supported by the research and advocacy of groups such as AEPA, the Alberta government made the commitment to work with communities to eliminate child poverty in five years and reduce overall poverty in ten years. Under the banner *Together We Raise Tomorrow*, public engagement on the development of an Alberta Children's Charter, a poverty-reduction strategy, and early childhood development took place from June to October 2013 (Alberta n.d.b). Subsequently, the ten policy domains identified in *Poverty Costs 2.0* were adapted into seven policy focus areas, and public input was once again invited in the development of a comprehensive, policy-focused strategy (Alberta n.d.a). At the time of writing, no further updates were available on the government's website on specific activities or progress in this area.

The Social Policy Framework

Arguably one of the most significant developments in the post-Klein social policy arena was the creation of Alberta's Social Policy Framework, first announced as part of Redford's campaign promises for the April 2012 provincial elections, to guide the future of Alberta's social policy and programs. Both the plan to end homelessness and the poverty-reduction strategy have been aligned with the principles put forward in this broad framework.

In 2010 the Alberta College of Social Workers (ACSW) published a thoroughly researched document that recommended the adoption of a new social policy paradigm for the province (ACSW 2010). When province-wide consultations were held between June and November 2012 to develop the social policy framework, the ACSW was able to use its own report to provide direct input into the draft framework and to encourage a wide range of affiliated and associated human services organizations to do the same.

The final version of the Social Policy Framework, released on 28 February 2013 (Alberta 2013a), mirrors many of the concerns raised by the ACSW. These include the growing complexity of and the need for organizational collaboration; the increasing cost of living; increasing income disparity; changing technologies and expectations of government; and demographic change and sustainability. The Framework's guiding principles are the need for dignity, putting people first, building healthy and strong communities, accepting mutual responsibility, promoting inclusion, and being proactive, collaborative, and accountable. The Framework articulates four overarching goals: protect the vulnerable; reduce inequality; create a person-centred system of high-quality services; and enable collaboration and partnerships. Individuals, families, communities, and the private, nonprofit, and government sectors are all seen as having important roles and responsibilities in contributing to the achievement of the Framework's outcomes. The roles and responsibilities identified for the nonprofit and voluntary sector, specifically, include: providing opportunities for citizen participation and inclusion; delivering social services and supports that are responsive to local needs; acting as a bridge between government and the public; providing a venue for collaboration and knowledge-sharing; assisting communities to develop localized responses; convening groups around shared interests and building community capacity; and championing the vision, principles, and outcomes of the Framework (Alberta 2013a).

Alberta's Social Policy Framework is a broad policy document that would have few detractors in the context of the Framework itself, particularly among the community human services sector, and reaction to it has been generally positive. In addition to the plan to end homelessness and the poverty-reduction strategy, other government programs, such as the transformation of services to adults with developmental disabilities (Alberta 2014b) have since been in the process of aligning their vision and activities with the new Framework.

These developments show that, when a government sets its mind to making a difference and allocating the necessary tools and resources to accomplish clearly defined goals, progress can be made – even in a seemingly hegemonic neoliberal regime. The examples support the argument that neoliberalism's manifestations are heterogeneous, capable of internal variety and complexity, depending on the changing socio-political considerations of political leaders and policymakers (Pierson 2000), as they are influenced – in these examples in particular – by the numerous and consistent efforts of nonprofit sector and community advocates.

Conclusion

The Klein reforms dramatically shaped the institutional landscape of Alberta's nonprofit sector, and left a policy legacy that profoundly affected the daily lives of average Albertans. Social and economic inequality grew even as the province enjoyed extraordinary economic growth. When faced with the challenging outcomes of the Klein reforms, Alberta's nonprofit organizations responded proactively by increasing their focus on marketing and public relations, working more closely with one another, and diversifying their funding sources by initiating commercial ventures to a greater extent than their counterparts in other provinces. In 2013 13 per cent of Alberta's nonprofits reported that they had increased their advocacy efforts in the previous year despite comments from federal ministers and senators questioning the legitimacy of charities participating in advocacy (CCVO 2013). This "can-do" attitude is embedded in the Albertan cultural psyche. The nonprofit sector also played important roles in pushing the government and supporting it to develop numerous progressive initiatives.

Are these developments evidence of a new social policy legacy for Alberta? Historical institutionalism tells us that positive feedback mechanisms that reinforce such changes are critical to the long-term adoption of a new regime, and that "critical junctures" are fraught with not one, but several policy alternatives vying for longevity and sustainability (Pierson 2000). Alberta's heavy economic dependence on volatile commodities for its revenues and a population historically opposed to taxes create a constant tension between prudent fiscal management and progressive social policies, making it difficult to predict the future of the province's social policy.

Now more than ever since the start of the Klein reforms, however, there are grounds for much optimism. On 5 May 2015 Albertans voted into power a majority New Democratic Party government under the leadership of Rachel Notley, emphatically ending forty-four consecutive years of PC Party dominance in the provincial legislature (*CBC News* 2015). Although the reasons for this historic shift in what has been considered Canada's most conservative province have yet to be analysed fully, many consider it to be the result of widespread anger at Premier Jim Prentice's "bad news" budget, which was seen as negatively affecting average Albertans and small businesses while leaving corporations unscathed (Johnson 2015).

For Alberta's nonprofit sector, this might be the right time to reinforce a new policy direction in both innovative and collaborative ways, with a government that, in theory, should have a socially progressive agenda. Given the sector's resource challenges, however, it will have to reach to seize this opportunity. It remains to be seen whether and how the province's nonprofit sector takes advantage of the opportunity present in the shifting sands of the current political landscape to forge a path to a new funding regime and a revitalized relationship with government.

NOTES

1 The Klein agenda may be seen as both neoliberal and neoconservative. Neoconservatives support public security, traditional morality, and hierarchical relations. Neoconservative manifestations include military intervention, tough law enforcement, attachment to "family values," and opposition to multiculturalism (Steger and Roy 2010). Many commentators (such as Albo 2002; Clark 2002; Harrison 2005) view neoliberal economic imperatives as the *primary* drivers and shapers underlying the overarching assumptions of, and approach to, the Klein reforms. Other commentators (such as Dacks, Green, and Trimble 1995; Denis 1995) rightly point to the neoconservatism in the application of the reforms to specific policy areas such social welfare, income support, and child care.

2 The increase in Alberta's cumulative per capita debt was at least 340 per cent, and even higher if one applies proper accounting to liabilities. The next-closest provincial increase over the same period was that of Quebec, at 42 per cent (Mansell 1997).

3 In fiscal year 1985/86 natural resource revenues accounted for 37 per cent
   of total government revenues; by 1990/91 this proportion had dropped
   significantly to just 19 per cent.
4 By 1992 the government had written off $2.4 billion in losses due to the
   failure of these initiatives (Mansell 1997).
5 The specific legislation was the Balanced Budget and Debt Retirement Act,
   requiring the elimination of the debt by fiscal year 2021/22; the Deficit
   Elimination Act, requiring the deficit to be eliminated by 1996/97; and the
   Alberta Taxpayer Protection Act, requiring a referendum to approve the
   introduction of a sales tax.
6 The amounts are obtained from Alberta (2006a), which reports the
   amounts in nominal dollars, restated on a 2005/06 basis. Per capita
   changes have been calculated using these amounts, divided by the annual
   population estimates for the relevant years provided by Statistics Canada
   (CANSIM database, table 051-0001).
7 The Alberta Sustainability Fund was established in 2003 to protect program spending from revenue volatility and annual cash deficits. Since
   fiscal year 2008/09, the fund has helped maintain funding for priority
   programs.
8 The presentation in this section of the chapter is derived primarily from
   ACSW (2010). Chapter co-author Lori Sigurdson was a member of the advisory committee for that document, and has been acknowledged as having provided significant input into its creation.

REFERENCES

Action to End Poverty in Alberta. n.d. "About Us." Calgary. Available online
   at http://www.actiontoendpovertyinalberta.org/about-us; accessed 26
   April 2013.
ACSW (Alberta College of Social Workers). 2010. *ACSW Social Policy Framework
   2010: Visioning a More Equitable and Just Alberta.* Edmonton: ACSW.
Alberta. 1997. "Economic Overview." In *Budget 1997: Building Alberta Together.*
   Edmonton: Alberta Finance. Available online at http://www.finance.
   alberta.ca/publications/budget/budget1997-2000/1997/economic.pdf;
   accessed 4 October 2012.
———. 2003. "Historical Fiscal Summary, 1985–86 to 2005–06." In *Budget
   2003: Making Alberta Even Better.* Edmonton: Alberta Finance. Available
   online at http://www.finance.alberta.ca/publications/budget/
   budget2003/fiscal.pdf; accessed 4 October 2012.

———. 2005. "Highlights of the Government of Alberta Annual Report 2004–05." Edmonton. Available online at http://www.finance.alberta.ca/publications/annual_repts/govt/ganrep05/highlights.pdf; accessed 4 October 2012.

———. 2006a. "Historical Fiscal Summary, 1985–86 to 2005–06." In *Government of Alberta Annual Report 2005-06. Executive Summary – Investing in the Next Alberta.* Edmonton. Available online at http://www.finance.alberta.ca/publications/annual_repts/govt/ganrep06/execsumm.pdf; accessed 20 May 2015.

———. 2006b. "Stelmach issues mandates for cabinet team members." News release. Edmonton. 19 December. Available online at http://alberta.ca/release.cfm?xID=209149C8DA42D-B5BD-1F00-52A0A0AB234256AE; accessed 10 February 2013.

———. 2007a. "Fiscal Plan 2007–10." In *Budget 2007: Managing Our Growth.* Edmonton: Alberta Finance. Available online at http://www.finance.alberta.ca/publications/budget/budget2007/fiscal.pdf; accessed 4 October 2012.

———. 2007b. *Government of Alberta Annual Report 2006–07.* Edmonton. Available online at http://www.finance.alberta.ca/publications/annual_repts/govt/ganrep07/execsumm.pdf; accessed 4 October 2012.

———. 2007c. "The New Royalty Framework." Edmonton. Available online at http://www.energy.alberta.ca/Org/Publications/royalty_Oct25.pdf; accessed 10 February 2013.

———. 2008a. "Annual Report 2007–2008: Preface, Accountability Statement and Executive Summary." Edmonton. Available online at http://www.finance.alberta.ca/publications/annual_repts/govt/ganrep08/execsumm.pdf; accessed 4 October 2012.

———. 2008b. Alberta Secretariat for Action on Homelessness. *A Plan for Alberta: Ending Homelessness in 10 Years.* Edmonton.

———. 2009a. "Annual Report 2008–2009: Preface, Accountability Statement and Executive Summary." Edmonton. Available online at http://www.finance.alberta.ca/publications/annual_repts/govt/ganrep09/execsumm.pdf.

———. 2009b. "Province announces three-point incentive program for energy sector." News release. Edmonton. 3 March. Available online at http://www.alberta.ca/release.cfm?xID=25402CDEFE818-F1BC-5D66-DF309066E457F2A4; accessed 10 February 2013.

———. 2010a. "Alberta stimulates new energy investment, new technologies." News release. Edmonton. 27 May. Available online at http://alberta.ca/release.cfm?xID=28441DB838B27-0336-BB5C-D5EDFEDE158ED1F6.

100   Sonpal-Valias, Sigurdson, and Elson

———. 2010b. "Consolidated Financial Statements of the Government of Alberta, Annual report 2009–2010." Edmonton. Available online at http://www.finance.alberta.ca/publications/annual_repts/govt/ganrep10/confinst.pdf; accessed 4 October 2012.

———. 2010c. "2010–13 Fiscal Plan." In *Budget 2010: Striking the Right Balance.* Edmonton. Available online at http://www.finance.alberta.ca/publications/budget/budget2010/fiscal-plan-overview.pdf; accessed 4 October 2012.

———. 2011. "Consolidated Financial Statements of the Government of Alberta, Annual Report 2010–2011." Edmonton. Available online at http://www.finance.alberta.ca/publications/annual_repts/govt/ganrep11/goa-2010-11-annual-report-financial-statements.pdf; accessed 3 October 2012.

———. 2012a. "Consolidated Financial Statements of the Government of Alberta, Annual Report 2011–2012." Edmonton. Available online at http://www.finance.alberta.ca/publications/annual_repts/govt/ganrep12/goa-2011-12-annual-report-financial-statements.pdf; accessed 4 October 2012.

———. 2012b. "Consolidated Financial Statements of the Government of Alberta, Annual Report 2011–2012: Executive Summary." Edmonton. Available online at http://www.finance.alberta.ca/publications/annual_repts/govt/ganrep12/goa-2011-12-annual-report-executive-summary.pdf; accessed 20 May 2015.

———. 2012c. "Dollars and Sense. Backgrounder B: Alberta's Current Savings Framework and Savings Accounts." Edmonton. Available online at http://www.finance.alberta.ca/business/budget/BackgrounderB-Alberta-Current-Savings-Framework-and-Savings-Accounts.pdf; accessed 3 October 2012.

———. 2012d. "Fiscal Plan Overview." In *Budget 2012: Investing in People.* Edmonton. Available online at http://www.finance.alberta.ca/publications/budget/budget2012/fiscal-plan-overview.pdf; accessed 16 February 2012.

Alberta. 2012e. "Fiscal Plan Tables." In *Budget 2012: Investing in People.* Edmonton. Available online at http://www.finance.alberta.ca/publications/budget/budget2012/fiscal-plan-tables.pdf; accessed 4 October 2012.

———. 2012f. Alberta Enterprise and Advanced Education. *Highlights of the Alberta Economy 2012.* Edmonton.

———. 2013a. *Alberta's Social Policy Framework.* Available online at http://socialpolicyframework.alberta.ca/files/documents/ahs-nonannotatedfrmwrk-webfinal.pdf.

————. 2013b. *Budget 2013: Responsible Change – Overview.* Edmonton. Available online at http://www.finance.alberta.ca/publications/budget/budget2013/fiscal-plan-overview.pdf; accessed 17 April 2013.

Alberta. 2013c. Alberta Human Services. "Building Families and Communities Act." Available online at http://www.qp.alberta.ca/documents/Acts/b07p5.pdf; accessed 1 November 2013.

————. 2013d. "Consolidated Financial Statements of the Government of Alberta, Annual Report 2012–2013: Executive Summary." Edmonton. Available online at http://www.finance.alberta.ca/publications/annual_repts/govt/ganrep13/goa-2012-13-annual-report-executive-summary.pdf; accessed 20 May 2015.

————. 2013e. Alberta Secretariat for Action on Homelessness. *A Plan for Alberta: Ending Homelessness in 10 Years, 3 Year Progress Report.* Edmonton.

————. 2014a. "Consolidated Financial Statements of the Government of Alberta, Annual Report 2013–2014: Executive Summary." Edmonton. Available online at http://www.finance.alberta.ca/publications/annual_repts/govt/ganrep14/goa-2013-14-annual-report-executive-summary.pdf; accessed 20 May 2015.

————. 2014b. Alberta Human Services. "Transforming the PDD Program within the Context of Disability Services." Edmonton. Available online at at http://humanservices.alberta.ca/documents/PDD/pdd-transformation-plan-august-2014.pdf; accessed 21 October 2014.

————. 2015. Alberta Human Services. "Alberta Interagency Council on Homelessness." Edmonton. Available online at http://www.humanservices.alberta.ca/homelessness/16051.html; accessed 25 May 2015.

————. n.d.a. "Policy Domains." Available online at http://povertyreduction.alberta.ca/Strategies/Policy_Domains; accessed 25 May 2015.

————. n.d.b. "Together We Raise Tomorrow: Alberta's Poverty Reduction Strategy." Available online at http://povertyreduction.alberta.ca/Main_Page; accessed 25 May 2015.

Albo, G. 2002. "Neoliberalism, the State, and the Left: A Canadian Perspective." *Monthly Review* 54 (1): 46–55. http://dx.doi.org/10.14452/MR-054-01-2002-05_4.

Baines, D. 2004. "Caring for Nothing: Work Organizations and Unwaged Labor in Social Services." *Work, Employment and Society* 18 (2): 267–95. http://dx.doi.org/10.1177/09500172004042770.

Bode, I. 2006. "Disorganized Welfare Mixes: Voluntary Agencies and New Governance Regimes in Western Europe." *Journal of European Social Policy* 16 (4): 346–59. http://dx.doi.org/10.1177/0958928706068273.

Boothe, P. 1997. "The new Approach to Budgeting in Alberta." In *A Government Reinvented: A Study of Alberta's Deficit Elimination Program*, ed. C.J. Bruce, R.D. Kneebone, and K.J. McKenzie, 216–30. Don Mills, ON: Oxford University Press.

Briggs, A., and C.R. Lee. 2012. *Poverty Costs: An Economic Case for a Preventative Poverty Reduction Strategy in Alberta*. Calgary: Vibrant Communities Calgary and Action to End Poverty in Alberta.

Brown, M. 2015. "AEPA February Update." Calgary: Action to End Poverty in Alberta, 10 March. Available online at http://www. actiontoendpovertyinalberta.org/news; accessed 25 May 2015.

Brownsey, K. 2005. "Ralph Klein and the Hollowing of Alberta." In *The Return of the Trojan Horse: Alberta and the New World (Dis)order*, ed. T.W. Harrison, 23–36. Montreal: Black Rose Books.

Calgary Homeless Foundation. 2009. *The Homeless among Us. Calgary Homeless Foundation. Report to Community 2009*. http://calgaryhomeless.com; accessed 3 November 2015.

CBC News. 2006. "Ralph Klein: Alberta's populist premier." 12 September. Available online at http://www.cbc.ca/news2/background/klein-ralph/; accessed 12 February 2013.

———. 2014a. "Alberta premier Dave Hancock stepping down from legislature." 12 September. Available online at http://www.cbc.ca/news/canada/edmonton/alberta-premier-dave-hancock-stepping-down-from-legislature-1.2764524; accessed 25 May 2015.

———. 2014b. "Alison Redford resigning as Alberta premier." 19 March. Available online at http://www.cbc.ca/news/canada/edmonton/alison-redford-resigning-as-alberta-premier-1.2579356; accessed 20 May 2015.

———. 2015. "Alberta election 2015 results: NDP wave sweeps across province in historic win." Available online at http://www.cbc.ca/news/elections/alberta-votes/alberta-election-2015-results-ndp-wave-sweeps-across-province-in-historic-win-1.3062605; accessed 25 May 2015.

CCVO (Calgary Chamber of Voluntary Organizations). 2013. *2013 Alberta Nonprofit Survey*. Calgary.

Clark, D. 2002. "Neoliberalism and Public Service Reform: Canada in Comparative Perspective." *Canadian Journal of Political Science* 35 (4): 771–93. http://dx.doi.org/10.1017/S0008423902778438.

Dacks, G., J. Green, and L. Trimble. 1995. "Road Kill: Women in Alberta's Drive toward Deficit Elimination." In *The Trojan Horse: Alberta and the Future of Canada*, ed. T. Harrison and G. Laxer, 270–85. Montreal: Black Rose Books.

Dart, R., and B. Zimmerman. 2000. "After Government Cuts: Insights from Two Ontario Enterprising Nonprofits." In *The Nonprofit Sector in Canada:*

Roles and Relationships, ed. K.G. Banting, 107–48. Montreal; Kingston, ON: McGill-Queen's University Press.

Denis, C. 1995. "'Government Can Do Whatever It Wants': Moral Regulation in Ralph Klein's Alberta." *Canadian Review of Sociology and Anthropology* 32 (3): 365–83. http://dx.doi.org/10.1111/j.1755-618X.1995.tb00777.x.

Kolkman, J., and Edmonton Social Planning Council. 2007. "Standing Still in a Booming Economy: Finding Solutions for Low Income Working Households." Edmonton: Edmonton Social Planning Council.

Emery, J.C.H. 1997. "New Directions? Government Spending Cuts and Alberta's Institutional Resilience in Advanced Education." In *A Government Reinvented: A Study of Alberta's Deficit Elimination Program*, ed. C.J. Bruce, R.D. Kneebone, and K.J. McKenzie, 340–68. Don Mills, ON: Oxford University Press.

Evans, B.M., and J. Shields. 1998. "'Reinventing' the Third Sector: Alternative Service Delivery, Partnerships and the New Public Administration of the Canadian Post-welfare State." Working Paper 9. Toronto: Ryerson University, Centre for Voluntary Sector Studies. Available online at http://www.ryerson.ca/~cvss/WP09.pdf; accessed 26 February 2012.

–––––. 2000. "Neoliberal Restructuring and the Third Sector: Reshaping Governance, Civil Society and Local Relations." Working Paper 13. Toronto: Ryerson University, Centre for Voluntary Sector Studies. Available online at http://www.ryerson.ca/~cvss/WP13.pdf; accessed 26 February 2012.

Evans, B., T. Richmond, and J. Shields. 2005. "Structuring Neoliberal Governance: The Nonprofit Sector, Emerging New Modes of Control and the Marketisation of Service Delivery." *Policy and Society* 24 (1): 73–97. http://dx.doi.org/10.1016/S1449-4035(05)70050-3.

Finkel, A. 2006. *Social Policy and Practice in Canada: A History*. Waterloo, ON: Wilfrid Laurier University Press.

Fong, P. 2009. "A 'wildrose' is blooming in Alberta: After nearly 40 years of Conservative rule, a new right-wing party is shaking up the province." *Toronto Star*, 24 December, A14.

–––––. 2012. "Undecided voters key to Redford's triumph: Turnout in election Monday was Alberta's highest in two decades." *Toronto Star*, 25 April, A6.

Gazso, A., and H. Krahn. 2008. "Out of Step or Leading the Parade? Public Opinion about Support Policy in Alberta, 1995 and 2004." *Journal of Canadian Studies* 42 (1): 154–78.

Gibson, D. 2007. *Spoils of the Boom*. Edmonton: Parkland Institute.

Hall, M.H., C.W. Barr, M. Easwaramoorthy, S.W. Sokolowski, and L.M. Salamon. 2005. *The Canadian Nonprofit and Voluntary Sector in Comparative Perspective*. Toronto: Imagine Canada.

Harrison, T.W. 2005. "Introduction." In *The Return of the Trojan Horse: Alberta and the New World (Dis)order*, ed. T.W. Harrison, 1–20. Montreal: Black Rose Books.

Harvey, D. 2005. *A Brief History of Neoliberalism*. Oxford: Oxford University Press.

Horne, T. 2005. "From Manning to Mazankowski and Beyond: Alberta's Fight to Privatize Health Care." In *The Return of the Trojan Horse: Alberta and the New World (Dis)order*, ed. T.W. Harrison, 215–35. Montreal: Black Rose Books.

Hudson, C. 2013. *Poverty Costs 2.0: Investing in Albertans*. Calgary: Vibrant Communities Calgary and Action to End Poverty in Alberta.

———. 2015. *Poverty Costs 2.5: Investing in Albertans*, rev. ed. Calgary: Vibrant Communities Calgary and Action to End Poverty in Alberta. Available online at https://d3n8a8pro7vhmx.cloudfront. net/actiontoendpovertyinalberta/pages/19/attachments/ original/1421860062/569b482d06.compressed.pdf?1421860062; accessed 25 May 2015.

Jenson, J., and S.D. Phillips. 2000. "Distinctive Trajectories: Homecare and the Voluntary Sector in Quebec and Ontario." In *The Nonprofit Sector in Canada: Roles and Relationships*, ed. K.G. Banting, 29–68. Montreal; Kingston, ON: McGill-Queen's University Press.

Johnson, T. 2015. "Business community mixed on Alberta budget." *CBC News*, 26 March 2015. Available online at http://www.cbc.ca/news/business/busi ness-community-mixed-on-alberta-budget-1.3011405; accessed 25 May 2015.

Kneebone, R.D., and K.J. McKenzie. 1997. "The Process behind Institutional Reform in Alberta." In *A Government Reinvented: A Study of Alberta's Deficit Elimination Program*, ed. C.J. Bruce, R.D. Kneebone, and K.J. McKenzie, 176–210. Don Mills, ON: Oxford University Press.

Kus, B. 2006. "Neoliberalism, Institutional Change and the Welfare State: The Case of Britain and France." *International Journal of Comparative Sociology* 47 (6): 488–525. http://dx.doi.org/10.1177/0020715206070268.

Lisac, M. 1995. *The Klein Revolution*. Edmonton: NeWest Press.

Mansell, R.L. 1997. "Fiscal Restructuring in Alberta: An Overview." In *A Government Reinvented: A Study of Alberta's Deficit Elimination Program*, ed. C.J. Bruce, R.D. Kneebone, and K.J. McKenzie, 16–73. Don Mills, ON: Oxford University Press.

Meinhard, A., and M. Foster. 2001. "Responses of Canada's Voluntary Organizations to Shifts in Social Policy: A Provincial Perspective." Working Paper 19. Toronto: Ryerson University, Centre for Voluntary Sector Studies. Available online at http://www.ryerson.ca/cvss/files/ WP19COVER.pdf.

National Council of Welfare. 2006. *Welfare Incomes 2005*. Ottawa. Available online at http://www.cmha.ca/public_policy/national-council-of-welfare-welfare-incomes-2005/.

Parkland Institute. 2012. "Fact Sheet: Women's Equality a Long Way Off in Alberta." Edmonton.

PC Party of Alberta. 2012. "Alberta by Design: The Progressive Conservative Party of Alberta – Election Platform 2012." Edmonton. Available online at http://www.auma.ca/live/digitalAssets/63/63837_ACFA9AB.pdf; accessed 20 May 2015.

Pierson, P. 1996. "The New Politics of the Welfare State." *World Politics* 48 (02): 143–79. http://dx.doi.org/10.1353/wp.1996.0004.

———. 2000. "Increasing Returns, Path Dependence, and the Study of Politics." *American Political Science Review* 94 (2): 251–67. http://dx.doi.org/10.2307/2586011.

Pratt, S. 2007. "Stelmach gov't takes first steps towards democratic reform; but will the changes really make the Tories listen to opposing views?" *Edmonton Journal*, 6 May, A16.

Public Interest Alberta and Edmonton Social Planning Council. 2009. *We Must Do Better: It's Time to Make Alberta Poverty-free*. Edmonton.

Ray, R., and J. Schmitt. 2007. *No-vacation Nation*. Washington, DC: Centre for Economic & Policy Research.

Sampert, S. 2005. "King Ralph, the Ministry of Truth, and the Media in Alberta." In *The Return of the Trojan Horse: Alberta and the New World (Dis)order*, ed. T.W. Harrison, 37–51. Montreal: Black Rose Books.

Scott, K. 2003. *Funding Matters: The Impact of Canada's New Funding Regime on Nonprofit and Voluntary Organizations, Summary Report*. Ottawa: Canadian Council on Social Development.

Shedd, M.S. 1997. "Family and Social Services, the Alberta Deficit Elimination Program, and Welfare Reform." In *A Government Reinvented: A Study of Alberta's Deficit Elimination Program*, ed. C.J. Bruce, R.D. Kneebone, and K.J. McKenzie, 250–74. Don Mills, ON: Oxford University Press.

Statistics Canada. 2008. "Aboriginal Population Profile, (2006 Census)." Ottawa. Available online at http://www12.statcan.ca/census-recensement/2006/dp-pd/prof/92-594/index.cfm?Lang=E.

Steger, M.B., and R.K. Roy. 2010. *Neoliberalism: A Very Short Introduction*. New York: Oxford University Press. http://dx.doi.org/10.1093/actrade/9780199560516.001.0001.

Taylor, A., L. Shultz, and D.W. Leard. 2005. "A New Regime of Accountability for Alberta's Public Schools." In *The Return of the Trojan Horse: Alberta and the New World (Dis)order*, ed. T.W. Harrison, 236–53. Montreal: Black Rose Books.

Terry, A. 2009. "Boom to bust: an economic timeline of Alberta."
    Global National, 7 April. Available online at http://web.archive.org/
    web/20090509201344/http://www.globaltv.com/globaltv/national/story.
    html?id=1474369; accessed 5 October 2012.
Thomson, G. 2010. "As years go, 2010 likely better off gone; Stelmach not
    predicting 2011 party – but maybe he'll get smoother ride." *Edmonton
    Journal*, 21 December, A16.
Wilkinson, R., and K. Pickett. 2010. *The Spirit Level: Why Greater Equality Makes
    Societies Stronger*. New York: Bloomsbury Press.
Wilsford, D. 1994. "Path Dependency, or Why History Makes It Difficult but
    Not Impossible to Reform Health Care Systems in a Big Way." *Journal of
    Public Policy* 14 (3): 251–83. http://dx.doi.org/10.1017/S0143814X00007285.
Wingrove, J. 2013. "Alberta's largest unions warn of cuts to public service."
    Globe and Mail, 4 March. Available online at http://www.afl.org/tags/
    collective_bargaining?page=3; accessed 20 May 20 2015.
Wingrove, J., R. D'Aliesio, and N. Vanderklippe. 2011. "Conservative
    showdown prompts Stelmach's resignation." *Globe and Mail*, 25 January.
    Available online at http://www.theglobeandmail.com/news/politics/
    conservative-showdown-prompts-stelmachs-resignation/article563505/;
    accessed 12 August 2012.
Yalnizyan, A. 2007. *The Rich and the Rest of Us: The Changing Face of Canada's
    Growing Gap*. Ottawa: Canadian Centre for Policy Alternatives.

5 Alberta's Persons with Developmental Disabilities Community Governance Act and the System to Provide Services

KEITH SEEL

One dimension of Alberta's social policy landscape that commands particular attention concerns people living with a developmental disability. This case study is presented through the specific lens of the Persons with Developmental Disabilities Act (PDD), a piece of legislation that, for a variety of reasons, has been under government and public scrutiny since its proclamation on 30 June 2006. The Persons with Developmental Disabilities Community Governance Act (RSA 2000) expired on 31 December 2010, but continued in force pending the results of an administrative review process undertaken by then-Minister Mary Ann Jablonski. It is this administrative review and its aftermath that underpins this case study.

In Alberta approximately 9,300 adult individuals qualify for services under the PDD Community Governance Act. On average across the six regions of the province, the annual cost per person covered by the Act is $63,274. For the fiscal year ended 31 March 2010, the PDD Community Boards spent $586.1 million, an increase of $21.7 million from the previous year (Alberta 2011b, 38). With provincial revenues falling and program costs increasing, the Alberta government reviewed human services costs with an eye to reducing expenditures. Management consulting firm KPMG was retained to conduct the administrative review of the PDD program for the minister responsible.

The PDD Administrative Review: Terms of Reference

The purpose of the administrative review, which commenced on 15 June 2010, was twofold (Alberta 2010, 1):

- to identify efficiencies and savings in PDD program administration (both internal and service provider administration) to address program cost pressures, so as to redirect funds to frontline services delivery; and
- to identify longer-term strategies to increase the PDD program's administrative effectiveness and efficiency.

The review had two expected outcomes. First, it was hoped that the ministry could ensure that program funding was being allocated specifically to include persons with developmental disabilities in community life as independently as possible. This effectively restated the expectation of the focus of funding stipulated in the PDD Community Governance Act. Second, it was hoped that the review could ensure that the ministry could deliver a PDD program that was sustainable.

KPMG was tasked specifically with examining "the internal administrative operations of the PDD program (including the six Community Boards and the PDD Program Branch), and the administration costs of PDD-funded agencies contracted to provide services to PDD clients" (Alberta 2015b, para. 2).Two dimensions were targeted: internal PDD program administration costs and service provider administration costs. Further, two sets of comparisons were to be made: one between the PDD Community Boards in each of the province's six regions and the other between service provider agencies. As part of the review deliverables, KPMG was asked to make both short-term strategic recommendations and recommendations on "longer-term system changes to increase effectiveness and efficiency" (Alberta 2010, 1).

Reactions to the Administrative Review

Although the administrative review process is normal within the Alberta government as pieces of legislation approach their expiry date, the review of the PDD Community Governance Act drew special attention from service providers in the nonprofit sector and families of individuals covered by the act. They were concerned that, given the worldwide recession then under way, the provincial government would use the process as a way to rationalize cost cutting. The Alberta Association for Community Living, a strong provincial advocacy group for individuals with developmental disabilities, stated, "With respect to those Review recommendations which called for increasing the size of service providers, consolidating services and/or tendering services ...

These are not supported by Alberta Association for Community Living and would not be in the best interests of individuals with developmental disabilities and their families" (Alberta Association for Community Living 2011a, 2).

During most of the administrative review, responsibility for the act was that of the Ministry of Seniors and Community Supports. This ministry also had responsibility for the Assured Income for the Severely Handicapped (AISH) program, which "provides financial and health-related assistance to eligible adults with a disability. The disability must be permanent and substantially limit the person's ability to earn a living" (Alberta 2015a, para. 1). The ministry effectively controlled the income of adults with disabilities and the type, duration, and frequency of services they would be eligible to receive. The power of the ministry sensitized service providers, families, and individuals with disabilities to the potential scale of changes that an administrative review could bring about.

Despite their sensitivity to the review, collective action by service providers – most of which are nonprofit organizations – was absent. The author was involved with providers in Calgary at this time and with two initiatives that exemplify their reaction. First, in conjunction with PDD Calgary Regional Board, the Institute for Nonprofit Studies at Mount Royal University convened sessions to explore creating system structures (such as multiple service organizations); collective action between service providers (such as bulk purchasing or joint staff training); and joint service delivery models. After nearly three years of work and support, there was no example of sustained activity between two or more service providers. The primary reason given was lack of time; however, when probed, senior management often spoke of reluctance by the board of directors to move away from an autonomous, agency-centric model.

Second, for eighteen months a group of eight board chairs and vice-chairs of service providers met regularly to accomplish two goals: to learn about similarities and differences between the organizations with a view to building a trusting relationship, and to plan a course of action prior to the April 2013 implementation of new contracting processes arising from the administrative review. After the first year, however, they had agreed only to share annual reports – documents that were public in any case – with one another.

These two examples from the author's experience leading up to and during the administrative review highlight a fundamental barrier to collective action by service providers: the near-total lack of trust on which to build a relationship. Without trust each provider exists in its own autonomous reality, as strong or as vulnerable as that might be. The prevailing notion that the nonprofit sector is collaborative by nature is not born out in these cases.

The ministry's style of consultation and pattern of review drew additional criticism. Public Interest Alberta (2012) commented on the province's approach to seniors care by stating, "[t]he concept paper is not a seniors' care proposal, but rather a business proposal … It is designed to off-load the government's costs onto those who require medically necessary services and to enrich insurance companies and facility operators in the process." The concerns of public and nonprofit service providers deepened with the consultations that followed the release of the KPMG report (KPMG 2010a), with the Alberta Disabilities Forum (2012, 7), for example, criticizing them as "not designed to seek solutions, but rather to ask participants which option they deemed more beneficial. There was no opportunity to suggest new ideas."

Legislative authority

With the election of Alison Redford as premier in 2012, Alberta moved to align and rationalize its human services legislation, regulations, and policies. Dave Hancock, Minister of Human Services, and Associate Minister Frank Oberle had the responsibility to fulfil this daunting task. Specific to PDD, Oberle was given a mandate to ensure "the integration of disability programs and services, so persons with disabilities receive appropriate supports in the most efficient and effective manner" (Alberta 2012b; see Appendix A to this chapter for the government's summary of the PDD program). In brief the PDD program arose from the Persons with Developmental Disabilities Community Governance Act, which was intended to emphasize the dignity and equal worth of individuals with developmental disabilities and their right to exercise self-determination and to be included in community life. To that end, the act enables funding for services – supplemental to what families, friends, and the community already provide – to assist qualifying individuals to live as independently as possible. Through a regional governance structure, services (family managed or those provided by community service organizations and PDD Community Boards) are delivered across the province.

Findings of the Administrative Review

Although the full report makes for interesting reading, it is useful to provide a summary of the main findings of the KPMG report.

Administrative costs

Compared with those of other programs in Alberta and other jurisdictions that support individuals with disabilities or provide a similar resource, the administrative costs of the PDD program were high, with $31 spent on administration for every $100 spent on direct supports to individuals. Other programs in the province ran on $24 on administration for each $100 of direct services costs, while programs in other jurisdictions in Canada and the United States spent between $6 and $20 on administration for each $100 of direct support (KPMG 2010b, 6).[1]

Regional cost variations

After analysing total administrative costs by region and delivery mechanism, KPMG found that the average annual cost per year per individual ranged from $3,000 to $31,000. Community Boards' annual administrative costs per individual were between $2,000 and $4,900, while those of service providers ranged from $200 to $45,000 per individual, and the larger the organization, the lower were the administrative costs per individual.[2] On average, service providers had administrative costs per individual of $8,800, of which $3,600 was for expenditures such as supervisory costs of frontline staff and $5,200 was for agency administration. Depending on the delivery mechanism, administrative costs per individual per year ranged from a low of $370 for family managed supports to a high of $27,000 for direct operations (KPMG 2010b, 6–7).

Lack of a systemic approach

In 2009–10 the PDD program had contracts with 257 service providers and 935 family-managed administrators (KPMG 2010a, 8). One finding in particular is noteworthy: "The number of service providers contributes to lower efficiency through the duplication of corporate services (e.g., finance, human resources, etc.)" (7). In other words, that each of the

257 service providers duplicates essentially the same internal administrative processes is a considerable inefficiency that could be addressed through common systems. Associated with this was the finding that many service providers had unique or purpose-built systems, and relied heavily on more costly and less efficient manual records and processes. This cost was most apparent when an individual accessed services from more than one provider, with multiple and unique records and processes for the same individual jumping the average administrative cost for these individuals to $18,000 per year (8).[3]

KPMG concluded that the lack of a system focus had resulted in a "significant overlap in responsibilities and duplication across all levels" (KPMG 2010a, 8). Specifically:

- Each Community Board had its own unique operating and staffing model, so that a PDD staff's caseload ranged from 57 to 290 individuals depending on the region (9), a variation that was inexplicable since program funding, units of support, and the general range of individuals receiving support did not vary between regions.
- The PDD program's roles and responsibilities were unclear, and varied across regions (9) for no apparent reason, again given the lack of variation in program funding, units of service, or the range of individuals receiving support.
- PDD program staff lacked consistent skills in finance, analytics, forecasting, budgeting, and information technology across regions (9).
- There was uncoordinated and unclear monitoring across the PDD program. Besides compliance activities and the needed monitoring within PDD program regulations and policy, other ministries and agencies – such as Occupational Health and Safety and the Workers' Compensation Board – also monitored service providers. KPMG found that "[t]he PDD Program has not defined what standards and performance indicators should be monitored, the frequency with which they should be monitored, or who should perform the activity" (10). There was also no consolidated report of monitoring results.
- Information technology needs were not being met by the system then used by the program. A system designed in the late 1990s for payment had had additional functions added to it over the years, but, "it does not have the capability to act as an effective case

management system" (10). As well, there were concerns about the system's data integrity. Because of the system's inadequacy, program staff duplicated case files and other records and tracking documents. There was no single source for information on a client.

• There was a lack of information on the PDD program, including a description of its core business.

Underutilization of low-cost services delivery methods

KPMG found that the family-managed delivery of services option was used by just 10 per cent of individuals (KPMG 2010a, 12). Given that its administrative costs, on average, were just $500 per individual, this option could deliver significant cost savings if it were more widely used.

Summary of the administrative review

To conclude its review, KPMG offered five recommendations, of which four were accepted (see Appendix B):

1. dissolve the Community Boards;
2. establish an organizational model for provincial program delivery;
3. clarify and enhance contracting processes with service providers;
4. improve access and support for family-managed services; and
5. improve information technology systems.

Consultation with Families and Service Providers, June 2011

Following the KPMG review and its recommendation to clarify and enhance the contracting process, the Alberta government launched another component of the administrative review. A broad consultation was held in June 2011 with service providers, families, and self-advocates accessing the PDD program. Focus groups were held in each of the six regions (a total of twelve were convened). A discussion guide for participants provided the questions the government wished to ask (see Box 5.1). To quote the final report (Alberta 2011c, 1–2):

The focus groups conducted across the province were undertaken to discuss and obtain feedback on the recommendation to introduce improved contracting strategies to enhance the efficiency and effectiveness of the service provider network. Participants were advised that a new contracting process might have the following characteristics:

- A clear definition of the results expected from the service provided, based on the individual's needs.
- A new model for service provider contracts to ensure the best possible services and best value.
- A service delivery model that allows for cooperation between service providers. It will be important to build this service network together, with an aim to streamlining administrative processes and making a range of services easier to access.
- Key performance measures and monitoring and reporting expectations for all service contracts.

The focus group conversations were divided into three parts:

- Getting better at being outcomes-based
- Developing the best kind of contracting process to deliver on outcomes
- Looking at performance measurement and communications about performance

---

BOX 5.1 QUESTIONS ASKED AT FOCUS GROUP SESSIONS

Outcomes

1. How can service providers and contracts enable an outcome-based focus?
2. What's getting in the way of being outcome-based?

Contracts

1. What are the most important aspects of a contracting process?
2. What are things to avoid in a new contracting process?
3. What are the advantages/ disadvantages of competitive bidding?
4. What do you think about cooperation among service providers?

Performance Measurement

1. What should be measured?
2. What should be reported?
3. What needs to change about the system in order to become more performance based?

Self-Advocate Questions

1. What helps you to have a good life?
2. What doesn't help you to have a good life (what gets in the way)?
3. Do you feel comfortable talking to your service provider about your supports and how well they're doing?
4. What is the one thing you wish you could receive from your service provider?

Source: Alberta (2011a, 3–4).

The focus group results are interesting in that they generally show a heightened expectation of accountability, outcomes, greater efficiency, and tangible changes in people's lives. Of particular interest are results showing an expectation that service providers be more responsive, that they specialize, coordinate transitions between agencies, and reduce the administrative burden, that the PDD program be proactive, rather than reactive, that it is planned well into the future, and that there is a common understanding of its goals and outcomes.

In terms of anticipated changes to the contracting process, participants expressed concern that competitive contracting could result in the selection of the lowest-cost option, rather than of the most effective option. Although competitive bidding was seen as a way to create a more consistent and efficient set of services, concerns about it included a focus on business goals rather than personal goals, potential for instability in the services offered, the risk that families would have no voice in the selection of service providers, and the potential of creating a selection process with a greater administrative burden. Longer-term contracts were felt to provide stability in program services available to individuals. Families were also interested in knowing the substance of the contracts service providers had with the PDD program.

There was strong support for measurement, especially of performance with respect to both personal and service provider goals.

Families wanted greater access to monitoring and accreditation information on agencies. Clear roles and responsibilities, better communication, reduced administration, and strong relationships were deemed important changes to the system.

What Does This Case Tell Us?

The case of government-funded services for adults with developmental disabilities through the PDD Community Governance Act provides an insight into how the Alberta government is thinking about human services.

Inherent tension in the PDD Community Governance Act

Legislation is a balancing act of public good, economics, and social responsibility. The PDD Community Governance Act is no exception. Box 5.2 presents the preamble to the act, which is clear about the public good to be created and the social responsibility of government to individuals with developmental disabilities. Economics are not directly addressed in the preamble, but are raised in the role of the relevant minister. In particular the minister has the responsibility to "ensure that there is reasonable access, comprehensiveness and portability across regions in the delivery of services to adults with developmental disabilities" (PDD Community Governance Act, 9(1)(e)).

BOX 5.2 PREAMBLE TO THE PDD COMMUNITY GOVERNANCE ACT

WHEREAS it is important that adults with developmental disabilities have opportunities to exercise self-determination and to be fully included in community life;

WHEREAS the individual needs of adults with developmental disabilities are most effectively met through the provision of services that are based on equitable opportunity, funding and access to resources;

WHEREAS the Government of Alberta recognizes, values and supports the ability of communities to respond to the needs of adults with developmental disabilities;

> WHEREAS the Government has ongoing responsibility to ensure and oversee the provision of statutory programs, resources and services to adults with developmental disabilities; and
>
> WHEREAS statutory programs, resources and services are best provided to adults with developmental disabilities in a manner that acknowledges responsibility to the community and accountability to the Government through the Minister.

As is often the case, "reasonable" access, comprehensiveness, and portability are a matter of debate. One emerging patterns is that it is "reasonable" to give priority to individuals who are at greater risk or are more vulnerable – for example, medically fragile individuals. The idea of what is reasonable, however, is affected by the economics of the day. For example, when reductions in services were introduced in 2009, discretion was removed from the PDD program and henceforth only individuals with an IQ of less than 70 would be eligible for funding (Alberta n.d.a). The KPMG report (KPMG 2010a) strongly suggested that the amount of resources being expended on redundant, duplicate, ineffective, and inefficient administration was unreasonable. Indeed, the Alberta government's approval of three of the report's recommendations concerning a more efficient delivery system – specifically, to establish an organizational model for provincial program delivery, clarify and enhance the contracting processes with service providers, and improve information technology systems – demonstrated its desire for reduced administration expenditures.

Moving to outcomes and best value

The question of how to achieve a combination of services delivered at a frequency and for a duration that actually results in positive outcomes for each individual is an enormous challenge. Facing tightening budgets, various Alberta regions began to introduce pilot instruments that could be objective measures of outcomes based on quantified kinds of services. In 2008–09, for example, the Calgary and Edmonton regions piloted the use of a Supports Intensity Scale (SIS) (Alberta 2009, 24), which "measures support requirements in 57 life activities and 28 behavioral and medical areas" (Supports Intensity Scale 2012). Another pilot program. Introduced in Edmonton, was the My Life: Personal Outcomes Index, which "provides direct feedback about how well [the] Persons with Developmental Disabilities [program] and service providers contribute to the quality of life of individuals with developmental disabilities" (Alberta 2012a).

The SIS pilot eventually was incorporated into the PPD program, so that all individuals receiving program funding or applying to receive funding must have completed an SIS review. According to the program, "[t]he Supports Intensity Scale is designed to measure the frequency, amount and type of supports and individual needs to participate in areas such as home living, community living, lifelong learning, employment, health and safety, and social activities. Information from the SIS will be used by the Individual, and/or their guardian, and the PDD Community Board to identify specific areas of support required by the Individual." The SIS is now a key component of the Individual Service Agreement, which "identifies the type and amount of services to be provided and the benefits of the services to the Individual" (Alberta n.d.a).

There is no doubt that, with an objective measurement tool to determine the frequency, type, and amount of services an individual needs, the Alberta government is better able to procure specific amounts and types of services from providers. Where the past model encouraged agency control of services delivery – or at least did not intervene in the agency's determining what services it would offer – the new model of procuring only those services determined as necessary puts the government in control. Agencies now must provide the amount and type of service that the government, through contract, has determined it needs annually. Any services not in the contract, but still delivered by providers, will be neither funded nor subsidized, leading to a potentially profound transformation of the services landscape.

Moving from agencies to systems

The evolving procurement model and the development of the organizational model for program delivery suggest that the Alberta government is moving to create a higher-order system. This system will retain the goals and objectives of the PDD Community Governance Act, and with government now controlling the purchase of services, agencies will have little choice but to accept the contracts they are offered. How much latitude there is for negotiation is not yet known, but there are several potential implications for service providers.

First, a system that is rationalized across the province will control costs better between agencies. It is reasonable to expect a standard schedule for costs that the government is prepared to pay – perhaps with variations to accommodate differences between urban and rural delivery costs. Second, with tight control over purchasing only what the SIS shows is needed to support individuals with developmental disabilities, the government is likely to reduce the number of agencies with which it contracts. Third, with a standard schedule of costs and service descriptions, the government will be able to put downward pressure on administrative costs since (1) all regions will use the same schedule, the same definitions, and be within the same cost bands; (2) reporting on the same services defined within a schedule will streamline monitoring and improve consistency in reporting and accountability across the regions; (3) fewer agencies are likely to be engaged in service provision, with the trend likely favouring larger, more cost-efficient agencies over smaller ones; (4) families and service providers are calling for increased accountability, which includes showing the impact of services on individuals; and (5) low administration models of services delivery, especially family-managed supports, are areas of focus for the government.

Moving from agencies to families

KPMG's recommendation to improve access and support for family-managed services, if fully implemented, will have a dramatic effect on service providers. The emphasis placed on talking to families and individuals during the Community Conversation process held in June 2011 is striking. During the twelve sessions there were no conversations specific to service providers; instead, providers were included in the six sessions with families, while the other six sessions were with individuals who were receiving support and services through the PDD program. MLA Genia Leskiw, who was responsible for the community conversations, commented: "I was particularly pleased to spend time with individuals receiving service. I gained great insight from speaking directly to these people who are, with dignity and determination, trying to build good lives for themselves with the support of the PDD program. Their comments were insightful, practical, and in many cases the input was deeply wise. I have tried to honour those contributions in this summary" (Alberta 2011c, i).

Leskiw's words, like the process itself, clearly privilege the voices of families and individuals over that of service providers. Although this could be viewed as the provincial government's taking a populist approach, it is more probable that there are more significant drivers for this focus on families and individuals. For example, service providers are unwilling to work collectively, cooperatively, and to change from an agency-centred to a person-centred model of service provision. As well, efforts to build a true system of service delivery starting with service providers has proven to be unworkable, and a new system of family-managed supports driven by families themselves would be less complicated to build. Finally, the emphasis on outcomes in the lives of individuals, rather than on service outcomes of agencies, naturally puts the highlight on individuals and their families.

Arising from the emphasis on families and individuals is the concept of family-managed services, the attraction of which to government is due at least in part to its very low administrative costs – because families are willing to absorb administrative costs in exchange for the freedom to choose and manage services for their family member.[4] In Calgary, the PDD Regional Community Board worked with the advocacy group Alberta Association for Community Living to create the Darrell Cook Family Managed Supports Resource Centre, whose primary role is to "assist families in becoming directly involved in managing services and supports for their family member with developmental disabilities" (Alberta Association for Community Living 2011a).[5] Specifically, the centre provides opportunities related to education, employment, recreation, and community living; assists with applications, approvals, planning, and administrative processes pertaining to family-managed supports; and offers workshops, a library, and web resources.

The KPMG recommendation went further by also calling for PDD-funded payroll service providers, tools for performance appraisals, and staff monitoring. The Alberta government's acceptance of the recommendation signaled a movement away from agency-controlled service structures to those controlled by families. There is an open question in the service provider community, however, as to whether families have the capacity to manage supports, especially as family members age.

More Recent Developments

The Alberta legislature began its fall 2013 session with a number of dramatic items affecting persons with developmental disabilities. First, on 23 October, Human Services Minister Dave Hancock announced that he was introducing legislation to repeal the PDD Community

Governance Act and dissolve the six regional PDD Community Boards. At the same time children's services would go through a similar process with the closure of its community boards and the ending of its enabling legislation. The act was not repealed because issues arising from the Redford government's failure to act responsibly side-tracked almost all legislative work and led to the premier's eventually quitting. The resulting delay in selecting a new premier followed quickly by the Jim Prentice government's calling a general election meant that the PDD Community Governance Act was never repealed. Hancock, as acting premier, did end the community board structure and set in place a process to create Family and Community Engagement Councils. The Prentice government suspended that action, so that, as of June 2015, the act has no board governance.

Given what has happened, it is interesting to note that the emphasis by Hancock, first as minister and subsequently as acting premier, on replacing two domains of legislation with one arose from his focus on implementing the Social Policy Framework released earlier in 2013. Another reason is that he was moving in this direction is that the new legislation was intended to make "services even more responsive and focused on individual needs" (Alberta 2013a), thus reversing the previous decision to reject the KPMG recommendation to dissolve the PDD Community Boards.

Another example of the power shift away from service providers to families and individuals with disabilities occurred with the announcement on 5 November 2013 by Frank Oberle, Associate Minister of Services for Persons with Disabilities, to strengthen the Premier's Council on the Status of Persons with Disabilities. The council includes individuals with disabilities and family members as well as educators and others representing the experiences of Albertans with disabilities. Its expanded mandate includes a "greater influence over policy and program development, as well as government business planning, and a larger role in supporting the relationship between government and community service providers" (Alberta 2013b), thus providing another instance of families and others advising government on its relationship with service providers.

The movement away from autonomous service providers to families and integrated systems is now well under way – even though there have been two years of delays due to the resignation of Premier Redford, the selection of Premier Prentice, and the general election that removed the Progressive Conservative (PC) government from power.

For service providers, most of which are nonprofit organizations, the wave of changes under the PC government was a clear move away from a model that had lasted for about thirty years. The PC government made it abundantly clear that its approaches, systems, and arguments for conducting the business of service provision in particular ways were no longer relevant. With the new NDP government, social issues will receive a much higher profile, and were referenced throughout the 2015 election campaign. The first sitting of the Alberta Legislature under the NDP government began in June 2015, and it remains to be seen if legislation that ensures services to persons with developmental disabilities is forthcoming. From the economic situation created by reduced revenues from oil and gas, Alberta is not in a position to fund redundant aspects of service provision such as duplicated administrative costs. Although the NDP might be more sympathetic, the new government's focus is more on the needs of individuals, and it would be reasonable to expect it to pay close attention to the KPMG review.

Conclusion

Alberta's PDD program is perhaps the most thoroughly examined human services program in recent years. As such, it provides a glimpse into the movements under way in government that are slowly coalescing into changes in both policy and regulations. Two of these are of particular significance. One is the movement away from an "agency unit of analysis" to a system-level analysis. Standardization of fees, service modes, and monitoring across the province are elements of structuring a consistent system of human services, of which service providers are a part but now subordinate to the system itself. The second significant change is the movement away from a focus on service providers to one on families, which are emerging as the most effective and efficient way to select and manage supports for individuals with developmental disabilities. With families expected to control increasing amounts of PDD program funding, the historic relationship of "PDD-service provider-family" is moving towards "PDD-family-service provider." Agencies thus might find themselves needing to market to families, rather than focusing on contract negotiations with the PDD program.

Both of these major shifts make it clear that the service provider role with respect to government and families will change. With families and rationalized systems in ascendancy, the power and influence of agencies are declining. Further, a rationalized system with clear evidence of the specific amounts, types, and frequency of needed services is likely to require fewer service providers. The larger providers are more likely to have the systems in place and enough resource "slack" to accommodate these changes; whether their governors will support the changes remains to be seen. Smaller service providers are vulnerable in this changing environment, though they have an opportunity to be nimble and draw support quickly to themselves through their more intimate connections with families and individuals with developmental disabilities. For all service providers, the signals are clear: unprecedented change is under way.

Appendix A: Summary of the PDD Program

The Minister [of Human Services] is responsible for the PDD program policy[, which] is developed and delivered under the authority of the Persons with Developmental Disabilities Community Governance Act. The Act identifies the following in relation to the provision of supports and services to adult Albertans with developmental disabilities:

- the people of Alberta honour and respect the dignity and equal worth of adults with developmental disabilities;
- it is important that adults with developmental disabilities have opportunities to exercise self-determination and to be fully included in community life;
- the individual needs of adults with developmental disabilities are most effectively met through the provision of services that are based on equitable opportunity, funding and access to resources;
- the Government of Alberta recognizes, values and supports the ability of communities to respond to the needs of adults with developmental disabilities; and
- the Government has ongoing responsibility to ensure and oversee the provision of programs, resources and services to adults with developmental disabilities.

PDD's Mission Statement

The PDD program works with others to support adults with developmental disabilities to be included in community life and to be as independent as possible.

Program Overview

The PDD Program funds, monitors and evaluates the provision of services for individual Albertans with developmental disabilities. These services supplement the support of family, friends and community members, and assist Individuals to live as independently as they can in the community. The PDD Program works with Individuals, their representatives and families, community members and service providers to provide supports throughout Alberta.

Services are provided to support Individuals in their home, work and social environments based on individual need. The PDD Program funds four types of services:

- Home Living Supports provide assistance to Individuals in their home environment;
- Employment Supports train, educate and support Individuals to gain and maintain paid employment;
- Community Access Supports promote community access and participation;
- Specialized Community Supports are generally short-term services to assist caregivers and staff in determining and delivering appropriate services.

The PDD program provides Individuals with opportunities to exercise self-determination. Individuals are the primary source for identifying the type of management and delivery of community-based services that best suit their needs.

There are three ways services can be provided:

- By the Individual and their family/guardian, known as Family Managed Services;
- By a Community Service Provider; and/or
- By the Ministry.

PDD regional staff will meet with the Individual and/or their guardian to identify the Individual's service and support needs and complete the PDD Service Plan. The PDD Service Plan will identify the types of PDD-funded services to be provided to the Individual and the desired service outcomes.

The service provider and/or funds administrator will lead the development of an Individual Support Plan in a collaborative process with the Individual/guardian and their support team. The Individual Support Plan will be provided to PDD regional staff by the service provider and/or field administrator not later than three months following the commencement of services.

Some Individuals, due to their disability, have legal representatives that act on their behalf in certain areas of their lives as defined in their *Guardianship Order*. An Individual may be represented by a guardian or trustee under the Adult Guardian and Trusteeship Act or an agent under the Personal Directives Act.

The PDD Program promotes supports and services that are responsive and flexible to Individuals, families, guardians, agents, and their communities. Recognizing the diversity of geographic boundaries among PDD regions, the PDD program ensures Individuals have reasonable access to the same or similar types of services across regions.

Source: Alberta (n.d.b.).

Appendix B: The Five KPMG Recommendations

The main focus of KPMG's recommendations involves consolidation and simplification of the PDD program. The review identified the need to view Alberta as one community. Within the context of the PDD program, the proposed vision would reflect one community of adults with developmental disabilities and their families served by one organization, a network of service providers, and one set of provincial policies. To achieve this vision, KPMG made the recommendations outlined below. The Alberta government accepted some of them and rejected others that might prove too disruptive to the individuals who depend on this important program (Alberta 2011c).

- *Dissolve the Community Boards*: this would include establishing an advisory council to reduce duplication of functions and inconsistency. (*Recommendation rejected*: the government believed that the Community Boards have an important role in keeping decisions as close to individuals as possible, and in providing feedback about community priorities; however, the minister would give the Boards written instructions to improve consistency and reduce duplication.)

- *Establish an organizational model for provincial program delivery*: this would involve establishing common roles and responsibilities from region to region to ensure both community engagement and the consistent application of policy and service delivery across the province. (*Recommendation accepted.*)
- *Clarify and enhance contracting processes with service providers*: this would involve establishing a new contracting process with clearly defined performance measures and administrative costs, and, where possible, individuals' being served by one service provider. (*Recommendation accepted*, but service providers, families, and other stakeholders were to be consulted about the new contracting process.)
- *Improve access and support for family-managed services*: this option could be encouraged through the development of resources such as PDD-funded payroll service providers, and access to tools and templates to assist family-managed administrators with hiring, performance appraisals, and staff monitoring. (*Recommendation accepted.*)
- *Improve information technology systems*: replace existing information technology with an integrated case management system to facilitate coordination between the PDD program and service providers, thereby reducing the administrative burden through automation. (*Recommendation accepted.*)

NOTES

1 There were nearly 1,300 Alberta government employees in the PDD program in 2008–09, a ratio of about one government employee for every nine adult Albertans covered by the act.
2 The costs dropped with the number of individuals receiving services. For example, 66 per cent of service providers serve fewer than fifty individuals at an average administrative cost of $9,418 per individual, while 1 per cent of service providers serve more than four hundred individuals at an average cost of $5,706 per individual.
3 More than three thousand individuals covered by the act – about one-third of all eligible persons – receive services from multiple service providers. The annual administrative cost of $18,000 per year for these individuals is two to three times as much as those for individuals receiving services from a single service provider.

4 KPMG examined the amounts paid to the 935 family managers and found that family-managed administration averages 2 per cent of support costs (2010a, 14). Roughly 10 per cent of all families accessing PDD program supports use the family-managed option.

5 The centre opened on 8 September 2011. The accompanying media release states: "The realization of this Centre will help to ensure families have equitable access to a source of funding that many find desirable as it enables them to hire and direct their own staff to support their family members with developmental disabilities and/or contract with an agency to provide needed supports. A recent government contracted review of the administration of PDD found[family-managed supports] to be a cost effective funding option and recommended further government investment in assisting families to access this funding. [Alberta Association for Community Living] would hope to see comparable developments in the provision of resources across Alberta."

REFERENCES

Alberta. 2009. "2008–2009 Persons with Developmental Disabilities Community Boards Consolidated Annual Report." Edmonton. Available online at http://humanservices.alberta.ca/documents/pdd-annual-report-2008-2009.pdf; accessed 1 May 2015.

———. 2010. Alberta Human Services. "PDD Administrative Review: Terms of Reference." Edmonton. Available online at http://humanservices.alberta.ca/disability-services/pdd-ar-terms.html; accessed 30 January 2013.

———. 2011a. Ministry of Seniors and Community Supports. "A Community Conversation about the Future: A Discussion Guide for Service Providers and Families." Edmonton. June. Available online at http://human services.alberta.ca/documents/pdd-ar-discussion-guide.pdf; accessed 1 may 2015.

———. 2011b. Alberta Human Services. "Persons with Developmental Disabilities Community Boards Consolidated Annual Report 2009–2010." Edmonton. Available online at http://humanservices.alberta.ca/documents/pdd-annual-report-2009-2010.pdf; accessed 1 May 2012.

———. 2011c. Ministry of Seniors and Community Supports. "Persons with Developmental Disabilities Community Conversation Report." Edmonton. Available online at http://humanservices.alberta.ca/documents/pdd-ar-community-conversation-report.pdf; accessed 1 May 2015.

——. 2012a. Alberta Human Services. "My Life Survey: The Personal Outcomes Index." Edmonton. Available online at http://humanservices. alberta.ca/disability-services/pdd-poi.html; accessed 4 September 2012.

——. 2012b. "Services for Persons with Disabilities Mandate." Edmonton. Available online at http://cpalberta.com/services-for-persons-with-disabilities-mandate/; accessed 10 July 2015.

——. 2013a. "Alberta creates new engagement opportunities for communities." Press release. Edmonton. 23 October. Available online at http://alberta.ca/release.cfm?xID=35215FE81DC4C-F3F8-CBFB-A481267CEF141DA8; accessed 8 November 2013.

——. 2013b. "Alberta to strengthen Persons with Disabilities Council." Press release. Edmonton. 5 November. Available online at http://alberta. ca/release.cfm?xID=35309A7215A15-B46A-06AB-9480E1EAEB759A58; accessed 8 November 2013.

——. 2015a. Alberta Human Services. "Assured Income for the Severely Handicapped (AISH)." Available online at http://humanservices.alberta. ca/disability-services/aish.html: accessed 14 June 2015.

——. 2015b. Alberta Human Services. "PDD Administrative Review – Terms of Reference." Available online at http://humanservices.alberta.ca/ disability-services/pdd-ar-terms.html#Purpose: accessed 14 June 2015.

——. n.d.a. Alberta Human Services. "PDD Program Policies." Edmonton. Available online at http://www.humanservices.alberta.ca/disability-services/pdd-policies.html; accessed 10 July 2015.

——. n.d.b. Alberta Human Services. "Persons with Developmental Disabilities (PDD) Manual: Program Purpose." Edmonton. Available online at http://humanservices.alberta.ca/pdd-online/program-purpose.aspx; accessed 10 July 2015.

Alberta Association for Community Living. 2011a. "Albertans Still Vulnerable." *AACL Connections* 4 (1): 2. Available online at http://www. aacl.org/clientuploads/documents/Connections%204%281%29.pdf; accessed 19 January 2013.

Alberta Disabilities Forum. 2012. "Persons with Developmental Disabilities Program – Summary of the Issues." Edmonton. Available online at http:// adforum.ca/files/download/181730b0385f207; accessed 1 May 2015.

KPMG. 2010a. *Report to the Minister, Ministry of Seniors and Community Supports, Administrative Review of the Persons with Developmental Disabilities Program.* Available online at http://www.humanservices.alberta.ca/ documents/pdd-ar-report.pdf; accessed 1 September 2012.

————. 2010b. "Summary Report to the Minister, Ministry of Seniors and Community Supports – Administrative review of the Persons with Developmental Disabilities Program." Available online at http://humanservices.alberta.ca/documents/pdd-ar-summary-report.pdf; accessed 1 May 2015.

Public Interest Alberta. 2012. "Closed-door government consultation revealed." Press release. Edmonton. 16 July. Available online at http://pialberta.org/content/closed-door-government-consultation-revealed; accessed 19 January 2013.

Revised Statutes of Alberta (RSA). 2000. Chapter P-9.5 (1 January 2014). Persons with Developmental Disabilities Services Act. Edmonton, AB: Alberta Queen's Printer.

Supports Intensity Scale. 2012. "Product Information." Available online at http://aaidd.org/sis/product-information#.VUN9omd0zIU; accessed 1 May 2015.

6 The Alberta Mentoring Partnership

LIZ O'NEILL, MARNI PEARCE, KEN DROPKO,
AND W.H. (WILMA) HAAS[1]

Introduction

In 2000, at a National Round Table on Mentoring in Toronto, research was presented that confirmed that mentoring was an effective approach to reducing risk and vulnerability for youth. The research concluded that, although mentoring is not the exclusively the role of government, the nonprofit sector and government can form an effective alliance to address youth at risk through mentoring. A subsequent survey in Alberta in 2001supported the formation of a provincial infrastructure for a province-wide mentoring initiative, which would evolve to become the Alberta Mentoring Partnership (AMP). This case study tracks the development of that initiative, and highlights important lessons related to government-nonprofit funding regimes.

As of fall 2012 the AMP quietly boasted a roster of ninety-four partners, consisting of provincial government ministries, government-funded agencies, community organizations, service organizations, and youth representation. The AMP publishes a public and open invitation for additional interested agencies to join the partnership (AMP 2012c). In place is a viable, supported, and funded three-year strategic plan; effective governance, operational and accountability structures; visible and credible champions and stewards; and an engaged and active membership committed to sharing resources and expertise. These elements are aligned collectively to realize shared goals and objectives. By all accounts, the AMP is a successful case study of community coalition building to achieve important societal outcomes.

Our study of the AMP consisted of an extensive review of historical and contemporary AMP-related documents; five semi-structured interviews with key informants, both current and founding nonprofit and provincial government members of the AMP; and a ten-member focus group of AMP co-chairs and representatives from provincial government ministries and the nonprofit sector.

In studying the AMP, one could be forgiven for concluding that initiative was the product of the happy coincidence of having the right opportunity, the right people, and the right resources all available at the right time – a social policy "big bang" event of sorts. Although it is true that many of the right ingredients were in place at an opportune time, the AMP story is more one of a successful evolution – a journey of continuous improvement involving iterative planning, implementation, evaluation, and improvement cycles. Realistically, the AMP is a case study of how hard work, dogged determination, patience, and unwavering commitment, by significant partners and champions, to an agreed vision are all critical for success. This is a story that illustrates the importance of both context and timing – particularly as they relate to political interfaces. And it is a case study of the critical need to align operational implementation with strategic vision within a culture that believes in what is possible given the right circumstances.

A History of Mentoring Organizations in Alberta

Although the AMP was officially launched in 2008, its roots were planted in 2000. Indeed, viable and successful mentoring organizations have long been a part of the Alberta social landscape. Many of these organizations are, relatively speaking, large agencies – for example, Big Brothers Big Sisters (BBBS) of Canada, Boys and Girls Clubs of Canada – for which mentoring is a fundamental component of their mandate. Numerous other organizations – such as Hull Homes, the Bent Arrow Traditional Healing Society – also offered mentoring programs that, while significant, were often just one component of a larger mandate. Largely established as nonprofit entities, most, if not all, mentoring organizations, by definition, face the ongoing reality of providing important community supports with finite resource capacity in the face of potentially unlimited demand for their services.

In the mid- to late 1990s, in addition to addressing the needs of their local communities, many mentoring organizations were being approached with requests to extend their services beyond their then-traditional client base and geographic region. Requests were arriving from other, typically rural and remote, communities to extend existing urban-based mentoring programs to their populations. Similar requests were also emerging from organizations such as school authorities and youth correctional centres for programs for their clientele. On the supply side of the equation, virtually every organization knew that the number of individuals interested in becoming mentors was not sufficient to fill the demand. It was increasingly obvious that many children and youth who could benefit from having a mentor could not be matched with one. And perceptions were emerging that these young people were more likely to be members of particular ethno-cultural groups and/or to be living in rural areas of Alberta.

In the broader Alberta context, one can speculate that provincial realities might well have contributed to the mentoring supply-and-demand challenges. The reader will recall – as profiled in Chapter 4 of this volume – that, in the early 1990s, Alberta was confronted with significant fiscal pressures. The energy sector "boom" had gone "bust," the unemployment rate was rising, and businesses and individual citizens alike were feeling the impact. Provincial revenues were down significantly, and government ministries were directed to undertake a significant round of program reviews to determine how best to direct their budgets in the post-boom fiscal cycle. Political key messages indicating that Alberta was dealing with a "spending problem, not a revenue problem" and that government should "get out of the business of business" were regularly heard. Resultant actions included significant outsourcing, privatization, and the planned sunsetting of many services previously delivered directly by a provincial government focused more on what it determined to be its core businesses – namely, policy development, legislative oversight, and so on. The provincial public service was also downsized as part of this refocusing and reduction of direct government services. Allegations that the province's actions effectively downloaded programs and services onto other levels of government and the nonprofit sector were not uncommon. Interestingly, too, a key message regularly heard from provincial politicians at the time was a commitment to ensuring that the needs of rural and remote Albertans were equitably addressed. Community and nonprofit direct service delivery organizations were feeling the pinch.

In the early to mid-1990s, in parallel with – or, arguably, in response to – the aforementioned events, community and interagency collaboration among mentoring and related organizations was emerging as a logical evolution to address common issues. For example, the Calgary Youth Mentoring Coalition emerged in approximately 1995. BBBS, in a working draft chronicling the history of agency collaboration, reported that "[t]he founding members of this coalition agreed that the cooperation and sharing of best practices would be of mutual benefit. Key goals arising from their strategic planning included the growth of mentoring and the capacity-building of agencies" (BBBS of Edmonton & Area n.d., 2). BBBS of Edmonton & Area was similarly engaged in discussions with other Alberta-based BBBS organizations and with other nonprofit agencies in Alberta's capital region to discuss the increasing need for mentoring programs and supports and how they might collaborate to support their populations. Individuals present at these early discussions reported some initial guardedness on the part of attendees and some evidence of turf protection. However, these cautionary behaviours apparently dissipated relatively quickly as the various groups built trust and came to acknowledge the merits of working collaboratively. The motivation and orientation of these local groups was solid. Tangible progress was, however, slow and difficult to achieve given limited resource capacity and the realities of competing priorities from the participants' home organizations. And the scope of the work remained largely focused on the needs of urban Alberta – particularly Edmonton, Calgary, and their surrounding suburbs.

Across the province, it was intuitively understood that mentoring works. As reported in a later AMP slideshow, "[m]entoring results in improved educational performance; healthier behaviours; improved social and behavioural outcomes; strengthened relationships; and improved resiliency" (AMP 2011a, slide 5). However, empirical data to support this understanding were not readily available. An early community agency champion of the AMP offered this perspective: "Research was beginning to emerge from the USA, in about 1997–98, providing compelling data that kids at risk who have mentors do better than those without. In Canada, there didn't seem to be much thinking about the science behind social policy initiatives. It was known that mentoring worked, but what wasn't known was how to scale it up into a broader social policy agenda" (interview respondent, 2012). And an early government champion of the AMP commented: "The ministry responsible for providing services to children (now Human Services) had been a long-time supporter of mentoring. Government interests were largely for the preventative value that mentoring relationships provide to young people – particularly young people in care or at risk of being taken into care. It was known, for example, that less than 1 per cent of aboriginal children in care had mentors" (interview respondent, 2012).

Events Leading to the Emergence of the AMP

If one were to try to identify a single catalyst for change within Alberta's mentoring landscape, it arrived in the form of the National Round Table on Mentoring, held in Toronto in March 2000. The event, sponsored by the federal government and BBBS, presented a platform for renowned authorities in the field to present their research findings. Each jurisdiction was allocated a limited number of seats for the event. BBBS organizations – in particular, BBBS of Edmonton & Area – were familiar with both the Alberta context *and* the way in which government organizations operate. They elected to go with a strategic approach to selecting the Alberta delegates. In addition to inviting the heads of the Edmonton and Calgary BBBS organizations, invitations were extended to a hand-picked group of influential individuals, including the deputy ministers[2] of the then-ministries of Children's Services, Learning, and Aboriginal Affairs and Northern Development. In retrospect this invitation list proved fortuitous; as one attending deputy minister reflected: "The Toronto National Roundtable presented irrefutable data-based evidence to confirm that mentoring works. It confirmed that we needed to do something in a more significant way in Alberta – not merely relying on the good works of disparate local mentoring organizations. Offering mentoring programs isn't the role of government. But we, in government, needed to work with the community, to support communities in collaborating amongst themselves to ensure more effective delivery of mentoring services for all children and youth in the province" (interview respondent, 2012).

Key champions at the provincial level were hooked, and the momentum to engage local communities and community organizations moved into a higher gear. The next step of what was later dubbed the "pre-AMP phase," was to invite Gary Walker, a key National Round Table presenter and renowned advocate of mentoring in the United States, to tour Alberta to promote mentoring in the province. Presentations were sponsored by the then-Alberta Alcohol and Drug Abuse Commission and the Edmonton-based Muttart Foundation[3] in six locations across the province (Lethbridge, Medicine Hat, Calgary, Red Deer, Edmonton, and Fort McMurray). Two additional presentations were also arranged: the deputy minister of children's services hosted a meeting with key Alberta business community leaders, and Children's Services and the Muttart Foundation co-hosted a presentation by Gary Walker for the Alberta Children and Youth Initiative (ACYI) partnering ministries.

Reference to the ACYI raises another important element in the Alberta government context as it relates to the AMP:

> Introduced in 1998, the Alberta Children and Youth Initiative … is a collaborative partnership of government ministries working together on issues affecting children and youth. Its vision ensures that Alberta's children and youth are well cared for, safe, successful at learning, and healthy. Children and youth issues cross many government ministries. This is both a challenge and an opportunity. The Alberta Children and Youth Initiative arose from recognition that a co-ordinated government-wide effort is critical for the effective and efficient support of children, youth and their families. Working together, government ministries and communities can more effectively address these issues. (Alberta 2013a, para. 2–3)

To put it more directly, the ACYI was established at a time when the Alberta government was determined to ensure that Albertans would be better served by ministries working together, horizontally, rather than focusing more narrowly on the specific mandates of their respective organizations.

The government's expectation of improved ministerial collaboration was reinforced through the establishment of facilitating mechanisms and accountability structures, such as ministerial mandate letters that specifically outlined the requirement to collaborate. Similar expectations were "trickled down" to deputy ministers – and, by extension, to other senior leaders in the ministries – through their performance contracts and associated compensation structures. Deputy ministers established a number of integrating (largely committee) structures – such as the ACYI partnering ministries – to ensure their ability to understand and address cross-ministry issues and linkages, to oversee progress on shared action plans, and generally to hold one another collectively accountable for results. Reflecting back on the list of Alberta delegates to the 2000 National Round Table on Mentoring, it was excellent strategy to invite three of the ACYI partnering deputies: the ACYI table became, and remains to this day, the primary source of AMP sponsorship and championship at the provincial government level.

The years between 2000 and 2007 were foundational for what ultimately became the AMP. This pre-AMP phase was characterized by coalition building and agency engagement, extensive research and planning, and small-scale (pilot project) implementations to achieve early successes. A chronology of activities and accomplishments during this time compiled by BBBS of Edmonton & Area (n.d., 2–11) highlights the following:

- In early 2001 the Edmonton Mentoring Partnership was established to develop more formally mentoring in Edmonton and area.
- In July 2001 a study funded by the Muttart Foundation and the provincial government on how to build support for sustainable mentoring in Edmonton and area revealed that Edmonton's needs and interests were comparable to those elsewhere in the province.
- In October 2001 representatives from across Alberta convened to assess interest in building a province-wide infrastructure to support mentoring. An employee was seconded from, and meeting facilitation support provided by, the Alberta government to enable the development of an initial business plan for a provincial mentoring entity.
- In 2002 meetings between agency and government representatives culminated in a planning retreat at which the AMP was established, along with an accompanying draft work plan. An initial structure for the new initiative was also put in place consisting of two co-chairs from the community (one from Edmonton and one from Calgary) to ensure broad provincial representation, a leadership committee consisting of the two community co-chairs and other members of the broader partnership to oversee implementation of the work plan and to ensure ongoing communication and collaboration with the larger partnership group. The draft work plan was further refined and completed in March 2002.
- In 2002 a pilot public awareness campaign was implemented to recruit more mentors in the greater Edmonton area. This work received government funding with the understanding that the knowledge gained and materials and methods developed would be relevant and applicable across the province.
- In 2002 three pilot projects, resourced through further government funding, were implemented to provide mentoring supports to Alberta youth with young offender or child welfare status. BBBS agreed to assume the role of fiscal agent for that funding and for any future funding to be received for the AMP.
- In 2003 came evaluation of the public awareness campaign and mentoring pilots; the launch of communication vehicles (such as newsletters) to keep AMP members connected; implementation of further pilot mentoring projects within Aboriginal and other

culture-specific communities; development and "soft launch" of the initial AMP public website; further research and environmental scanning; public presentations and awareness building; and further planning.

- In 2004 came the formal public, "hard" launch of the AMP website; development of standards and best practices; and convening of the first Provincial Mentoring Conference.
- From 2005 to 2007 the AMP was busy with ongoing and iterative cycles of planning, implementation, evaluation, reporting, and refining.

Throughout these years, awareness of and support for the AMP initiative grew. The community agencies, largely under the championship of their Edmonton and Calgary co-chairs, proved their willingness and ability to work together to achieve common goals. The Alberta government, under the continuing championship of a subset of the ACYI partnering deputy ministers and members of their staff, gained good returns on its various financial investments. The ACYI was able to demonstrate good pilot project outcomes and tangible evidence of successful cross-ministry collaboration. The time was right to move beyond pilot and other small-scale projects and seek a longer-term mandate and committed funding for the AMP.

The AMP membership came together in the latter half of 2007 to develop the AMP Leadership Team Strategic Plan 2008, an ambitious, "direction-setting document to provide a broad guide for the coordination, planning and delivery of mentoring services across Alberta over the next three years (2008–2011)" (AMP 2008, 3; see Box 6.1). The strategic plan also specified an ambitious eight outcomes, seventeen strategies, and ninety-one action items for implementation over the proposed three-year plan. The plan was presented to the full ACYI partnership table, and was endorsed and funded for implementation commencing in January 2008.

BOX 6.1 KEY ELEMENTS OF THE AMP LEADERSHIP TEAM STRATEGIC PLAN 2008

Vision:

Every child or youth at risk who needs a mentor has access to a mentor.

Mission:

The Alberta Mentoring Partnership Leadership Team will aid in the successful coordination, collaboration and implementation of strategies to grow sustainable mentoring across Alberta.

Goals:

1. Increase public awareness of the importance of mentoring;
2. Increase the recruitment and retention of mentors; and
3. Increase community capacity, training and the integration of strategies to grow sustainable mentoring across Alberta.

Source: AMP (2008, 6).

The AMP, 2008–11

At the time of the launch of the Leadership Team Strategic Plan, the AMP consisted of twenty-nine partners (members) representing ten Alberta government ministries, three agencies funded by the Alberta government, and sixteen community organizations and youth representatives (AMP n.d.). Leadership Team meetings were held regularly, and were facilitated initially by two co-chairs, one of whom, the executive director of BBBS Edmonton & Area, retained that role from the pre-AMP phase, providing essential continuity and strong community agency championship to the Leadership Team. The second co-chair role was assigned to an assistant deputy minister[4] from Alberta Children's Services. (A third co-chair, an additional assistant deputy minister from Alberta Education, was added in 2009.) Was it appropriate for government employees to assume this level of shared leadership for AMP? The following comment, provided by an AMP Leadership Team member, summarizes the team's consensus view:

> It made sense given the government's significant resource investment in AMP and the ongoing need to make sure the government was aware and supportive of AMP. The government representatives helped make sure we focused on the needs of all Alberta communities – not just the larger urban centers who can pretty much look after themselves. It was

also extremely helpful that these co-chairs behaved like true partners: they were respectful and didn't try to control things. I believe they learned as much from us as we did from them. (Interview respondent, 2012)

Was it a concern that all of the co-chairs were from Edmonton? Not according to this AMP Leadership Team member:

> I really don't think AMP could be the success it is if it wasn't primarily anchored – at the co-chair level – in Alberta's capital city. Our co-chairs had the network, the relationships *and* the proximity to our key government-level champions and decision-makers. It's difficult to maintain that level of "presence" if you're located somewhere else. And since our AMP Leadership Team 'culture' was one of trust, mutual respect, and effective relationship building, the location of the co-chairs has never been a problem. (Interview respondent, 2012)

To address the activities encompassed under the seventeen strategies in the Strategic Plan, six strategy groups were established – namely, on Public Awareness & Engagement; Integration into Education; Tools & Resources; Pilot Projects; Knowledge Transfer; and Evaluation & Resilience (AMP 2012a, 1). Each strategy was assigned a strategy lead, who had the option to appoint a project manager (or assume that role him- or herself) and considerable discretion on how to undertake the work, whether contracting for services, assembling a team internal to the strategy lead's own organization, or assembling a team consisting of multiple partner organizations.

The Leadership Team also benefited considerably from the efforts of a three-member Project Support Team provided by the co-chairs' home organizations. These individuals oversaw and coordinated the work of the strategy leads. They also handled the logistical and operational details involved in the planning and running of the Leadership Team meetings, supported the co-chairs, and generally monitored the implementation of the Strategic Plan.

An accountability framework was also implemented alongside the Strategic Plan. A "dashboard" format was adopted wherein each strategy – and its associated set of activities – was monitored and reported on in terms of both progress and adherence to assigned budgets by the strategy leads at each Leadership Team meeting. Strategy leads were required to explain any noted deviations from action plans and to indicate how they planned to get the initiatives back on target.

Individual members of the Leadership Team were held to high standards of personal and organizational accountability. Each member was oriented to the work of the AMP and the Leadership Team, and presented with an Orientation and Reference Manual. Active involvement and participation and regular attendance at meetings were strongly encouraged. Members who were unable to attend a specific meeting were welcome to send an alternate. That said, however, all alternates – as well as any new (incoming) partners – were required to attend a mandatory orientation briefing prior to attending a Leadership Team meeting. These steps helped to ensure that all attendees were informed and contributing members to Leadership Team discussions.

The information flow between the AMP and the ACYI was ongoing. The AMP website (both the public-facing site and the members' portal) was kept current, and regular update newsletters were circulated. Formal briefing notes were prepared for specific deputy ministers (and/ or ministers) addressing emerging issues and key milestones and highlighting progress on AMP activities and outcomes of particular relevance to individual ministries. Common briefing notes – for use in more than one ministry – were also generated as appropriate. Updates for the ACYI Partnering Deputy Ministers Committee collectively were also prepared on behalf of the entire AMP Leadership Team. These more formal briefings served two primary objectives: to fulfil normal accountability requirements (such as status updates on strategic plan progress and budget use), and to ensure that the AMP remained "front of mind" for ACYI partnering deputy ministers. In this way, these deputy ministers could better ensure the ongoing alignment and relevance of the AMP in both their own ministerial and shared cross-ministry issues and strategies. And the associated benefit of nurturing the ongoing support and championship of individual deputy ministers was deemed vital for the long-term sustainability and success of the AMP. As one of its early champions among deputy ministers said,

> I believed it critically important for AMP to have "political resonance." Through the Alberta Children and Youth Initiative partnering deputy ministers' understanding of AMP, its activities and results, we were able to provide our ministers with consistent, current, and timely information on how the work of AMP was directly aligned with the government's social policy agenda. Our elected officials were always keen to hear how AMP was contributing to their priorities in areas such as building safer

communities, enhancing the resilience of our youth or creating communities with active cultures of volunteerism, etc. (Interview respondent, 2012)

The referenced accountability and communication structures required some "adjustments" on the part of all AMP partners. Members of the AMP Leadership Team outlined some of their insights as follows: "It was a major 'aha' for me to realize it was inappropriate to suggest that the AMP website content and logos be approved through my [home] organization's [web] communications and approval channels" (interview respondent, 2012). Similarly: "It was a major learning for me, and for many of our other not-for-profit partners, too, to see how many briefings, levels of review, approval, and accountability reporting processes we had to complete to meet the needs of government departments. Sometimes I wondered if it would ever be possible for AMP to move forward given the potential bureaucratic obstacles" (interview respondent, 2012). And: "I believe it was important for us to be transparent around the government's structures, budgetary and planning processes, and accountability requirements. This was a degree of rigor that many of our agency partners weren't accustomed to. Yet I believe it provided them with invaluable learnings on how to work effectively with government organizations both now and down the road" (interview respondent, 2012).

Along with their approval of the AMP Strategic Plan, the ACYI partnering deputy ministers provided the critical financial resources required to achieve the planned outcomes. To this point in the AMP's history, individual organizations (including government ministries and agencies and the Muttart Foundation) had provided targeted funding in support of such specific activities as consulting services to conduct research or facilitate planning, and the purchase of media services for social marketing campaigns. The Strategic Plan, however, included a proposed budget of $3.2 million, which was presented to the ACYI partnering deputy ministers with the full understanding that no dedicated (voted) budget existed for this work and no one ministry had a vested interest in the full complement of proposed AMP activities and expected outcomes. The result was most interesting, and fully consistent with the intended rationale for establishing a cross-ministry entity such as the ACYI.

Some partnering ministries – specifically, those that either saw a limited alignment between the AMP plan and ministerial goals and objectives or had a very small budget overall – pledged modest contributions.

An early deputy ministry champion of the AMP expressed this comment: "My departmental budget gave me little flexibility to make a major contribution. But I recognized that our primary clients too would get benefit from successful implementation of some of the planned AMP initiatives and so I was determined we would find $50K to demonstrate our support" (interview respondent, 2012). In contrast, ministries that saw a strong alignment and had a larger base budget pledged much larger amounts. Another early deputy minister champion of the AMP provided the following perspective:

> My primary interest was in supporting the development of a mentoring capacity in every school and community in Alberta. I pledged big resources because I was interested in achieving big outcomes. While I had no hard financial projections to forecast an exact budget required to do this, I knew from prior experience that a significant investment would be required. I was not interested in supporting further small scale pilots: It was time to get serious about province-wide application of the best practices that our research evidence confirmed would make a difference. In my judgment and experience $1M was a reasonable investment to make. (Interview respondent, 2012)

In addition to concrete funding from the Alberta government, a number of AMP partners provide substantial "in-kind" contributions, consisting largely of staff time and expertise and the sharing of intellectual property such as mentoring-related tools developed by the partnering organization.

The timing of the budget request to the ACYI partnering deputies was highly relevant. Funds were requested in the third quarter of the government's fiscal year at a time when deputy ministers knew with a good degree of certainty what their year-end financial position would be and what they could, or could not, afford to pledge. Because the Strategic Plan was to be implemented over three years, it gave the partnering deputies the option to flow their proffered commitment either in one lump-sum payment or over two or three (annual) instalments. As well, the funds would go to the AMP by way of conditional grants, a structure that provided both financial certainty and fiscal accountability. And because BBBS Edmonton & Area had been approved to fill the role of fiscal agent for these funds, they would be effectively "in hand," contractually bound and beyond any risk of potential clawback in the event of future changes to the government's fiscal position.

With a detailed plan in place, and financial and other resources secured, the work of the AMP continued in earnest over the next three years. Much of the focus of the AMP Leadership Team moved into operational mode. The co-chairs, however, ensured that appropriate attention continued to be paid to strategic considerations. For example, recognizing that any potential intended extension of the AMP beyond 2011 would require evidence of the initiative's results, program evaluations and impact studies were commissioned. The executive summary of the AMP Report on Impact (AMP 2011b, 3), for example, highlights the following:

The Alberta Mentoring Partnership is an innovative and important collaborative initiative in Alberta. It has demonstrated impact across the province in a number of areas:

- AMP has increased the awareness of the importance of mentorship for young people;
- AMP has made resources and supports available to those organizations, schools and communities interested in increasing their capacity to offer mentoring programs;
- through the collaborative efforts of AMP, schools have more customized resources available to them to support mentoring programs and trainings; and
- AMP has supported the creation of a body of evidence around the use of strength-based mentoring approaches and the efficacy of this approach with children and youth (especially at-risk children and youth).

Anticipating that quantitative data would also be expected, the AMP selected the following statistical highlights for presentation to the ACYI partnering deputy ministers:

- An increased number of children and youth [are] being mentored:
  - 21% increase through BBBS agencies;
  - 20% increase in mentoring organizations outside of BBBS in Alberta (AMP 2011a, slide 7).
- [Between June 2010 and February 2011] 900 individuals have received the online training [developed for/provided via the AMP website] to become mentors.

- 14 organizations have developed new mentoring programs and two of the AMP mentoring pilot projects have secured longer-term funding.
- Three mentoring pilot projects [were launched] focusing on the unique and important needs of immigrant and Aboriginal children and youth in Alberta.
- Through the High School Teen Mentoring programs offered throughout the province, over 1000 youth have been trained as mentors using AMP resources.
- Five one-credit Career and Technology Studies mentoring courses [were developed] for schools in Alberta and one mentoring course at the University of Alberta.
- The ... AMP website that provides networking opportunities and access to the broad range of tools and resources created or sourced by AMP ... recorded 60,321 unique visitors between September 2009 and November 2010 with more than 1.5 million pages viewed. (AMP 2012d, 2–3)

As the end of the Alberta government's 2010/11 fiscal year approached, it was time for the AMP Leadership Team to brief the ACYI partnering deputy ministers on what their $3.2M investment had achieved and to begin planning the AMP next three years.

The AMP, 2012–14

In keeping with its previous approach, the entire Leadership Team was invited to participate in the next round of strategic planning. All aspects of the previous plan – from vision and mission statement to specific goals and strategies – were reviewed, discussed, and reworked, and a new Strategic Plan was drafted for a further three-year term (see Box 6.2).

BOX 6.2. KEY ELEMENTS OF THE AMP LEADERSHIP TEAM STRATEGIC PLAN FOR 2012–14

Vision:

Every child or youth who needs a mentor has access to a mentor.

Mission:

Grow sustainable mentoring across Alberta through a shared services approach.

Objectives:

1. Continue to increase the capacity of mentoring programs, organizations, and schools throughout the province to provide effective mentoring.
2. Continue to increase public awareness of the importance of mentoring.
3. Increase engagement of community partners in advancing the mission of AMP.
4. Ensure the sustainability of mentoring by collaboration among community agencies, schools, government, and AMP.

Source: AMP (2012d, 3–4).

The Leadership Team, throughout its planning processes, was mindful that the province's fiscal position for the term of the new three-year Strategic Plan was forecast to be significantly less buoyant than in the previous three years. This clearly suggested the need for a more modest plan. The Leadership Team also assumed that some of the partnering deputy ministers might take the hard-line position that it was time for the government to reduce or discontinue its funding altogether, and instead have the AMP approach the private sector for financial support or, alternatively, have member agencies that benefited from shared and other services available through the work of the AMP pay membership or other fees for future services received. The Leadership Team carefully considered these and other potential funding options, but determined that, although it was prudent for the AMP's budget request for the 2012–14 period to be more modest than the previous budget, the future of the partnership and its efforts would be jeopardized if its current efforts and activities were refocused towards fundraising, the outcome of which was highly uncertain.

Accordingly the Leadership Team co-chairs submitted a three-year, $1.2 million budget as part of the proposed 2012–14 Strategic Plan to

the ACYI partnering deputy ministers on 4 February 2011. As anticipated, the deputy ministers were particularly keen to hear what tangible results had been achieved in the three previous years and to learn
how the AMP proposed to continue that momentum over the next three
years. After careful consideration and extensive discussion, the deputy
ministers approved both the Strategic Plan and the proposed budget.
The AMP secured early resource commitments from the deputy ministers in attendance, who were also instrumental in securing the commitment of their colleagues in other ministries to fund the remainder
of the budget.

Follow-up discussions with key champions among ACYI partnering
deputy ministers about who should fund AMP were interesting. Two
such champions expressed the following comments:

> To suggest that an initiative like AMP should be funded by the corporate
> sector suggests to me a limited understanding of how the corporate sector
> works. The majority of the big corporations operating in Alberta aren't
> headquartered here and their major financial decisions aren't made here
> either. I agree that corporations can be very helpful in sponsoring parti-
> cular mentoring initiatives or supporting mentorship in specific commu-
> nities; and many companies have demonstrated wonderful community
> commitment in this way. But I don't believe corporate funding models
> will be effective in achieving our objective to have equitable mentoring
> opportunities available for all children, in all communities, in Alberta. (In-
> terview respondent, 2012)

And:

> If the government of Alberta doesn't financially support an initiative as
> important to our young people as AMP, then who will? We now have the
> data to confirm that mentoring works. We know that, from a preventative
> perspective, government investment in mentoring makes good economic
> sense. And AMP provides a fine example of how government investment
> can be directed to achieving good outcomes at the community level –
> without the need to build and maintain a new bureaucratic structure to
> achieve those outcomes. (Interview respondent, 2012)

Between the ACYI partnering deputy ministers' approval of the
2012–14 Strategic Plan and its subsequent implementation, a number
of significant events occurred in the Alberta political landscape. The

re-election of the Redford government in May 2012 and the premier's subsequent announcement of a new and somewhat smaller cabinet structure meant a number of changes relevant to the AMP. For example, some new ministers had no previous involvement with the ACYI and little, if any, familiarity with the AMP, while one key and previously involved minister was assigned to a new, more demanding portfolio and a number of the deputy ministers who had championed the AMP were replaced. As well, two new government co-chairs of the AMP were appointed, all three AMP Support Team positions saw a turnover of personnel, and a new full-time coordinator was hired.

These changes suggested an urgent need to plan for the orientation and familiarization of a significant number of elected officials and government personnel regarding the work of the AMP. Within the structure of the AMP itself, the 2008–11 Strategy Groups were refreshed (and many disbanded) to reflect the requirements of the 2012–14 Strategic Plan. As well, the number of AMP partners had grown from twenty-nine to ninety-four, largely reflecting both the Leadership Team's efforts to bring other "good fit" organizations into the partnership and effective partnership promotion (and published partnership criteria) through the AMP website (AMP 2012b). The tripling in the number of partners, however, made it no longer feasible to conduct the work of the AMP around one Leadership Team table and to have all partners automatically be members of the committee. As a result, general criteria were developed to guide the selection of a small Leadership Team, one that would reflect the diversity of the AMP's partner organizations.

Focus Group and Interview Findings

In the ten-member focus group we convened of AMP co-chairs and representatives from provincial government ministries and the non-profit sector, participants were invited to share their success stories by reflecting on the question: From your AMP experiences, what advice would you share with others interested in forming a successful partnership? The responses were highly consistent and included the following contributions:

- Pick the right people to be involved. Effective relationships – characterized by trust, openness, and mutual respect – are the cornerstone of a successful partnership (various interview respondents, 2012).

- "Together we're better: You can get a lot of work done if you don't care who gets the credit" (interview respondent, 2012).
- "Shared development of a compelling and unifying vision is the 'joining thread' that brings and keeps a partnership together" (interview respondent, 2012).
- "Partnership strategies and activities will change over time: Take the time to regularly pause, assess, re-evaluate, and adjust direction as required. Be dynamic and fluid. And be prepared to evolve" (interview respondent, 2012).
- "Have enough core funding and resources in place to do the work that needs doing: Partnership work can't be done off of the corner of people's desks" (interview respondent, 2012).
- "Ambitious coordinated outcomes won't be achieved through cautious implementation of a series of pilots and small projects. Real progress and traction is gained with the capacity and 'permission' to work on a grander scale over a longer time horizon" (interview respondent, 2012).
- "Integrate, collaborate, and communicate – horizontally and vertically – within and between involved and interested organizations" (interview respondent, 2012).
- "Credible, visible, and sustained championship, at all levels, is critical for long-term success" (interview respondent, 2012).

A similar question about what was needed to form the AMP partnership was directed to interview participants: current and former AMP co-chairs and ACYI partnering deputy minister champions. Their responses, while reflecting similar themes, add an additional level of insight. Embedded in their comments are important thoughts on how to sustain the AMP specifically and other partnerships generally into the future:

- Major initiatives sponsored by government need to have political "resonance." Such initiatives – their vision, goals, intent, and so on – need to be packaged in such a way that they resonate as "the right thing to do" with key funders and decision makers. These individuals need to fully understand the power of mentoring and, ideally, the role that the AMP plays so that they do not need ongoing reminding of the initiative; they will just know how it links to pressing policy and other priorities. Support for mentoring needs to be "spliced into the DNA" of the government. (Interview respondent, 2012)

- We must understand that the AMP partnership story is greater than the impact on individual kids. Although this might be the "glue" that keeps grassroots agencies at the table and collectively aligned, it is not enough to keep major funders committed. To truly gain – and keep – the commitment and sponsorship of major funding partners over the long term, decision makers need regular, current, and strategically focused information to keep them in the know as to how their individual/departmental support of the AMP is contributing to the achievement of "loftier" objectives – for example, mentorship training gives students of today and tomorrow important twenty-first-century skills; it redefines what "citizenship" means in our society; it contributes to the creation of safer, more resilient, and more caring communities; it is a critical and cost-effective preventive strategy to mitigate future, and higher, costs required for "curative" programs in health care, child protection, the justice system, and so on. (Interview respondent, 2012)
- The research data presented at the 2000 Toronto Roundtable on Mentoring cemented the case for eventual funding of the AMP. AMP partners need to agree on performance measures and have common and consistent data collection methods to maximize their ability to provide evidence of the return on the investments made by the funders. This will be critically important as the partnership approaches the end of its current 2012–14 Strategic Plan. Funders and key decision makers are more comfortable making decisions based on data, rather than on qualitative arguments. (Interview respondent, 2012)
- The AMP partnership is effective largely because it follows a values-based, rather than a rules-based, governance model. It is focused on assurance, rather than on compliance. As a result, the partnership has the flexibility to experiment and to "do the right thing," rather than being preoccupied with rigid adherence to predetermined rules and standards. This is critically important. (Interview respondent, 2012)
- Accountability is an important element not only for our government partners but for all AMP partners. It is very important for *all* AMP participating organizations (community and government agencies alike) to have their commitment to the AMP embedded in their business plans – and in their executive directors' performance contracts. As well, it is important for each partnering agency to promote the AMP brand in addition to their own organizational identity. (Interview respondent, 2012)

Discussion

In itself this edited book represents a contemporary scan of government-nonprofit funding regimes, of which the kind of partnership model envisioned and implemented in the AMP is but one example. As other chapters point out, the Alberta government's neoliberal orientation under the Progressive Conservatives was consistent with that of neoliberal governments everywhere – namely, "to make government's community collaborators more professional in their approach ... by influencing third sector organizations to adopt quasi-business models of organizational practice and accountability" (Aimers and Walker 2008, 14).

Connell, Fawcett, and Meagher (2009) define neoliberalism as "the project of economic and social transformation under the sign of the free market" (331), where "competition, choice, entrepreneurship and individualism" (333) are actively promoted. The increasing level of accountability to government resulting from this policy paradigm means that nonprofit organizations typically spend increasingly larger amounts of time tending to their relationship with the state, rather than to that with the community, and "risk overlooking a core part of their identity and purpose" (Aimers and Walker 2008, 14). Given how common is this imbalance of time allocation, this case study provides evidence of an alternative approach by both government and nonprofit stakeholders.

Alford and Hughes (2008) make the case that a government operating within a neoliberal framework typically tends to have a one-best-way orientation that limits effectiveness and innovation. They propose instead a "public value pragmatism" in which the best management approach is context dependent and includes being thoughtful about the kinds of value produced. Such thoughtfulness and context dependency is at the heart of "networked governance" – where many stakeholders work towards various ends and outcomes. Considine (2001) makes the case that contract-based relationships are slowly being seen as networked partnerships. Stoker (2006) observes that, although networked governance seems at odds with the one-best-way orientation of neoliberal governments, public value can be fully realized only when the motivation of community organizations to participate in networks and partnerships becomes part of the state's approach to assessing outcomes.

The AMP viewed itself as an important partnership with a social policy outcome – namely, that children and youth at risk would achieve the benefits of a solid relationship with an adult mentor. Operating in a social policy environment guided by the Alberta Progressive Conservative government's Social Policy Framework meant that the nature of advocacy for government support (not necessarily exclusively financial support) for mentoring had to evolve as the AMP did. DeSantis (2010, 40) notes that social policy initiatives (such as the AMP) "have life cycles characterized by fluidity over time." Assuming clarity and a one-best-way approach to social change is unworkable and unproductive.

In their discussion of the AMP, all interviewees expressed understandable pride in and satisfaction with the collective efforts and achievements of the partnership to date. Although interviewees conveyed considerable optimism about the AMP's potential, they also expressed a number of worries. Past and current AMP champions and partners spoke to the following themes, which provide food for thought and further planning consideration:

- The AMP has benefited greatly from the presence of strong co-chairs. The long and consistent tenure of the community agency co-chair has been a particular asset. Consideration should be paid to more deliberate succession planning for all AMP co-chairs and other key members of the leadership structure (that is, strategy leads and support team members).
- There has been so much change – at the government level, particularly – over the past year that I see considerable risk of the AMP's becoming "out of sight, out of mind." The social policy ministers, their deputy ministers, and members of their inner advisory circles are largely new to their positions and/or portfolios and do not yet have the benefit of a long or personal history with the AMP. The AMP co-chairs need good proximity to, and ability to influence, their boards, their ministers, deputy ministers, and departmental executive teams to ensure ongoing understanding of and support for the AMP.
- The AMP has moved quite heavily from a strategic focus to a focus on operational matters. This is understandable given that we are in the first year of our current three-year strategic plan. The magnitude of political and personnel changes in the AMP context, however, suggests that we need to chart an appropriate balance between operations and strategy.
- To help ensure the AMP's long-term sustainability, we need to keep the AMP and its accomplishments publicly visible. All partners

need to ensure that their organizations promote the AMP "brand," in addition to promoting their own organizational identity. And all partners – and their organizations' leadership – need to include the expectation of AMP involvement in their organizational business and performance plans.

Finally, individuals intimately familiar with the AMP raised several themes that warrant the continued attention, wisdom, and thoughtful consideration of the academic community:

One of the failings of big bureaucratic organizations, and governmental organizations are no exception, is that no one is specifically assigned responsibility for very big picture strategic thinking. In spite of ongoing emphasis on horizontal cross-ministry alignment and coordination, our focus continues to wander back to initiative-by-initiative discussions. Frequent changes of ministers and deputy ministers mean that what strategic thinking was done at this level gets lost and/or has to be redone. Continuity of key departmental personnel is helpful but reliance on the goodwill and best efforts of their grassroots employees to ensure the ongoing success of an initiative like AMP isn't enough. We need better models of how to build enduring horizontal integration into our large and complex organizations. (Interview respondent, 2012)

Our [government] financial systems don't lend themselves particularly well to funding complex initiatives [such as the AMP]. No one ministry has lead responsibility and therefore it is unlikely that any one ministry has a dedicated budget. One problem is our financial systems themselves: How do you financially justify "doing the right" thing when public dollars are involved? How do you place a value on community collaboration? How do you justify making financial expenditures when the emphasis so often hangs on the expectation of a short-term financial savings in return for those expenditures … or worse, the expectation that future savings should be more than sufficient to provide the up-front investments required? (Interview respondent, 2012)

I believe we need to influence a major sea change in our societies wherein our communities, collectively, acknowledge responsibility for our young people. A profound indicator of success for me would be a scenario where, in response to an event of youth violence for example, that public media's first question would go to the community: "Was this young person being mentored, and if not, why not?" rather than first going to the police to ask why they aren't keeping our streets safer, or to Child Welfare to find out where their systems broke down. (Interview respondent, 2012)

These themes then led to final comments from current and former AMP champions around the topics of values-based governance and future models for community building. Key discussion points were as follows:

As a concept, values-based governance is neither well understood nor entrenched. Governments, in particular, continue to focus on accountability, transparency, auditability, and risk mitigation – largely financial models focusing on efficiency and burdened with legislative requirements. Are social objectives, such as creating and sustaining healthy and resilient societies, well-served through traditional financial models? Could they be better served through adopting values-based governance models? If so, how should we build these models? How do we fund them? How do we assign accountability? (Interview respondent, 2012)

At the community level we are beginning to see new models of what community building and public service delivery could look like. AMP is a wonderful model of community partnership though its continuing success is quite dependent on one [traditional] funding model. What models of community-building might be applicable to the future initiatives like AMP to allow them to sustain themselves, and their positive outcomes for our communities, into the future? (Interview respondent, 2012)

Conclusion

The AMP continues to benefit from the passion and commitment of its membership, the relative security of having in place an approved three-year funded Strategic Plan, and appropriate structures and processes to support the work both in place and under development. The AMP benefits considerably from the continuing leadership of a large number of its founding members – including the ongoing tenure of one of its original co-chairs – as well as from the energy, ideas, and collective efforts of newer partners. Mentoring organizations, with their enhanced access to a plethora of tools, training, and other shared services, are now better positioned to focus their resources on their true value-added services. Alberta children and youth who need a mentor and who have increasing certainty of access to a suitable mentor are the ultimate net beneficiaries.

The Alberta Mentoring Partnership is making a difference in the lives of children and youth across Alberta. Its member organizations are working collaboratively around a shared vision: that every Alberta child or youth who needs a mentor has access to one. The AMP is a unique "made in Alberta" partnership with a leadership team representing various community agencies and service organizations, a number of Alberta government ministries, and the voice of Alberta youth.

Evidence of creating public value (Alford and Hughes 2008), networked partnerships (Considine 2001), and networked governance (Stoker 2006) exists throughout the pathway the AMP has taken. The Alberta government's ongoing, high-level engagement throughout the process leading up to the 2008–11 and 2012–14 Strategic Plans was significant, and might have contributed to the remarkable scope and direction of the Children First Act, passed in May 2013, which "updates and amends legislation and enhances the tools, process and policies that impact how government and service providers deliver programs and services for children and youth" (Alberta 2013b, para. 3).[5]

Having achieved its planned goals and objectives – including an impressive 20 per cent increase in the number of mentor-matches facilitated across the province, a reduction in barriers to mentoring, introduction of a number of shared supports and services, and more than tripling the number of partnering organizations – the AMP's initial phase (2008–11) was deemed an unqualified success. This record of accomplishments earned the AMP the financial support required to develop and implement a second three-year Strategic Plan (2011–14) focused on the further development of shared services between partner agencies and continued emphasis on enabling positive mentor matches – and positive outcomes – for Alberta children and youth.

NOTES

1 The authors would like to acknowledge the contribution of Dr Keith Seel for his assistance in the revision of the initial case study.

2 Deputy ministers are the most senior officials in the Alberta public service. Deputy ministers are not elected; rather, they are employees of the Alberta government, report to the cabinet minister assigned responsibility for a particular ministry, and are accountable to the minister for the administration of their department within the ministry.

3 The Muttart Foundation, a registered charitable organization, "supports
   the work of the charitable sector in Alberta and Saskatchewan as well as
   at a national level. Through its own charitable activities and its funding
   programs the Foundation works with other funders and charitable organizations to improve the early education and care of young children and to
   strengthen the charitable sector" (Muttart Foundation n.d.)
4 Assistant deputy ministers are senior executives (employees) of Alberta
   government ministries and report directly to a deputy minister.
5 A central element of the Children First Act is a Children's Charter (Alberta
   2013b) that focuses on:
   • dignity and respect for children;
   • recognition and respect for a child's familial, cultural, social, and reli-
     gious heritage;
   • the needs of children in the design and delivery of programs and
     services;
   • the fundamental roles of prevention and early intervention in address-
     ing social challenges that affect children;
   • the shared responsibility of communities, governments, parents, guard-
     ians, and families for the well-being, safety, security, education, and
     health of children.

REFERENCES

Aimers, J., and P. Walker. 2008. "Is Community Accountability a Casualty of
    Government Partnering in New Zealand?" *New Zealand Social Work Review*
    20 (3): 14–14.
Alberta. 2013a. Justice and Solicitor General. "Alberta Children & Youth Initiative
    (ACYI)." Edmonton. Available online at http://justice.alberta.ca/programs_
    services/safe/Initiatives%20Library%20%20Safe%20Communitites%20
    Secretariat/ACYI.aspx/DispForm.aspx?ID=4; accessed July 2015.
———. 2013b. Human Services. *Children First Act: Enhancing Supports and
    Protection for Alberta Children.* Available online at http://humanservices.
    alberta.ca/16594.html; accessed 11 November 2013.
Alford, J., and O. Hughes. 2008. "Public Value Pragmatism as the Next Phase
    of Public Management." *American Review of Public Administration* 38 (2):
    130–48. http://dx.doi.org/10.1177/0275074008314203.
AMP (Alberta Mentoring Partnership). 2008. *Leadership Team Strategic Plan –
    April 2008.* Edmonton.
———. 2011a. "Presentation to ACYI Partnering Deputy Ministers."
    PowerPoint slides. Edmonton. February.

———. 2011b. *Report on Impact: Executive Summary – 2008–2011.* Edmonton.

———. 2012a. *AMP Strategic Plan,* vol. 2 (Operational Structure): *Strategy Profiles 13.05.* Edmonton.

———. 2012b. "Becoming a Partner Agency." Available online at http:// albertamentors.ca/; accessed October 2012.

———. 2012c. "Map of AMP Partners." Available online at http:// albertamentors.ca/; accessed October 2012.

———. 2012d. *Strategic Plan 2011–2014.* Edmonton.

———. n.d. *Strategic Direction 2008–2011.* Edmonton.

BBBS (Big Brothers Big Sisters) Edmonton & Area. n.d. "Chronology of Events for the Creation and Maintenance of Infrastructure Support for Provincial Mentoring in Alberta." Edmonton.

Connell, T., B. Fawcett, and G. Meagher. 2009. "Neoliberalism, New Public Management and the Human Service Professions: Introduction to the Special Issue." *Journal of Sociology* (Melbourne) 45 (4): 331–8. http://dx.doi. org/10.1177/1440783309346472.

Considine, M. 2001. *Enterprising States: The Public Management of Welfare-to-Work.* Cambridge: Cambridge University Press.

DeSantis, G. 2010. "Voices from the Margins: Policy Advocacy and Marginalized Communities." *Canadian Journal of Nonprofit and Social Economy Research* 1 (1): 23–45.

Muttart Foundation. n.d. "About Us." Available online at http://www. muttart.org/about_us; accessed 22 November 2013.

Stoker, G. 2006. "Public Value Management: A New Narrative for Networked Governance?" *American Review of Public Administration* 36 (1): 41–57. http:// dx.doi.org/10.1177/0275074005282583.

7 Provincial Funding of Human Service Community-based Organizations in Saskatchewan

JOSEPH GARCEA AND GLORIA DESANTIS

The central objective of this chapter is to provide a description and an analysis of the provincial funding regime used to finance Saskatchewan's human service community-based organizations (CBOs, the common nomenclature used to describe nonprofit social service organizations in the province). We examine the past, present, and possible future of the funding regime, as well as the relationship between the Ministry of Social Services and CBOs.

Within this context we present an analysis of the configuration and refinement of the current provincial funding regime and provincial budgetary allocations for the provision of human services. This is followed by an analysis of the coordination and integration of human services planning, provision, and funding at the ministerial, regional, and intergovernmental levels. A funding regime typically comprises the approaches, strategies, mechanisms, instruments, and criteria used by government ministries (K. Scott 2003, 12–19; Smith and Lipsky 1993, 41–5). The decision to focus on the Ministry of Social Services, rather than on other human services ministries (such as Health, Education, Employment), is based, first, on the need to manage the scope of this case study and, second, on the substantial number of human service CBOs that fall within this ministry's reach. Blended into this funding regime analysis is the importance of policy voice, or lack thereof, of the very organizations that strive to both serve and articulate the needs of vulnerable people in their communities.

Evolution of the Funding Regime, 1905–45

A full appreciation of the funding regime for human service CBOs in Saskatchewan requires a brief overview of the historical legacy and factors that shaped not only the funding regime, but also the evolution of the CBO sector, since the policy, programming, and funding choices of the past influence present-day choices (Elson 2011).

The first four decades of Saskatchewan's existence as a province (1905–45) were formative years for the funding regime for human service CBOs. Martin (1985) explains that the entanglement of personal philanthropy, altruism, morals, religion, and politics all shaped the human service CBO sector as it ebbed and flowed over time. There was "movement back and forth" between CBOs and governments delivering various services, with no clear division of labour and an ambiguous relationship (Thériault, Gill, and Kly 2002, 141). Initially the responsibility for many human services lay with local municipalities, but over time the provincial and federal governments became directly or indirectly involved. Some services provided by CBOs were funded at least in part by multiple levels of governments. The 1929 annual report of the Department of Municipal Affairs, for example, shows that some CBOs received municipal funding (Saskatchewan 1930, 150), while the Saskatchewan Anti-Tuberculosis League, a CBO by today's criteria, began treating people in 1917 in sanatoria built and operated through provincial and federal government grants as well as private donations (Lawson and Thériault 1999). Funding through donations and other forms of fundraising was common among CBOs in this period. Community Chests, precedents of the United Way, were developed in the 1930s in larger urban areas as a central fundraising model (Canadian Welfare Council 1938), and became an important component of the early funding regime for CBOs (Tillotson 2008).

Early CBOs performed at least three key functions, which were shaped by numerous influences. One was a "service provision function" – for example, between 1908 and 1912, Children's Aid Societies were opened in urban centres (Dornstauder and Macknak 2009). These early CBOs also performed an "advocacy function" in the development of services (Fairbairn 1997) – for example, in the form of women advocating for health clinics and clothing exchanges through volunteer-led, church, and/or farmer groups, early Homemakers Clubs, and Women's Institutes (Saskatchewan Women's Institute 1988). Local voluntary groups also performed an important "convening function" by organizing meetings to discuss and develop collective responses to relief and welfare problems. For example, in 1935 the Community Council of Saskatoon, comprising forty member organizations, was formed "as a medium of cooperation and social planning for social agencies and public departments in all branches of welfare work" (Canadian Welfare Council 1938, 4). Influences such as economic problems (the Great Depression), natural disasters (prairie drought), and the rise of certain diseases spawned new CBOs, and forced government expansion into the funding and delivery of human services (Canadian Welfare Council 1938; Dusel 1990; Lawson and Thériault 1999). These early CBO functions and influences continued to shape the CBO sector in subsequent decades.

Human service organizations emerged, grew, matured, declined, disappeared, and sometimes reappeared to grow in a new cycle with new people in new environments. Different CBOs began at different times, grew at different speeds, and took on different forms depending on where they were located (whether urban or rural, northern or southern areas of the province), which populations they served (for example, First Nations women, children with disabilities, isolated seniors), and how they were perceived by the different levels of government that funded them.

Evolution of the Funding Regime, 1946–90

These early roots continued to mature and expand between the end of the Second World War and the latter part of the 1980s. In the immediate post-war period, the Saskatchewan government became more involved in planning, funding, and delivering human services than were its predecessors. This was fostered by the pan-Canadian movement to build a post-war welfare state and by the governing of Saskatchewan by the Co-operative Commonwealth Federation (CCF) between 1944 and 1963. The CCF is credited with fostering a positive role for the provincial government in building a more secure future, reducing social inequities, and fostering policy innovation (such as a social assistance plan in 1955 and medicare in 1962) (Marchildon and Cotter 2001). The CCF began with a democratic socialist orientation, and focused on public and cooperative services provision and ownership (Lewis and Scott 1943; Lipset 1950; J.T. Scott 1992), but it soon discovered there was not enough money to implement its ideas, so it approached sectors outside government (Larmour 1985).

During the three decades from the 1960s to the end of the1980s, successive provincial governments funded certain human service CBOs and provided direct services themselves. The following are some highlights of this era:

- Operating grants, capital grants, and maintenance grants were common in the annual reports of the then Department of Social Services until the mid-1970s, when "the co-ordination and development of programs necessitated the re-organization of the Community Grants and Standards Division" and the "purchase of services" concept arose (Saskatchewan 1975, 19, 22). Although the term "grants" continued to be used, the 1980s saw an evolution towards contracts, fees-for-services, subsidies for operations, and funding negotiations (Saskatchewan 1980, 11; 1985, 12). This period also marked a significant shift in the ministry's funding regime.
- The Federation of Saskatchewan Indians doubled its budget between 1969 and 1972, and went "from a lobby group to a program delivery organization" (Pitsula 2001, 359).
- Between 1966 and 1976 government spending on the elderly, the intellectually disabled, and the physically handicapped was greater than on children and people with mental health issues (Riches, Jeffery, and Kramer 1979).
- Between 1971 and 1982, when the New Democratic Party (NDP), the CCF's successor, governed the province, it "favoured community control of many social services," preferring the CBO sector as the delivery agent, as shown by a 25 per cent increase in spending on that sector (O'Sullivan and Sorensen 1988, 78), while the share of government spending under its own auspices dropped by nearly half (Riches and Maslany 1983). This orientation towards greater reliance on the CBO sector for service delivery was clearly evident in the 1979–80 annual report of the Department of Social Services, which articulated the following objective: "to develop and support community-based agencies which supplement and complement the Department's objectives" (Saskatchewan 1980, 10).
- A new source of funding became available to the CBO sector in 1969 when changes were made to the Criminal Code of Canada that legalized gambling. These changes led to the development of Saskatchewan Lotteries in 1974, and permitted licensed charitable organizations to earn money through casinos, bingos, and raffles (see Lynn Gidluck's in-depth analysis of this development in Chapter 8).
- When the 1982 recession surfaced and the Progressive Conservative Party took office, the government began cutting both government- and CBO-delivered human services, especially those designed for the "undeserving poor" (for example, adults who

were unemployed), and a shift away from comprehensiveness and universality occurred (O'Sullivan and Sorensen 1988, 80). These changes led to an increased demand for food banks and other human service CBOs (Warnock 2003).

It appears a consensus was never reached on the division of responsibility for human services between 1905 and 1990. O'Sullivan and Sorensen (1988, 79) state that "government and nongovernment agencies ... have played roles of varying importance in various fields of service delivery depending on the particular issue and on time and place" (see also Canadian Welfare Council 1938; Thériault, Gill, and Kly 2002). It also appears there was never an explicit consensus on the level or type of funding that CBOs could expect. Thus, by the end of the era, CBOs were cobbling together funding from diverse sources – governments, donations and fundraising, the United Way and other foundations, fees for services, and sales of products – to serve people in need.

Evolution of the Funding Regime, 1991–2012

The Ministry of Social Services funds hundreds of CBOs. Its main programs and services are offered through three divisions: the Child and Family Services Division, the Income Assistance and Disability Services Division, and the Housing Services Division. Although a few programs and services (such as income support) are delivered directly by staff in these divisions, many are delivered by CBOs and other organizations, including First Nations and Métis organizations on a program contract basis or fee-for-service basis.

Between 1991 and 2012 the ministry undertook three important initiatives related directly or indirectly to the funding regime for human service CBOs: configuring and refining the current funding regime; establishing budget allocations for the provision of human services; and improving the coordination and integration of human services planning, provision, and funding.

Configuring and refining the contract-funding regime

In the mid-1970s the then Department of Social Services, along with other departments, started shifting from a "core-funding regime" to a "contract-funding regime" (Saskatchewan 1975, 1980, 1985; K. Scott 2003, 35–61) to fund human service CBOs. Under the former regime the provincial government transferred funds to CBOs largely through operating grants for their general operations as well as for programming and service provision. These transfers were subject to some relatively basic terms and conditions, including the number and precise needs profile of people the CBOs served, as well as reporting and accountability requirements. Under the contract-funding regime, in contrast, the government transfers funds to CBOs through what are essentially services-based or fee-for-service contracts, with more detailed and substantial terms, conditions, and reporting and accountability requirements than under the core-funding regime.

The contract-funding regime now prevails, not only in the Ministry of Social Services, but in many jurisdictions in Canada and elsewhere. During the past two decades, however, and particularly in recent years, the ministry has undertaken several strategic initiatives to refine the contract-funding regime (Saskatchewan 2010, 2012a) – in particular by focusing on standardizing and improving the contracting authority and negotiations of contracts; the format of contracts; the duration of contracts; contract compliance and accountability; and contract evaluation.

Authority: The contracting authority of the social services minister and officials is derived from the Government Organization Act. Current contract approval regulations stipulate that any contracts worth $50,000 or more require cabinet approval through an Order in Council, which allows the cabinet to have oversight and control of all sizable contract funding. The Ministry of Social Services negotiates contracts with individual CBOs as well as with umbrella organizations. Funding agreements with human service CBOs typically are negotiated individually; in 2012 approximately 1,350 different service contracts were negotiated (Wihlidal 2012).

Format: Contracts negotiated with CBOs generally have essentially the same format and elements, and so might be described as "template contracts." Every contract contains one or more sections and subsections dealing with its general elements – for example, the names of the contracting parties, key definitions, the contract's general purpose, and key provisions. Also included are one or more schedules or appendices specifying important matters related to the programs or services to be provided by the CBO, the timelines in providing them, the payment system, and the reporting requirements. The precise provisions of these sections and schedules differ, of course, to accommodate specific CBOs.

Duration: The ministry uses a mix of single- and multiyear contracts. The latter are only for a maximum of two or three years – the precise duration is related primarily to the CBO's accountability rating – and funding is provided on an annual basis. The rationale for shorter-term contracts is that it makes it easier for the ministry to ensure the services system is responsive to changes in clients' needs by being able to adjust the precise services it funds and the level at which it funds them, without long-term encumbrances.

Compliance and accountability: CBOs must comply with the terms and conditions of their contract, including with respect to the services they provide, the use of funding for specified purposes and within specified expenditure categories (salary and nonsalary budgets), and reporting periods (usually monthly, quarterly, or semi-annually). Contracted CBOs are also required to provide audited annual financial statements as part of their accountability framework.

Performance evaluation: In recent years the ministry has attempted to standardize and improve contract performance evaluation based on outcomes, rather than on outputs. In attempting to measure outcomes, however, CBOs face such difficulties as identifying the appropriate evaluation criteria (for example, direct and indirect costs and benefits) and a shortage of the human and financial capacity to perform program evaluations. As well, individual CBOs often hold more than one contract, receive funding from multiple sources, and, in some cases, receive only a small proportion of their total funding from the Ministry of Social Services or other provincial ministry or agency. Despite these challenges, the ministry continues to include some outcomes-based reporting requirements in all contracts. In April 2013 the ministry embarked on a joint venture with CBOs to develop outcome measures in three program categories: family support, intensive in-home support, and counseling support and education.

Current Funding of CBOs

Today, as in the past, the human service CBO sector is funded by a diversity of sources (Hall et al. 2004), including, as Mann (2012, 5) notes, "different programs within one ministry, different ministries, federal and municipal governments, community foundations, United Ways, Saskatchewan Lotteries, Community Initiatives Fund, as well as fundraising and fee-for-service (e.g., a Regina CBO received revenues through 43 different sources)."

During the past two decades provincial funding for CBOs has fluctuated from time to time, but the overall trend has been to increase it, particularly in recent years, rising from $112 million in fiscal year 2008/09 to $206 million in 2012/13, $206 million for 206 CBOs. However, the significance of this increase is diminished somewhat when adjusted for inflation and the increased cost of living; moreover, the available funding has had to be spread over an increased number of agencies and services offered. Thus, the following observation, made more than two decades ago, is still relevant today in Saskatchewan: "nonprofit organizations that seek or receive government funding operate in an environment marked by competition for finite resources, evolving public policy, periodic turnover of elected officials, government restructuring and differences within and across government departments and jurisdictions" (McFarlane and Roach 1999, 2).

The Provincial Government Service Coordination and Integration Movement, 1991–2012

In addition to institutionalizing and refining the contract-funding regime, during the past two decades the Saskatchewan government has also undertaken initiatives designed to improve coordination and integration of the provision and funding of human services. As a document prepared for the provincial government explains, "[s]ervice integration is any approach to providing services to the public that streamlines and simplifies client access and bridges traditional organizational or program boundaries" (Myers 2012, 5). As Box 7.1 shows, initiatives aimed at improving coordination and integration have been undertaken at the interministerial, regional, and intergovernmental levels.

Interministerial coordination and integration

Several initiatives were undertaken over the past two decades to improve coordination and integration at the interministerial level. These initiatives started in 1991, when representatives from the provincial government's Family Foundation joined with representatives from human service ministries to form the Integrated Services Planning Committee. Over time this committee became the Associate/Assistant Deputy Ministers' Forum, which was restructured in the mid-1990s to become the Human Services Integration Forum, consisting of senior officials from eleven ministries. During the subsequent fifteen years the Human Services Integration Forum led the service integration initiative (Myers 2005, 2012).

BOX 7.1 SERVICE COORDINATION INITIATIVES AND THE INTEGRATION MOVEMENT, 1991–2012

1990   2012

Interministerial level

1991	Early 1990s	Mid-1990s	2010-2011
- Family Foundation - Provincial Government Integrated Services Planning Committee	Associate/Assistant Deputy Ministers' Forum formed	Human Services Integration Forum (HSIF) formed	Senior Inter-Ministry Steering Committee formed; HSIF disbanded

Regional level

1996–present day
Ten regional intersectoral committees formed and continue today; every region of the province covered

Intergovernmental level

2010-2012
Ministry of Social Services Letters of Understanding with First Nations and Métis governments

Major Influences on Service Coordination and Integration Movement

- fiscal pressures on government in recent decades;
- shift towards minimalist state;
- new localism, subsidiarity, and devolution movement;
- increase in number of CBOs;
- collective advocacy work of CBOs;
- 2002–07 Premier's Voluntary Sector Initiative;
- 2008 and 2012 regional summits across the province.

In 2010 and 2011 the provincial government continued to develop and refine interministerial mechanisms, with the formation of a Senior Inter-Ministry Steering Committee – comprising representation from ten ministries, the Executive Council, and the Public Service Commission – a Cabinet Committee on Children and Youth, and a Deputy Minister's Committee on Children and Youth. The Deputy Minister's committee was later merged with the Human Services Deputy Ministers committee, and the Human Services Integration Forum merged with the Senior Inter-Ministry Steering Committee.

The shared mission of these committees was to apply the "enterprise approach" and related intersectoral coordination strategies to reduce barriers to service provision at the governmental and nongovernmental levels, and to improve "integrated services and supports for children, youth and families, and those at risk or living in vulnerable circumstances" (Saskatchewan 2011). Initially, the enterprise approach was to be used in relation to the following four strategies: Child Welfare Review Investments; Autism Strategy and Fetal Alcohol Spectrum Disorder Strategy; Saskatchewan Policy and Partners Strategy to Reduce Crime and Violence; and First Nations and Métis Education and Employment Strategy. The enterprise approach, inspired by principles of new public management, is a strategic management framework designed to ensure that policymaking, decision-making, and programming systems are seen as an interconnected set of enterprises and operated in an enterprising or entrepreneurial manner. This includes "the adoption of integrated strategies to support better targeting of services and identification of strategic, government-wide outcomes" (Saskatchewan 2011).

Regional coordination and integration

The regional dimension of the coordination and integration initiative is reflected in the creation of Regional Intersectoral Committees (RICs), ten of which, covering the entire province, were established by 1996. Each RIC consists of representatives of participating ministries, local and regional agencies such as health and school boards, and some CBOs. A provincial ministry manages the RIC system. The precise composition of the membership of RICs varies by region. The RICs' principal role is to facilitate consultation and coordination for a wide range of human service agencies at a regional scale in order to identify needs, establish priorities, design evaluation frameworks, and assess outcomes (Myers 2012).

RICs also perform an adjudication function for the Community Initiatives Fund, a funding agency created by the provincial government, as well as for Student Summer Works and the Childhood Development and Nutrition Program, which are outside the scope of the Community Initiatives Fund. The RICs do not actually grant the dollars, but they do bring a regional perspective to the review of applications and make recommendations to the various funding agencies (Mann 2012; Wihlidal 2012). The RICS' contribution to policy and program coordination and integration at the regional level is not always as clear, however, as the structure would imply. As well, some RICs acknowledge that they have not been successful at service integration work with many First Nations and Métis communities.

Intergovernmental coordination and integration

In recent years some human services coordination and integration initiatives have also been undertaken between the provincial government and First Nations and Métis governments. More specifically, the Ministry of Social Services has signed Letters of Understanding and agreements with the Federation of Saskatchewan Indian Nations (FSIN) and the Métis Nation–Saskatchewan (MN–S), and contracts with some of their agencies. This includes two historic Letters of Understanding signed in August 2011 with the FSIN and the MN–S, respectively, on the goals and protocols for collaborative engagement following extensive consultations on these matters (Saskatchewan 2012a, 14). Among the most significant agreements are those that delegate to numerous First Nations Child and Family Services agencies responsibility for the provision of child protection services and services for children in care on-reserve. As of March 2011, eighteen such Delegation Agreements had been signed concerning agencies serving a client base of 1,139 children. Within the scope of these agreements, the Ministry of Social Services performs a quality assurance role. The ministry also helps to build capacity – for example, with respect to home assessment, custom adoption, and therapeutic crisis intervention – in First Nations communities (Saskatchewan 2012a). Under the terms of these agreements, responsibility for ensuring the safety and well-being of children on-reserve is shared between First Nations Child and Family Services agencies and the ministry, although ultimate responsibility for child protection rests with the minister.

Influences on coordination and integration

The provincial government's service coordination and integration work has been influenced by several interrelated economic and ideological changes. One is the fiscal pressures that reached crisis proportions during the 1990s, forcing the government to reduce funding to CBOs.

Another is the growing influence of the neoconservative view that the footprint of government should be reduced to a minimalist state, which the communitarian values embedded in Saskatchewan's political culture tempered, but did not completely overcome (Carbert 1996). A third influence has been movements in other countries towards "new localism" (Corry et al. 2004; Corry and Stoker 2002), "place-based policymaking" (Bradford 2005), and "subsidiarity" (Brouillet 2011), which refers to the devolution of planning and service provision to the lowest levels of government and authorities (such as health boards and school boards) capable of performing them.

Saskatchewan's coordination and integration initiatives have also been influenced by the CBO system itself, including the increasing number and types of CBOs, the services they provide, especially for people with complex needs, and the increasing social policy and funding advocacy undertaken by some of the larger and more powerful CBOs and umbrella organizations (DeSantis 2008) – for example, Elmwood Residence Inc., and the Saskatchewan Association of Rehabilitation Centres, which has a membership of eighty CBOs.

Finally, although the Premier's Voluntary Sector Initiative (VSI), established in 2002 by NDP premier Lorne Calvert, was not about service coordination and integration specifically, it was launched to strengthen the cooperative relationship between the provincial government and the voluntary sector and to build capacity within the voluntary sector. It facilitated meetings between the government and the CBO sector that increased mutual awareness regarding a variety of issues (Saskatchewan 2002). In this, the basic goals and objectives of the Premier's VSI were very similar to those of the federal government's Voluntary Sector Initiative, established two years earlier (Phillips 2003). The Premier's VSI Steering Committee consisted of fourteen community representatives and eleven representatives from government departments, and the government hosted three forums with CBOs over the period between 2002 and 2007.

The VSI was dissolved in 2007 after the election of the Saskatchewan Party, but in 2008 the new government hosted five regional summits in major centres across the province to encourage conversations about human services in general, as well as issues related to existing and future social policies and funding issues for human services. In November 2012 the government organized another four sectoral summits with funded CBOs to broach these issues again in an effort to continue exploring issues and options on potential reforms designed to improve not only the funding regime, but also working relationships between government agencies and CBOs.

CBO Perceptions of the Contract-Funding Regime

The perceptions of CBO officials regarding the evolving funding system for human services were articulated in the five regional summits the province hosted in 2008, the purpose of which was "to develop a new social policy direction for Saskatchewan" (Saskatchewan 2008). Invited to offer their thoughts, ideas, questions, and recommendations to that end, CBO officials discussed four main themes: elements of the contract-funding regime, paid human resources and volunteers, accountability and transparency issues, and relationship and collaboration issues. These issues were not prioritized during the summits, and we do not present the highlights here in any particular order; moreover, the list is not an exhaustive one. It is noteworthy that CBOs' conversations did not focus solely on the provincial government or on the Ministry of Social Services.

CBO officials expressed concerns about a number of elements of the contract-funding regime. In a province of rural and urban communities separated by great distances, considerations of space and place – in the form of, for example, mileage compensation and travel costs of clients and staff – are critical elements that funding formulas should take into consideration. Concerns were also expressed about the lack of pay equity between CBO workers and government workers, the instability of funding, the need to refocus on operational funding, and the need for broader categories of what should be "fundable." Officials also raised the issue of the timeliness of access to agreed-upon funding – for example, many CBOs do not have surplus funds to "carry" staff until the government sends the cheque. In general, there was a sense of competition for government funding among CBOs that works against service integration and partnership building for service delivery. In addition, some CBO officials indicated that government funders seemed to feel they were entitled to interfere in CBO operations. To address these concerns, CBO officials suggested moving towards standardized funding agreements – with respect to the contents and length of forms, equitable funding for salaries, and standard budget requirements across funders – multiyear contracts, multiyear funding (a minimum of three years), standardized final reports across funders, and a system to ensure that funding serves community needs, not government needs.

In discussing the issue of human resources, CBO officials noted that, since some CBOs' services are delivered entirely by volunteers, there was a need for resources and time to attract, support, train, and celebrate volunteers, whether they deliver services or sit on boards of directors. Officials also lamented the difficulty of recruiting and retaining staff, citing low and inequitable wages, the lack of benefit packages in many organizations, the lack of affordable training opportunities, and few opportunities for advancement, all of which lead to high staff turnover. Staff burnout was also a concern, with officials indicating they spent an inordinate amount of time on the paperwork involved in seeking funding, especially on the part of CBOs with multiple funders. They also noted there was a stigma attached to the type of people who work for CBOs, who are often regarded as uneducated and unskilled; moreover, the sector tends to be female dominated and therefore undervalued. Among the suggestions to address these issues were the hiring of more First Nations and Métis people and the creation of a central agency to train and develop staff, assist with payroll needs, and share staff with similar job descriptions across agencies.

With respect to accountability and transparency, CBO officials noted that, although they expected to be held accountable for the public money they were given, demands for greater accountability were increasing but were not being matched by increased funding for such extra administrative work. Officials felt that the amount of paperwork required should reflect the amount of funding received – for example, a CBO that received $5,000 should not be expected to complete the same amount of paperwork as one that received $500,000. Suggestions to address these issues included clearer funder performance criteria, the need for accountability and transparency on the part of both CBOs *and* funders, and the use of outcome indicators to demonstrate accountability, with longer-term funding (5–10 years) for CBOs with demonstrated positive outcomes.

On CBOs' relationships with governments, officials expressed the need for partnerships, collaboration, and networking with respect to public policy development, service planning and delivery, funding priorities, evaluation, and mutual learning. Officials noted that the nature of funding relationships could be cooperative, collaborative, and consultative, or full of friction. They also recognized that partnerships with other CBOs were vital, but were concerned that the provincial government did not realize how much time was required to cultivate these partnerships. Further, CBOs did not experience "service integration" and "service collaboration" in the way the government might intend – for example, despite all the government-driven service integration work, CBOs described a funding and service delivery system that was fragmented.

Among other challenges CBO officials cited at the summits were self-contained "silos" in different ministries and across different levels of government that made it difficult for CBOs to communicate and coordinate their program planning and that required additional resources; government policy choices made without CBO dialogue or collaboration – especially early enough in the process – and that did not actually meet community needs; and the need for policy development to be a partnership of managers, clients, government decision makers, and families. CBO officials suggested that CBOs themselves should establish a united front, instead of competing with one another for funding, that successes, such as "joint task teams," should be expanded in number and scope, and that a more balanced relationship, including formal agreements between the voluntary sector and all levels of government, should be created.

Since these 2008 summits, some welcome changes have taken place, including the introduction of multiyear funding contracts and cost-of-living adjustments (Mann 2012), and the launch – after a decade of discussions, a feasibility study, surveys, and a CBO-only meeting held in November 2012 – of the Saskatchewan Nonprofit Partnership (SNP 2012), but there is still much to be done.

Discussion

The contract-funding regime for CBOs in Saskatchewan operates within a system of evolving organizational frameworks and relationships. Change is constant, as human service organizations continue to emerge, grow, mature, decline, disappear, and sometimes reappear, and as multiple, complex, and highly differentiated relationships between the provincial government and CBOs persist.

Given government annual reports, the results of CBO summits, and discussions with CBO and government officials, it is clear there are diverse types of relations between the Ministry of Social Services and CBOs. Where the CBO is powerless and dependent on government funding, the relationship is highly unbalanced; where the CBO is more powerful and self-sufficient, the relationship is better balanced (see Boudreau 2006). As Coston (1998) explains, the typology of the

CBO-government relationship ranges from repression and rivalry to supportive and collaborative, and includes three main dimensions: the degree of government resistance to or acceptance of CBOs and the people they serve, the distribution of power in the relationship, and the degree of formality. Indeed, these relationships are reflected across the spectrum of CBOs in Saskatchewan.

Culture and characteristics of the funding regime

The culture and characteristics of the contract-funding regime today is different than it was several decades ago. As noted earlier, a fundamental shift began to occur in the mid-1970s, when, over the course of fifteen years, the core-funding regime was replaced by a contract-funding regime, a move that brought about a more business-like relationship between the provincial government and CBOs. The shift to a contract-funding regime also produced a more competitive culture among CBOs looking for scarce funding. There appears to be an understanding on the part of both the government and CBOs that they are in an interdependent relationship, but this relationship is often imbalanced, with CBOs having to position themselves carefully regarding advocacy for funding and advocacy for more progressive and productive public policy. Although the series of summits held in 2008 and 2012 were intended to build mutual awareness and understanding and improve working relationships between the government and CBOs, and although reforms to the funding regime were intended explicitly to pave the way for the government and CBOs to meet their respective objectives, clashes continue to occur due to the inherently different nature, focus, and locus of power between them.

Since the early 2000s, the Ministry of Social Services has focused its efforts on institutionalizing and refining the contract-funding regime. To this end, the ministry has engaged in three main areas of work. First, it has set out to improve a number of components of the funding regime, including a higher degree of standardization within and across government departments and a move towards outcomes evaluation for services provided by CBOs. Second, the ministry has focused on improving both the funding regime and its own strategic planning and management processes, and has encouraged CBOs to do the same. Third, the ministry has increased the level and distribution of funding across certain types of CBOs. For example, in December 2012 the minister announced that an additional $17.34 million per year would be directed to front-line workers in Saskatchewan Association of Rehabilitation Centre agencies and to other agencies that provide critical services to vulnerable adults and children (Saskatchewan 2012b).

Yet unease among CBOs lingers. The Premier's VSI document offers a glimpse of the government's funding philosophy that leads to this unease: After the Second World War Saskatchewan saw a "rapid increase in the number and scope of these organizations. CBOs often developed and evolved to provide more specialized services that were not fully addressed within the public sector ... The government of Saskatchewan began to develop programs to fund *targeted* CBOs. *The funding was intended to enhance existing resources from fundraising and donations*" (Saskatchewan 2002, 5; emphasis added). The statement raises the question of whether the provincial government ever intended to provide core funding for human service CBOs or only to top up CBO budgets.

Implications of the current contract-funding regime for CBOs

There are at least four main implications of the current contract-funding regime for CBOs: stability, reporting and accountability requirements, government fiscal and program policy alignment, and advocacy and voice.

Stability: CBOs are concerned that the current funding regime, even with multiyear contracts, does not provide an adequate assurance of mid- to long-term stability, particularly for CBOs that depend heavily upon, among other things, the decisions of ministries on such highly discretionary matters as the amount of contract funding a CBO receives, the number of organizations that will be funded in any community in any given year, the number of clients a CBO must serve to receive various levels of compensation, and the actual financial compensation formulas used for various types of service contracts. It is because of such uncertainties that many CBOs rely on a diversity of funding sources. More specifically, models such as "social entrepreneurship" might become more attractive to CBOs as either a supplement to or a complete replacement for government funding (Pitsula 2005).

Reporting and accountability: CBOs expect to be held accountable for the public money they receive to deliver services to people in need. In some instances, however, demands for reporting and accountability do not take into consideration the extraordinary amount of administrative work required to apply for funding and prepare reports. Most CBOs thus welcome a shift to multiyear contracts that reduce the time staff and volunteers spend on administration. The shift away from reporting solely on inputs, activities, and outputs towards reporting on outcomes is not new to CBOs; many of them began measuring outcomes in the early 2000s, after the United Way of America released its groundbreaking document, *Measuring Program Outcomes: A Practical Approach* (Hatry et al. 1996). Nonetheless, there is great variation in outcomes measurement across the CBO sector. Mann (2012) cautions CBOs and funders not to focus just on "efficiency" in service delivery, but to consider outcomes related to citizen engagement and social inclusion – an important reminder that CBOs need to be accountable to the communities they serve as well as to those who fund them. It is also a reminder that governments, too, have to be accountable both to the community and to CBOs. In the case of CBOs, the prevailing view articulated at the 2008 summits was that accountability and transparency between CBOs and the government should be bidirectional.

Alignment of government fiscal and program policies: More than twenty years ago the provincial government spawned a human services coordination and integration movement that had both bureaucratic and political structures and processes. Its focus, however, was explicitly on relations among ministries, rather than on links with the CBO sector – although some regional intersectoral committees have since created mechanisms for CBO engagement in human services planning.

The 2008 summits indicated that different CBO subsectors were engaged with the provincial government to different degrees and in different ways in human services planning – in other words, the participation of CBOs in the setting of government program policies and priorities development was uneven. For example, some alignment appears to take place in the work of the Ministry of Social Services and the Federation of Saskatchewan Indian Nations and between the ministry and some umbrella disability organizations, but comparable efforts are not evident with other organizations. Direct CBO participation in the evolution of the contract-funding regime is also not formalized, even though the government has implemented some changes based on recommendations that arose from the summits. It also appears that numerous service coordination and integration structures and processes are not aligned with the funding regime, which can create serious problems. For example, several decades ago the provincial government announced deinstitutionalization policies for people living with mental disabilities, but failed to shift funding from government-run psychiatric hospitals to community-based programs (Crocus Cooperative,

Saskatoon Mental Health Association, and Saskatoon Housing Coalition 1987), which resulted in hundreds of deinstitutionalized people living in communities without adequate community-based supports such as housing, and facing multiple crises that in turn strained the CBO system (Dickinson 1989).

Advocacy and voice: It is noteworthy that Saskatchewan does not have an umbrella organization for the nonprofit sector generally or for the nonprofit human services sector specifically to advocate for funding and policy changes. Instead, such advocacy comes from numerous subsectoral organizations such as the Saskatchewan Association of Rehabilitation Centres (serving people with disabilities), the Provincial Association of Transition Houses of Saskatchewan (serving women leaving domestic violence situations), and the Disability Income Support Coalition (which advocates for a dignified welfare legislation for people with disabilities).

In the absence of an umbrella organization for the sector as a whole, the provincial government has been known to use the power of the purse to influence CBO planning, service delivery, and advocacy work (Council on Social Development Regina 1993; Dickinson 1989; Kly and Thériault 2001). For example, in 2010 and 2011 the government pulled its funding of a number of individual welfare and human rights advocacy organizations, forcing some CBOs to close their doors (such as the Regina Welfare Rights Centre) and others to scale back their operations. Officials of some CBOs involved in the 2008 summits indicated that the funding regime had diminished the sense of power and voice of their organizations regarding their funding deliberations with the Ministry of Social Services and constrained their public policy advocacy work. This combination of factors appears to have led a group of CBOs to launch the province-wide Saskatchewan Nonprofit Network (SNP 2012).

Prospects and directions for reform of the funding regime

Consensus is emerging among CBOs and within the provincial government itself that both the funding regime and government-CBO relationships need to change. Such recognition of the need for reform comes largely from consultations at the provincial summits, planning sessions hosted by the provincial government with umbrella organizations such as Saskatchewan Association of Rehabilitation Centres and the Saskatchewan Association for Community Living, the government's twenty-year human services integration movement, committees of senior administrators and cabinet members, and the creation of the SNP.

CBOs and the government differ, however, on what the precise focus and direction of reforms should be (Mann 2012). Since the status quo does not appear to be an option for either side, what directions might funding reforms take? There are two possibilities. One would be to continue refining various components of the existing contract-funding regime, using the same combination of stable incrementalism and punctuated equilibrium that has been employed for the past two decades (Howlett, Ramesh, and Perl 2009, 202–8). The other direction would entail a shift from a relatively "fragmented" to a more "integrated" contract-funding regime in which funds would be allocated to various priorities and to the CBOs involved in working on them based on a system-wide, comprehensive, and coherent client-centred – or citizen-centred – planning, budgeting, and funding framework. Such a shift would require funders and funded alike to demonstrate cogently and persuasively, based on reliable evidence, how the funding CBOs receive for services will improve outcomes.

A more integrated contract-funding model likely would be based on a system-wide strategic planning system involving provincial officials, CBO officials, and other participants (for example, private sector stakeholders and public-private partnerships) who have instrumental roles in the human services system. Such a model likely would be rooted in what might be termed "neorationalism" and based on a complex, multilevel governance system (for more details, see Brock 2003; Brock and Banting 2001; Hall and Banting 2000). This reform direction appears to be the provincial government's preference. The challenge will be to develop and implement the requisite participatory processes to implement this model, given the ongoing challenges posed by the plethora of complex relations between the government and myriad CBOs and the existence of financial constraints even during economic booms.

While the Ministry of Social Services is engaged in reforming the contract-funding model, the CBO sector continues to reform its funding mix of donations, earned revenue, and government grants. Historically, the sector has adapted to changes in its environment, and has altered its programs and services to meet the changing needs of its communities. Within the scope of these sources of funding, there are at least three ways CBOs could generate revenues at the community level. One is through the "social entrepreneurship model," which was born out of the fee-for-service and product commercialization movement and which has been gaining traction among CBOs in Saskatchewan and across the country. Another way is through the emergence of "funders consortiums." In one such consortium, in Saskatoon, funders are involved in roundtable discussions on the creation of common application forms, the setting of funding priorities, and the coordination of funding approaches. A third way to generate revenues is to rely more heavily on the cooperatives model – an attractive option for some types of CBOs in a province with a long history of the use of cooperatives – health cooperatives, in particular – to meet the needs of individuals in many communities.

Although key questions remain unanswered, the provincial government and the CBO sector are probably better prepared today than ever to tackle them (Canadian Welfare Council 1938; O'Sullivan & Sorensen 1988; Thériault, Gill, and Kly 2002). For example, what are *essential services* and who should be responsible for funding and delivering them? In what areas should CBOs *supplement* government services? And in what areas should CBOs be a *complete substitute* for government-delivered services?

Conclusion

A central goal of reforms to the human services system in Saskatchewan remains improvements in efficiency and effectiveness and in transparency and accountability by, among other things, reducing fragmentation and improving coordination and integration. There appears to be a consensus that the human services system in Saskatchewan, much like that in Manitoba (see Frankel and Levasseur, in this volume), is a patchwork system that runs along a continuum from extreme fragmentation to certain degrees of integration, depending on the particular population being served, the location of service delivery, and the available resource base, to name but three factors. The province's Regional Intersectoral Committees appear to reduce this fragmentation, although some are more successful than others. CBOs and the provincial government do not, however, have a clear division of labour across the board in the delivery of all human services. As noted earlier, the provincial government funds CBOs to provide specific services (such as group homes), while government ministries provide a direct services to people in need (such as counselling). In many cases, referrals back and forth between government staff and CBOs happen regularly.

There also appears to be a consensus that the contract-funding regime, too, is fragmented and in need of refining. Considerable resources have been devoted to establishing and enhancing policies, processes, mechanisms, and instruments for contract-funding purposes. CBOs have noted the challenges that provincial government organizational and funding silos create insofar as they constrain CBOs to communicate and coordinate their program proposals across multiple provincial ministries, and in some instances even between the various levels of government. Despite twenty years of human services coordination and integration work, much remains to be done, particularly since CBOs and the provincial government are often not the only partners involved in funding relationships. Most CBOs cobble together funding from multiple sources, including provincial government ministries, federal government agencies, municipal governments, community-resident donors, corporate donors, and fees for services. The challenges posed by such a fragmented funding system are compounded by the constantly evolving CBO-government funding regime and relationship. Both parties are operating in a dynamic, fluid system that can change either slowly (for example, slow ideological change over decades regarding where people with cognitive disabilities should live) or rapidly (for example, the sudden housing crisis that hit Saskatchewan during the recent economic boom).

Both the fragmented service delivery system and fragmented funding regime have important implications for the nature of CBO-government relations. Stretched, strained, tiring, concerning, and uneven are some of the words that describe these relations. The 2008 summits appear to have been a good start towards building mutual awareness and understanding. The explicit and formal service delivery and funding agreements negotiated and signed by the Ministry of Social Services with two major Indigenous organizations in the province and with some disability CBOs constitute valuable precedents for that ministry's capacity to coordinate and integrate service planning and funding. They are also good examples of the human services co-production and policy co-construction concepts that are already common in Quebec (Vaillancourt 2009). The examples further reflect the direction in which the broad-scale coordination and integration of CBOs – including the less powerful, smaller ones – needs to go. Future summits, we suggest, should not be "consultation" mechanisms; rather, they should be moulded into collaborative mechanisms, with more defined and explicit goals for service coordination, integration, and funding.

REFERENCES

Boudreau, R. 2006. "Rehabilitating the Voluntary Sector Initiative: Rethinking Accountability and Creating Capacity." *Saskatchewan Institute of Public Policy, Student Policy Essays* (4): 25–41.

Bradford, N. 2005. *Place-based Public Policy: Towards a New Urban and Community Agenda for Canada*. Ottawa: Canadian Policy Research Networks.

Brock, K., ed. 2003. *Delicate Dances: Public Policy and the Nonprofit Sector*. Montreal; Kingston, ON: McGill-Queen's University Press.

Brock, K., and K. Banting, eds. 2001. *The Nonprofit Sector and Government in a New Century*. Montreal; Kingston, ON: McGill-Queen's University Press.

Brouillet, E. 2011. "Canadian Federalism and the Principle of Subsidiarity: Should We Open Pandora's Box?" *Supreme Court Law Review* 54 (2): 601–31.

Canadian Welfare Council. 1938. *A Study of Community Welfare Services in Saskatoon*. Ottawa: Council House.

Carbert, L. 1996. "Governing on the Correct, the Compassionate, the Saskatchewan Side of the Border." In *In the Presence of Women: Representation in Canadian Governments*, ed. J. Arscott and L. Trimble, 57–77. Toronto: Harcourt Brace.

Corry, D., W. Hatter, I. Parker, A. Randle, and G. Stoker. 2004. *Joining-up for Democracy: Governance Systems from the New Localism*. London: New Local Government Network.

Corry, D., and G. Stoker. 2002. *New Localism: Refashioning the Centre-Local Relationship*. London: New Local Government Network.

Coston, J. 1998. "A Model and Typology of Government-NGO Relationships." *Nonprofit and Voluntary Sector Quarterly* 27 (3): 358–82. http://dx.doi.org/10.1177/0899764098273006.

Council on Social Development Regina. 1993. *Forging Responsible Partnerships: Human Services Review. A Report on the Relationship between the Saskatchewan Government and Non-Government Organisations in the Human Services Sector*. Regina, SK: Western Institute for Public Policy.

Crocus Co-operative, Saskatoon Mental Health Association, and Saskatoon Housing Coalition. 1987. *Community Support Research Project*. Saskatoon, SK.

DeSantis, G. 2008. "A Critical Exploration of Voluntary Sector Social Policy Advocacy with Marginalized Communities Using a Population Health Lens and Social Justice." PhD diss., University of Regina.

Dickinson, H. 1989. *The Two Psychiatries: The Transformation of Psychiatric Work in Saskatchewan 1905–1984*. Regina, SK: University of Regina, Canadian Plains Research Centre.

Dornstauder, F., and D. Macknak. 2009. *100 Years of Child Welfare Services in Saskatchewan: A Survey*. Regina: Saskatchewan Association of Social Workers.

Dusel, S. 1990. "An Analysis of NGOs in Saskatchewan." Presentation to Non-Governmental Organizations Conference, Controlling Our Agenda, Regina, January.

Elson, P. 2011. "The Emergence of Structured Subnational Voluntary Sector-Government Relationships in Canada: A Historical Institutional Analysis." *Voluntary Sector Review* 2 (2): 135–55. http://dx.doi.org/10.1332/20408051 1X583823.

Fairbairn, B. 1997. "The Social Economy and the Development of Health Services in Canada: Past, Present and Future." Presentation to the International Conference on the Social Economy in the North and in the South, Ostend, Belgium, 7–8 March.

Hall, M., and K. Banting. 2000. "The Non-Profit Sector in Canada: An Introduction." In *The Nonprofit Sector in Canada: Roles and Relationships*, ed. K. Banting, 1–28. Montreal; Kingston, ON: McGill-Queen's University Press.

Hall, M., M. de Wit, D. Lasby, D. McIver, T. Evers, C. Johnston, J. McAuley, K. Scott, G. Cucumel, L. Jolin, et al. 2004. *Cornerstones of Community: Highlights of the National Survey of Nonprofit and Voluntary Organizations*. Cat. no. 61-533-XIE. Ottawa: Statistics Canada. Available online at http://www.statcan.gc.ca/pub/61-533-x/61-533-x2004001-eng.htm; accessed 11 May 2015.

Hatry, H., T. van Houten, M. Plantz, and M.T. Greenway. 1996. *Measuring Program Outcomes: A Practical Approach*. Alexandria, VA: United Way of America.

Howlett, M., M. Ramesh, and A. Perl. 2009. *Studying Public Policy: Policy Cycles and Policy Subsystems*. Don Mills, ON: Oxford University Press.

Kly, Y., and L. Thériault. 2001. "Human Rights and the Situation of Third Sector Mental Health NGOs in Saskatchewan." Social Policy Research Unit working paper. Regina, SK: University of Regina, Faculty of Social Work.

Larmour, J. 1985. "The Douglas Government's Changing Emphasis on Public, Private, and Co-Operative Development in Saskatchewan, 1944–1961." In *Building the Co-operative Commonwealth: Essays on the Democratic Socialist Tradition in Canada*, ed. W. Brennan, 161–80. Regina, SK: University of Regina, Canadian Plains Research Center.

Lawson, G., and L. Thériault. 1999. "Saskatchewan's Community Health Service Associations: An Historical Perspective." *Prairie Forum* 24 (2): 251–68.

Lewis, D., and F. Scott. 1943. *Make This Your Canada: A Review of CCF History and Policy*. Winnipeg: Central Canada Publishing.

Lipset, S. 1950. *Agrarian Socialism: The Cooperative Commonwealth Federation in Saskatchewan*. Berkeley: University of California Press.

Mann, T. 2012. "Saskatchewan Community-Based Organizations'
Perspectives." Presentation to the Forum on Funding Policies and the
Nonprofit Sector in Western Canada, Calgary, 15 October.

Marchildon, G., and B. Cotter. 2001. "Saskatchewan and the Social Union."
In *Saskatchewan Politics into the Twenty-First Century*, ed. H. Leeson, 367–80.
Regina, SK: University of Regina, Canadian Plains Research Center.

Martin, S. 1985. *An Essential Grace: Funding Canada's Health Care, Education,
Welfare, Religion and Culture*. Toronto: McClelland and Stewart.

McFarlane, S., and R. Roach. 1999. "Strings Attached: Non-profits & Their
Funding Relationships with Governments." Alternative Service Delivery
Project Research Bulletin 4. Calgary: Canada West Foundation.

Myers, T. 2005. *Human Services Integration Forum (HSIF)/Regional Intersectoral
Committees (RICs)*. Regina, SK: Ministry of Education.

———. 2012. *Interconnected: Community-Human Service Engagement in
Saskatchewan*. Bulyea, SK: Terry Myers Consulting.

O'Sullivan, M., and S. Sorensen. 1988. "Saskatchewan." In *Privatization and
Provincial Social Services in Canada: Policy, Administration and Service Delivery*,
ed. J. Ismael and Y. Vaillancourt, 75–93. Edmonton: University of Alberta
Press.

Phillips, S. 2003. "In Accordance: Canada's Voluntary Sector Accord from Idea
to Implementation." In *Delicate Dances: Public Policy and the Nonprofit Sector*,
ed. K. Brock, 18–61. Montreal; Kingston, ON: McGill-Queen's University
Press.

Pitsula, J. 2001. "First Nations and Saskatchewan Politics." In *Saskatchewan
Politics into the Twenty-First Century*, ed. H. Leeson, 349–66. Regina, SK:
University of Regina, Canadian Plains Research Center.

———. 2005. *The Saskatchewan Voluntary Sector in the Context of Social
Enterprise: A Case Study of Family Service Regina*. Regina, SK: University of
Regina, Saskatchewan Institute of Public Policy.

Riches, G., B. Jeffery, and M. Kramer. 1979. *Spending Is Choosing: Restraint
and Growth in Saskatchewan's Personal Social Services 1966–77*. Regina,
SK: University of Regina, Faculty of Social Work, Social Administration
Research Unit.

Riches, G., and G. Maslany. 1983. "Social Welfare and the New Democrats:
Personal Social Service Spending in Saskatchewan 1971–81." *Canadian Social
Work Review* 1: 33–54.

Saskatchewan. 1930. Department of Municipal Affairs. *Annual Report for the
Financial Year 1929–1930*. Regina: King's Printer.

———. 1975. Department of Social Services. *Annual Report 1974–75*. Regina.

———. 1980. Department of Social Services. *Annual Report 1979–80*. Regina.

———. 1985. Department of Social Services. *Annual Report 1984–85*. Regina.
———. 2002. *The Premier's Voluntary Sector Initiative: A Framework for Partnership between the Government of Saskatchewan and Saskatchewan's Voluntary Sector*. Regina.
———. 2008. Ministry of Social Services. "CBO Summits 2008: What Saskatchewan Community-Based Organizations Are Saying about Human Services in Saskatchewan." Regina.
———. 2010. Ministry of Social Services. *Annual Report 2009–2010*. Regina: Government of Saskatchewan.
———. 2011. Senior Inter-Ministry Steering Committee. "Saskatchewan Child and Youth Agenda: Terms of Reference." Available online at http://northwestric.ca/wp-content/themes/nwric/images/sims-sept15-2011.pdf; accessed 11 May 2015.
———. 2012a. Ministry of Social Services. *Annual Report 2011–2012*. Regina: Government of Saskatchewan.
———. 2012b. Ministry of Social Services. "Government investing in care for vulnerable people." News Release, 17 December. http://www.saskatchewan.ca/government/news-and-media/2012/december/17/government-investing-in-care-for-vulnerable-people.
SNP (Saskatchewan Nonprofit Partnership). 2012. *Provincial Summit: Summary of Proceedings*, Saskatoon, 5–6 November. Available online at http://www.cifsask.org/uploads/SNNO%20Nov2012.pdf.
Saskatchewan Women's Institute. 1988. *Legacy: A History of Saskatchewan Homemakers' Clubs and Women's Institutes, 1911–1988*. Regina, SK: FOCUS Publishing.
Scott, J.T. 1992. "Voluntary Sector in Crisis: Canada's Changing Public Philosophy of the State and Its Impact on Voluntary Charitable Organizations." PhD diss., University of Colorado at Denver.
Scott, K. 2003. *Funding Matters: The Impact of Canada's New Funding Regime on Nonprofit and Voluntary Organizations*. Ottawa: Canadian Council on Social Development and Coalition of National Voluntary Organizations. Available online at http://www.ccsd.ca/index.php/research/funding-matters.
Smith, S., and M. Lipsky. 1993. *Nonprofits for Hire: The Welfare State in the Age of Contracting*. Cambridge, MA: Harvard University Press.
Thériault, L., C. Gill, and Y. Kly. 2002. "Personal Social Services and the Third Sector in Saskatchewan." In *Social Economy: Health and Welfare in Four Canadian Provinces: Interprovincial Perspectives*, ed. S.A. Stilitz, Y. Vaillancourt, and L. Tremblay, 135–61. Halifax, NS: Fernwood.
Tillotson, S. 2008. *Contributing Citizens: Modern Charitable Fundraising and the Making of the Welfare State, 1920–66*. Vancouver: UBC Press.

Vaillancourt, Y. 2009. "Social Economy in the Co-Construction of Public
    Policy." *Annals of Public and Cooperative Economics* 80 (2): 275–313. http://
    dx.doi.org/10.1111/j.1467-8292.2009.00387.x.
Warnock, J. 2003. *The Structural Adjustment of Capitalism in Saskatchewan.*
    Saskatoon, SK: Canadian Centre for Policy Alternatives.
Wihlidal, B. 2012. "Ministry of Social Services Perspectives on Funding of
    Community-Based Organizations." Presentation to the Forum on Funding
    Policies and the Nonprofit Sector in Western Canada, Calgary, 15 October.

8 Funding Policy and the Provincial Lottery: Sport, Culture, and Recreation in Saskatchewan

LYNN GIDLUCK

Saskatchewan's volunteer sport, culture, and recreation sectors have a unique funding regime and delivery system. When the provincial lottery was established, the Saskatchewan Lotteries Trust Fund for Sport, Culture and Recreation was created to grant funds to eligible nonprofit volunteer organizations, as designated by the provincial ministry, which manages the relationship with Saskatchewan Lotteries. Today twelve hundred sport, culture, and recreation groups, Tribal Councils, and First Nation Band Councils receive direct lottery funding. In turn these organizations distribute funding to more than twelve thousand affiliated organizations in Saskatchewan. Volunteer committees from the three sectors review all funding requests, and play a central role in the oversight, direction, and management of the Trust Fund.[1] For the fiscal year ending 31 March 2015, the net profit to the Lottery Trust Fund, after prizes and retailer commissions, federal and provincial taxes, and operating expenses, was $57.2 million (Sask Sport Inc. 2015). Funding from the Trust Fund is allocated in fixed proportions to sport (50 per cent), culture (35 per cent), and recreation (15 per cent).

Since 1974 the lottery has been operated on the provincial government's behalf by the nonprofit amateur sport federation Sask Sport Inc., which is the umbrella organization for seventy-eight member organizations, including sixty-four provincial governing sports bodies such as Football Saskatchewan and Special Olympics Saskatchewan. Providing direction on program and policy for the cultural component of the lottery is SaskCulture, which, in 2015, funded 140 member-based organizations involved in delivering arts, heritage, multicultural, and other cultural programs or initiatives (SaskCulture 2015). The recreation portion of the Trust Fund is managed through the Saskatchewan Parks and

Recreation Association (SPRA), whose membership consists of cities, towns, villages, rural municipalities, First Nations and Métis communities, provincial recreation associations, and regional and urban park authorities, among others (SPRA 2015).

Saskatchewan is hardly the only jurisdiction where a government has chosen to dedicate portions of the revenue it receives from state-led or -supported lotteries and other forms of gaming to sport, culture, and recreation. Indeed, when the laws concerning gambling were liberalized in Canada in 1969, directing profits from lotteries to these sectors was the prevalent choice of most provinces because this revenue stream initially was seen as volatile and unpredictable. The first national lottery in Canada was organized to raise money for the 1976 Olympic Games in Montreal (LaBrosse 1985; Morton 2003). With the formation of the Western Canada Lottery Foundation (WCLF), revenue was distributed through agencies to sport, culture, and recreation (WCLF 1975) in the western provinces. Other regional and provincial lotteries were later organized, including in Ontario, where profits from its government-run lottery were distributed to nonprofit organizations in the cultural and recreational fields (Vance 1986, 106).

What makes Saskatchewan's situation unique is that the volunteer community was given the opportunity to develop its own fundraising mechanism, the lottery system, and it continues to have direct oversight and management of the system. Other provinces, in contrast, chose to create a Crown corporation to oversee lotteries or to appoint government representatives to provincial or regional lottery entities such as the Western Canada Lottery and the Atlantic Lottery. Revenue from these entities then flows into the provinces' general funds, and the provincial governments determine how the money will be spent through their regular budgetary processes (Cosgrave and Klassen 2009, 10).

A variety of institutional arrangements are in place throughout the country to distribute government revenues to sport, culture, and recreation. Manitoba, for instance, provides funds to sport through a nonprofit umbrella organization, Sport Manitoba, that is similar to Sask Sport. Other provinces have established nonprofit Crown corporations, such as the Alberta Sports, Recreation, Parks and Wildlife Fund and the Trillium Foundation in Ontario, and charged these entities with devising methods for granting funds. In British Columbia civil servants in the Ministry of Finance work to create grants programs and administer funds. Arrangements vary as to the degree of involvement, if any, of sport, culture, and recreation communities in developing the programs or grants they receive and how they are held accountable for the funds.

The Saskatchewan Lotteries Trust Fund is a distinctive collaborative relationship between government and the nonprofit sector to both raise and deliver funds to support public priorities in the areas of sport, culture, and recreation. Those knowledgeable about this arrangement – staff, volunteers, civil servants, and politicians charged with developing, maintaining, and improving the system – believe the sport, culture, and recreation sectors in Saskatchewan are fortunate relative to their counterparts in other parts of the country. The funding regime is characterized by long-term, stable funding from the Trust Fund and by volunteers' control and management of the system. The provincial government is given credit for empowering the voluntary sector with a fundraising mechanism that enables it to foster community development, and for encouraging and rewarding efficient management and high standards of accountability by giving volunteers a feeling of "ownership" and grassroots control.

This chapter presents the preliminary findings of a case study of Saskatchewan's lottery-based funding of sport, culture, and recreation. I begin by examining the historical context of and rationale for the provincial government's taking an approach to lottery funding that was so different from that of other jurisdictions. I explore the original public policy issue that was being addressed, how the problem was defined, and the solution that was offered through this novel experiment in government–voluntary sector collaboration. I then discuss the strengths of the regime in the context of the institutional structure that was developed to administer the program. I show the steps that were taken to ensure that all members of the partnership understood the need to work together and move along a strategic pathway based on research and community consultation that cultivated and demonstrated widespread public support for the lottery system. By developing and maintaining a strong collective voice and initiating sustained and coordinated educational efforts, the voluntary sport, culture, and recreation sectors were able to resist a number of attempts to change the system over the years.

Methodology

I used a number of sources for this study, which allowed me to triangulate and validate the research data. Sask Sport was generous in providing unfettered access to its files, including policy papers, organizational plans, minutes, and other material dating back to the late 1960s, when the idea of creating a federation to act as the collective voice of amateur sport was still in its infancy.

My ability to develop a rich and nuanced description of how Saskatchewan's lottery system developed and evolved was enhanced by access to the original source material of three researchers, Ernie Nicholls, Roy Ellis, and Elva Nixon, who undertook studies in areas that touched on some of the historical background of the system (Ellis and Nixon 1986; Nicholls 1982). I also examined the archival papers of two former Saskatchewan premiers and three cabinet ministers who were responsible for the lottery portfolio; and conducted semi-structured and open-ended interviews with eighty individuals – including staff, civil servants, volunteers, and political leaders from the early 1970s to the present – who are knowledgeable about the origin, evolution, strengths, and weaknesses of the Saskatchewan Lotteries system.

In analysing the interviews, I identified two general types of data. The first type is generally historical or descriptive in nature (information about specific programs, historical context, and biographical information about key agents), which helped piece together the historical narrative or sequence of events. The second type reflects the interviewee's perspectives on the strengths and weaknesses of amateur sport, culture, and recreation in Saskatchewan.

The Historical Context

Prior to 1969 almost all lotteries were a criminal offence under the Criminal Code of Canada. Religious and charitable organizations could hold small raffles and bingos, parimutuel betting was allowed at race tracks, and gambling was permitted at agricultural fairs, but any efforts to convince Parliament to allow larger-scale or state-directed gambling ventures such as lotteries traditionally were handily defeated (Campbell 2000; Osborne 1991). It was not until Quebec and Montreal, faced with the enormous debt that had accrued from the 1967 World's Fair, began lobbying for the introduction of a provincial lottery that the idea gained momentum (Derevensky and Gillespie 2005). Proponents also argued that Canada should allow lotteries to prevent the loss of revenue to jurisdictions that permitted them (Klassen and Cosgrave 2002) – the United States, for example, had lifted its prohibition on lotteries in 1964. Accordingly, in 1969, the Criminal Code of Canada was amended to allow the federal and provincial governments to become involved in gambling ventures. Provincial governments, whose powers of taxation are limited, quickly saw the advantage of this new source of nontax revenue, and by 1976 all the provinces, territories, and the federal government were directly involved in lotteries (Klassen and Cosgrave 2002; Mcauliffe 2006; Vance 1986). In 1985, after a protracted series of federal-provincial jurisdictional disputes, the provinces gained exclusive rights to control lotteries and other forms of gaming (Morton 2003, 194–5).

In Saskatchewan, by the early 1970s, the provincial government was looking for a way to keep the profits from these activities in the province, while limiting its own participation in them. The government of the day – particularly Premier Allan Blakeney – saw lotteries as a tax on the poor, and wanted as little as possible to do with raising money in this manner.[2] When Bill 122, An Act respecting Lotteries, was first introduced in 1974, Blakeney declared that the approach his government had devised for managing lotteries was "as good a compromise as we can get since neither Government nor private individuals would be promoting the sale of lottery tickets in order to get revenue for themselves." The only benefit to government would be indirect in the sense that organizations that would receive funding from the provincial lottery system might otherwise lobby government for money (Blakeney 1974, 2729).

The Western Canada Lottery Foundation was incorporated as a nonprofit organization authorized to conduct and operate lottery and gaming-related activities as on behalf of its members, the governments of British Columbia, Alberta, Saskatchewan, and Manitoba. The WCLF was set up as an equal partnership to extract the most out of economies of scale by sharing expenses and collaborating on such things as central systems, ticket printing, and game design. By-laws stipulated that the provinces could sell tickets only within their own boundaries, but each province retained the right to distribute and market tickets in its own way. Profits sold in each jurisdiction would stay in that province. British Columbia, Alberta, and Manitoba chose to have a much more direct role in lottery operations, with government employees liaising and overseeing the activities of the WCLF in their provinces. Saskatchewan opted to leave the running of the lottery to Sask Sport (WCLF 1975).[3]

In Saskatchewan, unlike in the other provinces, no government money was invested in setting up the infrastructure for the lottery, and in its early years the lottery licence was kept to a nominal fee – in its first year of operation, it was just $3,000. The nonprofit community has been able to earn money from the lottery in two ways. At first, any incorporated nonprofit organization (not just those from sport, culture, and recreation) could earn a commission by selling lottery tickets. Those who chose to stick strictly to volunteer sales forces could earn up to 20 per cent of every ticket sold. Some groups hired individuals to sell tickets on their behalf, keeping 10 per cent and using the other 10 per cent as a sales incentive. This was a very high commission compared with what other provinces paid – Ontario, for instance, paid less than eight cents on the dollar in total commissions to retailers and distributors – but Saskatchewan saw the lottery as a way for everyone in the voluntary sector to benefit.[4]

When electronic lottery games such as LOTTO 6/49 emerged in the early 1980s, there was no longer a need to have a large network of nonprofit distributors. In recognition of the support and hard work the original distributors underwent to build the network, Sask Sport negotiated an agreement with these groups whereby they would receive a share of lottery proceeds in perpetuity, as long as they maintained their nonprofit status and provided annual follow-up reports.[5] Sask Sport and the Saskatchewan government regularly negotiate the terms of the lottery licence agreement, which then must be passed through an Order in Council by the provincial legislature. The licensing fee for the agreement that ends in 2019 was 3.75 per cent of lottery ticket sales (Government of Saskatchewan 2014).

When the provincial government first licensed Sask Sport to run the lottery, net revenues were intended to fund only organizations that were provincial in scope. An extensive list of other sport, culture, and recreation organizations and programs continued to be funded from general revenues, and civil servants delivered programs aimed at increasing participation in these activities at the community level. Department staff would attend Lottery Trust Fund meetings to make sure that its funding decisions did not duplicate those of the government.[6] Funding might be allowed to go to some of the same organizations that the government supported directly, but only for extras it was not already covering. Over the years, as lottery funds continued to increase and the government faced growing fiscal pressure, the province devolved its program and funding responsibilities in these areas almost exclusively to the lottery system. Today, the government does no programming in these areas, focusing exclusively on providing policy leadership. As a senior Sask Sport employee described it, "the government could have gone and done like other provinces – in other governments they kept sport inside their shops and built up a bureaucracy. Here, this government pushed it out into the community. They devolved responsibility based on a strategy that would see the community empowered to do some of the stuff themselves. The plan worked."

Until 1993 legislation and the terms of the regularly negotiated licence agreements made only vague references to the lottery's public policy objectives. One civil servant who worked on the updated partnership agreement said: "The legislation regulations were revised and the Lottery Agreement was a much different looking document, a much more living document now. Not only did it have a fiscal side to it but it had a policy side to it." Another civil servant described the policy framework of the licence agreements as "a shared perspective on what needed to happen with the system," the benefits, in his perspective, being that Sask Sport's leaders now had firmer terms of reference to take back to their board and to their umbrella partners about policy objectives the province wanted them to meet. In this sense, then, the licence agreement is related not just to money, but to the priorities of the system.

The System's Strengths

The overarching theme that emerged from the interviews for this study is that the relationship between the voluntary sector and the provincial government through the Saskatchewan Lotteries system is something that all parties are proud to be associated with and that they believe is the subject of envy from their counterparts in the sport, culture, and recreation sectors in other provinces. As one elected official put it, "people from other provinces that understood anything about our system [are] really envious about the way it works." The pride reflected in the interviews is based on a number of perceived strengths and outcomes of the system.

Stable, flexible funding

A key strength of Saskatchewan's lottery-based sport, culture, and recreation sectors is the relative stability and flexibility of this core funding source. As one former deputy minister put it, "you have strong organizations that have on-going funding. Many of them are able to actually hire staff to supplement the volunteers that work. There's a chance to do more planning here as a result of that certainty." Another senior civil servant, with a background in community development, emphasized how important this ongoing funding is for these groups: "I've seen organizations that are dependent only on project funding, and they're always chasing at least half a dozen pots of money, and rather than creating access and opportunity, they spend 50 to 80 per cent of their time chasing money."

A study of gambling granting programs conducted by the Canada West Foundation reinforces this perception. An executive director of an arts organization in Saskatchewan interviewed by Berdahl (1999, 37) described the benefit of the lottery system as follows: "With lotteries, we know what we're eligible for, and unless we do a poor job of accounting for the spending of the money the previous year, we know we are going to get that money." Another nonprofit employee interviewed by Berdahl emphasized that "it is all run by volunteers in terms of adjudication. And it's people who know the system from within and have a real sense of when organizations have a tendency to veer off … So they can monitor and challenge them to accountability" (59).

Funding of these sectors has also been more stable because it is tied to a formula related to net lottery proceeds, and does not have to be voted on in the legislature every year during the annual budgetary process. As numerous interviewees said, this is especially advantageous during times when the province is experiencing fiscal difficulties. One executive director of a provincial sport governing body said that, when she meets her counterparts across the country, they marvel at the Saskatchewan set-up: "The fact that I know my funding from two years out ... It's almost unheard of in other provinces. They just basically have to go year to year to year ... Their funding comes through direct from government, so it's very political." Another individual, working for a lottery-funded multisports organization, agreed that the sports community in Saskatchewan is fortunate: "Other provinces, if they need more money, have a bureaucracy to go through that's mind-boggling. We're pretty thankful that we have one step and that's Sask Sport and they make the decision, whereas in Manitoba, when they want to increase funding, they've got to go through about four hoops before they can even begin to find a process or begin to get extra funds."

Grassroots, volunteer involvement

From the beginning volunteers have been heavily involved in the development of new programs, funding oversight and adjudication, and monitoring system needs and priorities. One long-serving volunteer was quick to highlight the meaningful role she felt she had in working with Sask Sport to develop programs that respond to community needs. "It's more than sport, actually," she stressed. "It's participation that most people would not have a chance to take part in unless they were some senior policy analyst or some elected official."

Because volunteers serving on the board of directors of the three umbrella organizations are elected by and accountable to the member-based provincial bodies that receive lottery funding, they are in a good position to identify the need for new programs that meet the changing requirements and priorities of the communities they represent. As one retired arts administrator said, "one of the strengths of the lottery system is that it allows volunteers, people who care passionately about those disciplines, to be not only involved but to actually make the decisions and to be part of the whole planning process for how that development will take place." Understanding the needs of member organizations has also resulted in the development of more efficient and flexible application and accountability processes that ease administrative burdens without sacrificing responsible oversight.

A sense of ownership

Another key strength of the Saskatchewan Lotteries system is the sense of responsibility and ownership that the volunteer community has in it. As one senior government administrator put it, having responsibility for the administration of the revenue base as well as the granting side ensures that the system is extremely responsible and accountable for its activities because the volunteers understand where the money comes from and have a personal stake in seeing the operation thrive.

Volunteers and staff have always understood that the government can alter or annul the relationship at any time. One former minister believed this tension has served a useful purpose: "They have never taken their system for granted. They've always been extra, extra careful with what they do." This belief was confirmed by comments from staff and volunteers.

Efficient, highly accountable, and nonpartisan

A key reason the Saskatchewan government, even during times of serious fiscal problems, has never seriously considered making fundamental changes to the way the lottery system is run is that administration costs have always been kept to a minimum. As one senior civil servant put it, "Sask Sport is more efficient at running the lottery system than the government would be as a Crown agency."

Another major strength of the lottery system is its ability to transcend politics. "Part of the strength of the system," one minister said, "was and still is that it is not partisan – because the decisions are not being made by elected officials." As this elected leader saw it, volunteers, who have a better understanding of the needs of their sector, are in a better position to judge the relative merit of individual grant applications. Furthermore, as he and others noted, getting involved in these types of processes brings more political headache than benefit. One former deputy minister recalled a conversation he had with a colleague, who said, "the only person happy is the one who receives the grant … [Y]ou don't want to get into this little grants game. You don't want to have this kind of fight for the ability to say no to a whole bunch of people."

Community development

One minister believed that a key strength of the funding regime is that the money builds community in a way that tax dollars are unable to do: "Tax dollars are seen as somebody doing something for you. With this system, it's the community doing it themselves and building their own institutions." Another minister, from a different political administration, expressed a similar perspective, adding that lottery funds have always represented "seed money": "It doesn't fund their whole budgets. For every dollar they can get say in grant money they raise ten themselves among their members, and supporters … That's a big multiplier effect on the economy of the province."

A senior Sask Sport employee pointed out that "our programs are all based on the same principle. The volunteers own it. They raise the money. They give the money away … If it's going to be successful, it'll be successful because you did the work." When the leadership at Sask Sport was first made aware of the serious inequities between Aboriginal and non-Aboriginal communities when it came to opportunities for sport, culture, and recreation, they realized they would have to play an even bigger community development role than they had in the past: "We were used to working with groups of people who volunteered to do work, so putting money in their hands to do programs worked. In the beginning we followed the same approach with the Aboriginal community. We had to learn that those systems, those volunteers, didn't exist in Aboriginal communities. Poverty had stripped that community of any capacity to be effective in doing anything. We had to train people to be role models and mentors." This understanding and way of operating has been applauded by many people from Saskatchewan's Aboriginal community. As one First Nations leader saw it, "the only reason Aboriginal sport has got from A to B right now is because we're in control of our own destiny here. We can allocate these pots of money the way we see as experts around the table, that it's going to benefit our communities." Another First Nations leader and former Sask Sport employee said, "they [Sask Sport] were willing to overlook the everybody's the same policies, get some Aboriginal people in there to help them and break down the cookie-cutter policy approach."

Maintaining the System

When the Blakeney government decided to experiment with a new model for running the provincial lottery and for funding the sport, culture, and recreation sectors, it led to what theorists such as Pierson (2003) and Thelen (2003) refer to as a path-dependent public policy direction. As Elson (2011, 10–11) explains, this means that the likelihood of moving in the same direction increases with each step down the path because positive feedback mechanisms make it more difficult to change course. The Saskatchewan Lotteries regime is no exception to this general rule. By allowing the voluntary sector to develop, control, and benefit from the lottery, the provincial government instilled a sense of ownership in the recipient groups. In turn this strong feeling of ownership led the community, along with the civil servants charged with working with it, to do everything in their power to make the experiment work. By proving they could come up with programs that responded to *real* community needs in a manner that was efficient, transparent, and well managed, they were able to make a powerful argument to continue down the same path. Having such strong proponents in communities throughout the province also made the government aware that changes to the lottery system could lead to serious political repercussions.

Despite these powerful feedback mechanisms, which made it difficult to change the policy direction, there *have* been a number of times when what Kingdon (2011) refers to as "policy windows" opened up and the lottery system in Saskatchewan came under threat. During each case when the system was under scrutiny and susceptible to change, the partners responded with creative solutions that kept this increasing revenue stream flowing to the sport, culture, and recreation sectors instead of being diverted to general revenues as most governments have done with lottery profits. Knowing *how* threats to the lottery system were resisted can provide valuable insight into how voluntary sector and government partners can maintain and expand community-based programming and delivery of public services.

The strategic umbrella structure

Although the provincial government dictated that the sport, culture, and recreation sectors would have to work together and determine how to benefit mutually from lottery revenues, it left to them how best to do this. The lead party in the arrangement, Sask Sport, was itself still a fledgling operation, almost completely reliant on volunteers, with very little to bind organizations together under its umbrella other than the promise that, if they worked together and the lottery was a success, they might raise money for sport programming. The other major player in the lottery system, the cultural community, was even more fractured and less inclined to come together in unity of purpose. When the lottery agreement was signed, there was no umbrella organization representing arts organizations, and it was left to Sask Sport to try to determine accountability measures that garnered support from a community it knew little about. The recreation sector would prove challenging to manage for different reasons. Because the province had invested a lot more resources in community-based recreation in the past than it had in sport, and because Sask Sport was taking more risk in actually running the lottery, recreation was granted only a 10 per cent share of the net revenues – an amount the sector would be perennially looking to increase.

The sports federation appointed the members to the cultural committee, something they did reluctantly because they recognized that this was not their area of expertise. They turned to civil servants in the Department of Culture and Youth to help find members for the committee, and employed a staff person to provide administrative support for them. Sask Sport was quick to realize, however, that, if it was to gain widespread support in the cultural sector, arts organizations needed to get organized and develop their own collective voice. As one long-serving employee said, "Sask Sport was doing its best, but the reality was that we were sports people – the sports federation was in charge of handing out grants to the cultural world ... We appointed some great people to the Trust Committee that awarded the grants – folks who were just as dedicated and hard working as our sports volunteers were. But I always thought it would be better if they had their own organization making these kinds of decisions." A prominent cultural volunteer who was one of the founders of the Saskatchewan Council of Cultural Organizations (renamed SaskCulture in 1997) said: "Sask Sport told us you have to get your act together. They pushed us, for our own good."

The longevity and success of the lottery-based sport, culture, and recreation sector in Saskatchewan can be attributed at least in part to the fact that these three sectors worked very hard to put in place a formal structure that meets most of the criteria Elson (2011, 155) identifies as necessary for optimum institutional effectiveness. These criteria include

- building a broad representative membership link across the breadth and depth of organizations in the sector;
- developing reporting and accountability structures that hold representatives to account to both the membership and the general public;
- unity in dealings with government;
- understanding the importance of basing policy requests on strategic research; and
- engaging in broad consultations with the communities they represent.

A strong collective voice

Having a strong collective voice has served the lottery partners well over the years. As Sask Sport's general manager said, "It's one thing that we ran an efficient system, but how much money we made and how much money we spent on administration was not what really resonated with the politicians. They knew that there were 12,000 plus volunteers out there who valued the lottery as *their* fundraiser [speaker's emphasis]. When it mattered, they made the phone calls. They organized telephone trees, and called their local MLAs or people they felt were in positions of influence. It was, and still is, a powerful network."

The secret to successfully maintaining this strong collective voice, one civil servant believed, is the approach Sask Sport took to ensure that culture and recreation felt like equal partners in the relationship. Although Sask Sport serves as the primary point of contact with the relevant ministry and is the lead partner in the negotiations for the lottery licence, it has always taken care to ensure that its sister organizations, SaskCulture and the SPRA, are well versed on all discussions and are at the table when there is a need to demonstrate solidarity and unity of purpose. This really impressed one senior government official, who commended Sask Sport for never using its position inappropriately: "They've made sure that they have processes that allow all three globals to be on top of all the issues they have to be on top of ... Everyone gets their say, even if they might not like what the others are saying."

It was no easy task to keep the three groups working together, especially in the early days of the partnership. As one of the first employees of Sask Sport said, "there were those who said you'd never put those three groups of people together and have them get along." Time has proved early sceptics wrong. One of the hallmarks of the success of the Saskatchewan Lotteries system has been the ability of the three sectors to work together for the benefit of their collective membership. As one former civil servant said, "they kept their disagreements to themselves. They spoke as one. I think they understood that, if the government had to make the decision, that would be the wrong place to do it." Like most partnerships that have survived the test of time, all parties in the Saskatchewan Lotteries system have had to work hard to make the relationship work. Open and ongoing communication among the three partners was seen as crucial to maintaining and continuing to make improvements to the system.

Strong and reasoned arguments to keep the funds

Lottery partners have long understood the importance of having solid research to back up their claims that the funds directed to sport, culture, and recreation are being put to good use and serve the interests of the broader Saskatchewan community. Never was this more important than during the late 1970s and early 1980s, when lottery revenue was increasing at a dramatic pace and many people in the provincial government began to think that some of these funds should be diverted to other priority areas. Pressures were also felt from the mid-1980s to the mid-1990s, when the government was facing tremendous fiscal pressures due to mounting debt and deficits.

Although volunteers and staff in the three global organizations and the department could acknowledge that amateur sport, culture, and recreation had witnessed tremendous expansion and growth because of lottery funding, they knew that their sectors still had many unmet needs. To keep the provincial government comfortable with allowing all the lottery dollars to continue to go to sport, culture, and recreation, Sask Sport and senior government officials, knew they had to work with the Saskatchewan Council of Cultural Organizations and the SPRA to make a clear case for additional funds. To do this, a consultant was hired to do a needs assessment. "The study was undertaken in a fairly short period of time, but it was pretty extensive," said a civil servant who helped oversee the research. "Information was gathered from regional associations, representative communities, and provincial organizations." Not surprisingly, needs at the grassroots level were identified as having the greatest priority. Until this time, the only groups eligible for lottery funding were provincially based sport, culture, and recreation organizations (Ellis and Nixon 1986, 102). As a Sask Sport employee said, "we were doing a good job of funding the provincial groups, but limited dollars were getting to the grassroots, and those were the groups that were really struggling."

The result of these deliberations was the Trust Initiative Program, introduced in 1982 and later renamed the Community Grants Program. Through this program, every regional association, zone advisory council, or community with a recognized recreation board was able to apply for lottery dollars. An advisory group for the program, consisting of volunteers from each of the three organizations, was set up as a subcommittee of the Saskatchewan Lotteries Trust Fund. Sask Sport's general manager believed that much of the credit for the new program should go to the SPRA and recreation volunteers in communities throughout the province who recognized the needs at the local level.

Another way to give the government more control over how lottery dollars were spent while ensuring that the money was still directed to the sport, culture, and recreation sectors was to create a special pool of funds within the department, to be distributed at the minister's discretion. Accordingly, the Minister's Directed Fund was created in 1987 as a way for the department to fund sport, cultural, and recreation activities that fell outside the original narrow scope of beneficiaries of lottery funding – namely, only province-wide organizations. As Sask Sport's general manager explained, this posed a problem because "just as soon as we got going, there was a lineup of people going to government's door every day. It wasn't a nefarious thing. It was just, how do we handle all these people? They're not an organization with province-wide membership, so they don't quality for funding from the Lottery Trust Fund. The answer became: send them to the department. The department already had a process set up where they were giving out grants – this was just a logical extension of that." Sask Sport's assistant general manager added: "Creating this special fund was also a way to extract a licence from the lotteries but at the same time ensure that the money remained directed to sport, culture, and recreation." If Sask Sport had just paid a licence fee, he argued, there was no guarantee that it would have been directed to sport, culture, and recreation: "It could have gone to health, education – a million places."

In time, the Minister's Directed Fund came to be criticized by the provincial auditor for not meeting standards of transparency and public accountability. As one former elected official assigned the critic portfolio to the lotteries file put it, "I didn't find that recipients from that minister's discretionary fund were inappropriate. I don't want to accuse [the minister] or the government of the day of using that fund for partisan purposes, but it did offer that minister a certain political advantage where you can just whip a cheque out of your pocket. Somebody's got a problem? You can solve it."

Eventually the government addressed such criticisms by devolving responsibility for distributing money from the fund to the Saskatchewan Lotteries system for the umbrella partners to distribute to the sport, culture, and recreation sectors. Over time, the government would divest itself of all responsibility for program funding to Saskatchewan Lotteries.

Cultivating political support and being open to change

Since 1974, when the Saskatchewan Lotteries system was established, it has witnessed five changes in government, been housed under eleven government departments, and reported to twenty-four different ministers. One reason for the system's longevity is that its leaders have understood the importance of cultivating and maintaining good relationships with the provincial government at both the bureaucratic and political levels. They have also gone to great lengths to work with civil servants to educate new ministers and their staff, as well as Treasury Board and Finance officials, as to why the lottery should continue to be run by Sask Sport to benefit the province's sport, culture, and recreation communities. As a long-time cultural sector employee said, "over the years I think the umbrellas have done an excellent job in educating the politicians (especially the Ministers responsible for lotteries) about the system, and as governments and ministers change, that work must always continue." A senior-ranking bureaucrat still working for the provincial government remarked: "Lots of systems and networks that get set up become ... almost insular. They are not open to discussion and change. They ... protect the status quo. I think the people in the Lottery system are very much open to discussion and they're there for the right reasons. They're not there thinking about 'what happens to my job?' They're thinking about their network and how it benefits the Saskatchewan people."

Conclusion

Saskatchewan's sport, culture, and recreation sectors are supported by a funding regime that empowers people at the community level to shape public policy and develop innovative programs that meet the unique needs of individual communities. Numerous informants for this study expressed the strong belief that the funding regime puts the these sectors in an enviable position relative to their counterparts in other jurisdictions. The following words of a former civil servant summarize the sentiments expressed by a wide cross-section of the individuals who shared their experiences for this study:

> With the lotteries and government it is a really good example of how people can work very effectively together by embracing community, giving them the means to do their work but still having lines of accountability, still making sure that regular communication and dialogue is there that allows whatever the changing public policy parameters of the day might be, they're communicated, they're understood, there's feedback, and there's give and take as to what can be ... accomplished ... Government can get a lot done in terms of its public policy mandate through an enormous community-based group like the lottery system.

One thing that was clear in talking to people who have been central to the success of this funding regime is that it took a lot of hard work and commitment by all parties to get to the point described above. The relationship was not always as smooth as the parties would have liked; there were times when trust was at a low point. According to Elson (2011, 158), this is to be expected. As he suggests, government and voluntary sectors working together within similar institutional regimes, such as is the case with the Saskatchewan government and the sport, culture, and recreation sectors, "must expect to step on each other's toes a few times in learning how to tango."

Many of the volunteers who were interviewed for this case study – particularly those who served as presidents of Sask Sport when lottery revenues were increasing at a rapid rate during the 1980s – did not understand or appreciate the role ministry officials had to play. They resented what they felt was government interference. In the words of one volunteer, "once we started doing our programs, they were sitting on their hands and basically they were trying to get into the programs to do something – it was the fact that they didn't have anything to do." A senior civil servant responsible for managing the overall relationship during this period believed the volunteers had reason to be upset with government: "The community was feeling really held back because they weren't able to do anything without the government officials either giving the nod or feeling they had to be personally involved. Government officials were trying to manufacture the agenda at a time when the community felt empowered."

As this astute observer noted, most of the civil servants were as passionate about sport, culture, and recreation and the Saskatchewan Lotteries system as the volunteers were. They felt a sense of ownership because they had helped build the system. Most had started their careers putting together sport and recreation structures at the community level and delivering programs that originally were funded by government but were later devolved to the Lotteries system. At one time, for instance, civil servants trained volunteers to be coaches and officials, and organized and managed most aspects of the province-wide participation in the Saskatchewan and Canada Games movement and many other hands-on sports activities. As more and more of these types of activities were devolved to volunteer-based sport organizations, the government's role was downsized. And as much as senior bureaucrats and the leadership of Sask Sport believe this was done in a planned and strategic manner, it did not always appear this way to some of the civil servants who were left behind after their colleagues were let go. One government official, while supporting and appreciating the devolution of programs to the volunteer sector, said, "as a person who has worked at the community level, the transition wasn't really that well done because some of the things we [government] used to do all of a sudden weren't happening. It was tough to work through those first few years, and the corporate knowledge was gone just like that."

Despite bumps along the way, policies, procedures, and institutional structures were put in place to facilitate communication and to demonstrate that the lottery-funded sport, culture, and recreation sectors were working in consort with the government to develop public policy and programs rooted in the community and responsive to community needs. Strong leadership was required to keep everyone on the same path and to convince sector partners and volunteers of the need to put aside personal or organizational agendas to respond to the needs of the larger community and to ensure the long-term viability of the lottery program. Clearly, governments, nonprofit organizations, and policymakers looking to develop collaborative partnerships between the voluntary and public sectors have much to learn from this Saskatchewan experiment, which began in 1974 and shows no signs of stopping anytime soon.

NOTES

1 See the website of Saskatchewan Lotteries at http://www.sasklotteries.ca/about-us/who-we-are.htm.
2 Author's personal communication with A.E. Blakeney, 15 March 2011.
3 British Columbia withdrew from the WCLF in 1986, choosing to set up its own Crown corporation to oversee government gaming activity. The WCLF then became the Western Canada Lottery Corporation (WCLC). Today the WCLC is governed by a board of directors consisting of two representatives appointed by each of the member provincial governments; Yukon Territory and Nunavut participate as associate members.
4 B. Clarke, interview with E. Nicholls, 13 October 1977.
5 Author's e-mail correspondence with S. Barry, Chief Financial Officer, Sask Sport Inc., 24 September 2013.
6 In Saskatchewan, government "departments" became "ministries" with the election of the Saskatchewan Party in 2007.

REFERENCES

Berdahl, L. 1999. *Gambling in Canada: Triumph, Tragedy, or Tradeoff? The Impact of Gaming upon Candian Non-profits: A 1999 Survey of Gaming Grant Recipients.* Calgary: Canada West Foundation.
Blakeney, A.E. 1974. *Bill 122: An Act respecting Lotteries.* Second Reading, 29 April, 17th Legislature, 4th Session, vol. 14, Part 4. Regina.

Campbell, C.S. 2000. "Lawlessness: Gaming Policies in British Columbia, Canada." Paper presented at the 3rd National Gambling Conference, Sydney, Australia, 11–12 May. Available online at http://www.aic.gov.au/conferences/gambling00/campbell.pdf; accessed 9 May 2010.

Cosgrave, J.F., and T.R. Klassen. 2009. *Casino State: Legalized Gambling in Canada*. Toronto: University of Toronto Press.

Derevensky, J.L., and M. Gillespie. 2005. "Keynote Address: Gambling in Canada." *International Journal of Mental Health and Addiction* 3 (1): 3–14. Available online at http://youthgambling.mcgill.ca/en/PDF/Publications/2005/Gambling%20in%20Canada%202005.pdf; accessed 17 May 2015.

Ellis, R., and E. Nixon. 1986. *Saskatchewan Recreation Legacy: A Perspective from the Saskatchewan Parks and Recreation Association*. Regina: Saskatchewan Parks and Recreation Association.

Elson, P.R. 2011. *High Ideals and Noble Intentions: Voluntary Sector-Government Relations in Canada*. Toronto: University of Toronto Press.

Government of Saskatchewan. 2014. Saskatchewan Community Will Benefit from Renewed Lottery Agreement. https://www.saskatchewan.ca/government/news-and-media/2014/January/13/renewed-lottery-agreement.

Kingdon, John W. 2011. *Agendas, Alternatives and Public Policies*, 2nd ed. London: Pearson Higher Education.

Klassen, T.R., and J. Cosgrave. 2002. "Look Who's Addicted to Gambling Now." *Policy Options* (July/August): 43–6.

LaBrosse, M. 1985. *The Lottery…From Jacques Cartier's Day to Modern Times*. Quebec City: Loto-Québec.

Mcauliffe, E.W. 2006. "The State Sponsored Lottery: A Failure of Policy and Ethics." *Public Integrity* 8 (4): 367–79. http://dx.doi.org/10.2753/PIN1099-9922080404.

Morton, S. 2003. *At Odds: Gambling and Canadians 1991–1969*. Toronto: University of Toronto Press.

Nicholls, E.A. 1982. "An Analysis of the Structure and Function of Three Provincial Sports Collectives in Western Canada, 1977–78." PhD diss., University of Alberta).

Osborne, J.A. 1991. "The Evolution of Public Lotteries in British Columbia: The Genesis of a Modern Lottery Scandal." In *Gambling and Public Policy: International Perspectives*, ed. W.R. Eadington and J.A. Cornelius, 285–302. Nevada: University of Nevada, Reno, Institute for the Study of Gambling and Commercial Gaming.

Pierson, R. 2003. "Big, Slow-Moving, and ... Invisible: Macrosocial Processes in the Study of Comparative Politics." In *Comparative Historical Analysis in the Social Sciences*, ed. J. Mahoney and D. Rueschemeyer, 177–207. Cambridge: Cambridge University Press.

SPRA (Saskatchewan Parks and Recreation Association). 2010. *Saskatchewan Recreation Strategy Environmental Scan: A Summary of the Key Issues and Trends Facing Recreation in Saskatchewan.* Regina.
———. 2015. "Membership: Categories and Fees." Available online at http://www.spra.sk.ca/membership/categories-and-fees/; accessed 17 May 2015.
SaskCulture. 2015. "Member Directory." Available online at http://www.saskculture.ca/network/members/member-directory; accessed 17 May 2015.
Sask Sport Inc. 2015. *2014–2015 Annual Report.* Regina.
Thelen, K. 2003. "How Institutions Evolve: Insights from Comparative Historical Analysis." In *Comparative Historical Analysis in the Social Sciences,* ed. J. Mahoney and D. Rueschemeyer, 208–40. Cambridge: Cambridge University Press.
Vance, J. 1986. "Canadian State Lotteries: 1970–1984." PhD diss.; Carleton University.
WCLF (Western Canada Lottery Foundation). 1975. *Annual Report 1974–1975.* Winnipeg.

9 A Patchwork of Funding Relationships in Manitoba: From Principal-Agent to Co-governance

SID FRANKEL AND KARINE LEVASSEUR

Introduction

Nonprofit organizations in Manitoba, as elsewhere, play an important role, not only in service delivery, but also as agents for the expression of interests and values (Hall et al. 2005, 3). Each of these functions aligns with different levels of collaboration between the state and nonprofit organizations. If nonprofit organizations are conceived solely as delivery agents, then there is less room for collaboration than if they are understood to be vehicles for the expressions of the values, norms, and interests of some palpable community. The level of collaboration is significantly determined by the funding regime the state uses to finance nonprofit organizations, presumably based on views related to their roles. This funding regime is characterized by the kinds of funding instruments used, how they are implemented, and the accountability interactions between government departments, agencies, and programs and the nonprofit organizations they fund.

The most recently available survey data indicate that Manitoba has the second-largest nonprofit sector in Canada proportional to its population. This, coupled with the fact that the provincial government is the largest funder of the nonprofit sector in Manitoba (Frankel 2006, 24), makes an inquiry into how Manitoba finances nonprofit organizations an important issue.

Based on interviews with fifteen experienced nonprofit and government leaders, this chapter describes the regime that characterizes the funding relationship of the Manitoba government with nonprofit community social service organizations. Following from Krasner (1982) and Scott (2003), we define the funding regime as the principles, norms, rules, and decision-making procedures that structure the funding relationship. Therefore, our interest goes far beyond formal agreements.

In a landmark edited volume, Salamon (2002) articulates a typology of instruments by which governments provide funding to nonprofit organizations. These are referred to as "tools" (although more commonly denoted as funding instruments) (Imagine Canada 2006), and three types are relevant to our analysis. The first is the purchase-of-service contract, which refers to an agreement under which a government agency enlists a private entity to deliver a service to an eligible group of clients in exchange for money (DeHoog and Salamon 2002). This implies a principal-agent relationship between funder and funded (Broadbent, Dietrich, and Laughlin 1996). Grants, the second tool, are defined as payments from a donor government to a recipient organization that are characterized as gifts (Beam and Conlan 2002). Their purpose is to stimulate or support a service activity, and the recipient organization is not required to provide a specified service on behalf of the granting government. The third relevant tool involves loans and loan guarantees to encourage funding for borrowers (Stanton 2002). These tools are ideal types, and distinctions among them might hinge on subtle judgments about the degree of autonomy experienced by funded organizations and expectations of loan repayment by governments. Our analysis characterizes funding instruments by this typology, as well as by the constructions articulated by interviewees.

Funding is inherently linked to accountability. Our analysis of accountability regimes is based on a two-dimensional typology developed by Goodin (2003) as displayed in Table 9.1. The first dimension involves the focus of accountability: Are agents being held accountable for their actions (outputs), results (outcomes), or motives (plans)? The second dimension involves the mechanisms of accountability, which include hierarchical systems of command and control, competitive discipline, and cooperative networking. Again, these are ideal types, and an accountability regime might include several elements of each dimension. Goodin argues that command-and-control systems focused on actions are most characteristic of the public sector. This is seen as an extension of the internal vertical accountability mechanisms of parliamentary government (Aucoin and Jarvis 2005).

For our conceptual framework for understanding instances of cooperation we rely on Brandsen and Pestoff (2006). In their review of cooperation between the nonprofit sector and government, they conceptualize three modes, two of which involve the organizational level

Table 9.1. Dimensions of Accountability

Accountability mechanisms	Outputs	Outcomes	Intentions
Hierarchical command and control	Public sector norm		
Competitive discipline		Private sector norm	
Cooperative networking			Nonprofit sector norm

Source: Authors' compilation, based on Goodin (2003).

of interest here – namely, co-management, which involves coopera-tion in the implementation of service production, and co-governance, which involves mutual planning and policy formulation. These may be contrasted with investing (Phillips, Laforest, and Graham 2008) at one extreme, which involves support for capacity maintenance or building, with relatively little engagement between funder and funded, and, at the other extreme, shopping, which involves the purchase of services through relatively highly specified contracts that allow little space for organizations to shape service offerings or how they are produced. The relationship is one of principal-agent, rather than of participants in col-laborative management, planning, or policy formulation.

The relationships among the elements of the theoretical frame-work are complex and contingent. For example, purchase-of-service contracts might be seen as theoretically aligned with command-and-control accountability mechanisms and a shopping mode of coopera-tion, but contracts can be implemented in a manner that provides space for cooperative networking in accountability. Similarly, purchase-of-service contracts can be associated with co-management, or even co-governance, based on the intentions and level of functional autonomy of the contracting parties.

Historical Context

Funding regimes do not emerge in a vacuum, but are heavily influ-enced and structured by the broader economic, social, and political/ ideological landscape in which they are embedded. As a result, outlin-ing the historical context is an important way to understand the evolu-tion of funding in the keystone province.

A complete historical review is not possible here, but a good starting point is the Progressive Conservative government of Gary Filmon, since the public management reforms introduced by the Filmon government yielded significant changes in the relationship between the provincial government and the nonprofit sector. These reforms were motivated by both ideological and fiscal factors, and the implementation of some of them preceded decreases in federal transfer payments. Leader of a minority government elected in 1988 and then of a majority government elected in 1990, Filmon was viewed as "an urban progressive in a party whose political centre of gravity was rural, fiscal and social conservatism" (Thomas 2010, 237). His government's initial leaning towards social conservatism did not last long, however, given the economic and political realities of the mid-1990s. Starting in 1994 the federal government initiated a series of program reviews to identify areas suitable for expenditure reduction as a means to respond to deficit concerns. Part of this exercise included accommodation to significant cuts in federal transfer payments to the provinces.

Transfer payments, especially to have-not provinces such as Manitoba, are an important influence on what a province can and cannot do to support the nonprofit sector (Miller 1998). The reduction in transfer payments amounted to approximately one-third of Manitoba's provincial revenues (Thomas 2010, 237). This fiscal reality, coupled with the passage of balanced budget legislation in 1996, led to reduced spending in a number of policy areas, including health and social services. By extension, Thomas (2010) contends that these events led the Filmon government to transform public sector management with a preference for the ideals entrenched in New Public Management (NPM) (see also Sonpal-Valias, Sigurdson, and Elson, in this volume). As a political theory that promotes a smaller and leaner state – for example, privatization of publicly owned assets, devolution, and alternative service delivery – NPM also espouses the public sector's adoption of private sector management techniques, such as the emphasis on competition and the contracting out of services. This fervent movement towards NPM did not go unnoticed, especially in a province that is generally known for its pragmatism and moderate approaches to governing (Wesley 2011). Indeed, Thomas concludes that the Filmon era was largely "ideological, radical, extensive and aggressive that was outside the tradition of past Manitoba governments" (2010, 242).

It is thus perhaps no surprise that, given this context, the relationship between the province and the nonprofit sector shifted in three noticeable ways. First, reductions in provincial funding of nonprofits led to their constrained capacity to deliver services adequately. Second, consistent with the promotion of competition under NPM, funding was increasingly delivered via contracts, with a reduction in the availability of grant funding, which is thought to be less administratively burdensome to the sector. Third, grant funding of fifty-six advocacy groups, such as Girl Guides and Indian Friendship Centres, was also reduced, by $3 million in 1993 (Roberts 1993, A4).

As a case in point in understanding the complexity of the evolution of these arrangements, Evenson (2001) studied the funding instruments of fourteen mental health organizations five years after the 1993 initiation of funding arrangements with the provincial government for service delivery. Seven were funded by purchase-of-service agreements – an intermediate instrument between grants and purchase-of-service contracts – that referenced specific services, but were not competitively awarded and involved limited accountability. Six other organizations were funded by grants and one by a purchase-of-service contract. Regardless of funding instrument, competitive tendering was limited, with government officials selecting and approaching particular organizations. Although agreements were annual, they were all continued after a cursory review. Across funding instruments, accountability reporting was limited to standardized reporting of program inputs and outputs, with no evaluation of effectiveness. Distorted organization goals, reduced service accessibility, diminished advocacy, bureaucratization, devoluntarization, and decreased service integration were not generally reported. By 1998, however, stagnant or reduced funding levels had compromised the organizations' ability to recruit and retain appropriate staff.

In part because of the deep cuts to frontline services, notably in health care, the Progressive Conservatives lost the 1999 election to the New Democratic Party (NDP) led by Gary Doer. Deemed to be a pragmatist, rather than an ideologue (Thomas 2010, 243), Doer is credited, or blamed, depending on one's viewpoint, for shifting the party from its left-leaning social democratic principles to a more centrist position reflective of Third Way principles. As conceived by Anthony Giddens (2000), the Third Way rejects the domination of governing through large-scale bureaucratic machinery advocated by the left and the reduction of government's responsibility to govern as advocated by the right. Rather, the Third Way attempts to balance the pursuits of social justice and economic gain, with an emphasis on the role of the community and organizations in the governing process. Although there might be debate as to the degree to which the NDP has moved to Third Way principles,[1] this framework presumably allows for more opportunity for nonprofit organizations to become involved in the governing process.

Woolford and Curran (2011, 590) contend, however, that "Manitoba's New Democratic Party ... government has imported British Third Way discourses as a means to smuggle in neoliberal policy objectives that include offloading services, individual responsibilization, and risk management. The Manitoba NDP carries these tasks out by aligning them with social democratic concerns, such as by reframing service offloading as a form of community-building." On the basis of interviews with twenty-five selected nonprofit managers of community social service organizations in Winnipeg's inner city in the summer of 2009, Woolford and Curran conclude that these discourses have entered the bureaucratic field, partly through funding regimes, and have led these organizations to replace welfare dispositions with neoliberal dispositions. Welfare dispositions are characterized as focused on meeting service users' needs and addressing proximate social conditions leading to disadvantage. Neoliberal dispositions relate to a business approach to organizational management, an entrepreneurial approach to funding (including enthusiastic acceptance of offloading), accountability regimes that marketize the relationship between the state and nonprofit organizations, and replacement of an orientation of meeting needs with one of managing risks. The authors also find that these new technologies of management and accountability create relational distance between service providers and service users (Woolford and Curran 2013).

The Manitoba Voluntary Sector Initiative

In 2000, during the Doer era, the Manitoba Voluntary Sector Initiative (MVSI) was organized by the nonprofit sector to identify, over a three-year period, challenges and opportunities facing the sector and its relationship with government. Initially funded by the Winnipeg Foundation, funding for the MVSI later came from the Thomas Sill Foundation and three levels of government, including the province. The provincial government also created a Minister Responsible for the Voluntary Sector, and it participated in developing what Carter and Speevak Sladowski (n.d., 3) call a formal deliberate relationship with the nonprofit sector to "build a more effective working relationship, and having built it, to maintain and use it into the future to produce better outcomes for governments, for sector organizations and ultimately for communities." In 2003, the province, along with the City of Winnipeg, the Manitoba Federation of Labour, the Volunteer Centre of Winnipeg, the Manitoba Chamber of Commerce, the Winnipeg Chamber of Commerce, and Downtown Winnipeg BIZ, signed a declaration indicating how they could support the work of the nonprofit sector. The declaration was nonbiding, and, although none of the signatories has withdrawn its support, there is also no evidence that the declaration has influenced their actions.

In 2002 the MVSI conducted an omnibus survey of chief executive officers of 1,286 Manitoba nonprofit organizations (Frankel and Rodgers 2003). More than 80 per cent indicated that the advantages of government funding outweighed the disadvantages, more than 68 per cent indicated they did not have enough influence over government funding decisions, and almost 20 per cent thought that securing government funds had distorted their organization's purpose. More than 52 per cent felt that too many organizational resources were expended in meeting government financial reporting requirements, and more than 42 per cent indicated that too much board and staff time was spent securing government resources. Collectively, these findings suggest a principal-agent relationship with government, at least from the point of view of these organizations.

Data from the 2003 National Survey of Nonprofit and Voluntary organizations also point to similar implications of government funding in Manitoba, Saskatchewan, and the territories (Frankel 2006). Of organizations that received more than half of their revenue from government sources, 69 per cent indicated an overreliance on project funding from external funders, 74 per cent reported unwillingness on the part of external funders to fund core operations, 56 per cent indicated a need to modify programs to obtain funding, and 51 per cent said they had problematic reporting requirements. These results imply limited power sharing between external funders and nonprofit organizations.

In a study of eight community-based social service nonprofits operating under purchase-of-service contracts, Kao (2006) reports an extreme imbalance in the contracting relationship with government and little scope for collaboration. Unlike federal government contracts, however, Manitoba government contracts supported a portion of core administrative costs. The imposition of service standardization and government control was limited, but the treatment of one organization demonstrated the potential for control in the contracting arrangements. Most organizations reported that contracts had positive impacts, including stable core funding, service expansion, enhanced credibility, and improved coordination.

Current Realities

In October 2009 Greg Selinger replaced Doer as premier and his government was reelected with a majority in 2011. Dubbed the "Manitoba Miracle" for its ability to insulate itself from the recessionary storm that arose in 2008, Manitoba now finds itself wrestling with increased deficits, including one of $518 million in fiscal year 2013/14. In our interviews conducted in fall 2012, many informants anticipated a difficult funding environment for the nonprofit sector. As we will see later, however, the Selinger government has indicated that it is serious about trying to improve the administrative process that underpins the funding regime in Manitoba and to maintain and increase the nonprofit workforce.

In January 2013 twenty nonprofit sector leaders met at a policy roundtable on "Financing Our Organizations to Support a Stable and Quality Workforce," sponsored by the Manitoba Federation of Non-Profit Organizations. Without specifying which order of government they were referring to, attendees characterized government funding as unstable, short term, and insufficient, leading to precarious work arrangements, with low salaries, absence of benefits, few training opportunities, and limited tenures. Some, therefore, characterized the nonprofit sector as a training ground for the public and corporate sectors.

These perceptions are consistent with a 2009 survey of the health and social services subsectors conducted by the Manitoba Bureau of Statistics, which found that the sector is characterized by low wages: "The overall annual salary for full-time employees is just under $30,000, with 21 per cent of the organizations paying less than $20,000, another 32 per cent paying between $20,000 and $30,000, 25 per cent paying between $30,000 and $40,000 and the remaining 22 per cent paying between $40,000 and $63,000, on average" (Stevens 2010, 5). Roundtable attendees also broadly characterized government as lacking respect for and knowledge of the nonprofit sector, and inappropriately micromanaging in a way that erodes organizational governance. Some expressed concerns that co-management could provide government with the capacity for increased intrusion.

A Patchwork Funding Regime

Manitoba's central agency policy provides a framework, articulated in the *Grant and Other Funding Accountability Guide* (Manitoba 2005, i), to support the funding of nonprofit organizations: "This guide provides a general grant and other funding accountability framework ... Departments should ensure that their granting practices are consistent with the accountability framework." Despite this framework designed to prescribe more centralized control over the funding regime, interviews with civil servants and nonprofit sector leaders revealed that funding is "silo based," with some respondents suggesting there is considerable variation in funding practices from one department to another and even across programs within departments. What this means, in essence, is that one cannot speak of a single large-scale funding regime per se, but of multiple and sometimes overlapping or contradictory regimes that have emerged over time at a middle level that involves departments and sometimes programs and even in the context of relationships with individual nonprofit organizations.

Perceptions of the funding instruments

The *Grant and Other Funding Accountability Guide* distinguishes among purchase-of-service agreements, memoranda of understanding, and letters of intent. The first involve payment for a particular defined service and clear accountability, reporting, standards, and deliverables. Memoranda of understanding are based on a defined purpose, apply to nonessential services, provide a component of support for a specific service, and involve some accountability, reporting, and a definition of deliverables. In terms of the theoretical framework, memoranda of understanding are intermediary between purchase-of-service agreements and contracts. Letters of intent might not apply to specific services and accountability might be nonspecific. In this sense, they equate with grants. According to one senior government official, a grant may be allocated when there is little concern about the product or when the product is difficult to evaluate. By way of example, an arts group might receive a grant, rather than a contract, because the end product (art) does not lend itself to evaluation.

Government officials perceived the instruments in terms of two dimensions – namely, factors that determine the amount and the specificity of deliverables – rather than to the form of agreements per se. In terms of the first dimension, most interviewees distinguished between grants and per diems, with purchase-of-service agreements being used for both. On the second dimension, per diems involved the specification of deliverables, and grants varied from very specific volumes and types of outputs to identification of a general purpose. The most common instrument used for all was a purchase-of-service agreement.

Accountability regimes and government funding

The focus of accountability generally involves actions, specifically program outputs, client characteristics, compliance with expenditure requirements, and compliance with privacy requirements, not program outcomes and impacts. Interviewees indicated that the amount and level of detail required varied by department. The mechanism of accountability was generally command-and-control reporting, but there was significant variation in the flexibility and specificity of targets in deliverables. In addition, in some cases, when requirements were not met, there was negotiation as to how to respond. In others, funding was adjusted.

Collaboration between government agencies and nonprofit organizations

Thinking back to the theoretical framework outlined earlier, funding relationships can be classified into several modes of cooperation, and our data provide evidence that all these various modes are at play in the funding relationship between the province and the nonprofit sector.

The first mode really does not speak to cooperation per se, but to the absence of cooperation. A principal-agent funding relationship occurs when the principal (in this case, a provincial government department) hires an agent (here, a nonprofit organization) to complete a specific set of tasks on behalf of the principal. In this type of funding relationship, control is exerted by the principal largely through a contractual arrangement that specifies deliverables – such as which populations will be served, how many clients will be served, expected outcomes, expenditure types, program elements, and so on.

One nonprofit organization revealed a funding relationship of this nature. This nonprofit receives 100 per cent of its revenues from provincial sources to provide training services. This funding stems from two line departments that will be referred to as Department "A" and

Department "B" to protect the confidentiality of the interviewee. Although this nonprofit is engaged in a contractual arrangement with two departments, the funding relationships and opportunities for collaboration differ significantly. As the nonprofit's senior staff person explains, "I think it is the way the funding is delivered and [I tell you] the difference ... is absolutely striking ... between how [Department A] works with us and how [Department B] works with us. [Department B] is building up ... a structure of control, and [Department A] has always worked with us, so it's a consultative relationship between [Department A] and ourselves." In essence the controlling factor of government funding is a function of how the funding is delivered. In this example the funding delivered by Department B is command-and-control driven, whereby the department dictates what the organization delivers and how the services are to be delivered, with little space for consultation, let alone collaboration.

The principal-agent mode contrasts with the co-management mode of cooperation. Recall that co-management refers to funding models that support nonprofit organizations to deliver goods and services cooperatively. So, although the same funding tool – namely, a purchase-of-service contract – might be used in both the principal-agent and co-management modes, there is an element of cooperation in the latter that is absent from the former. In the example provided above, Department A is more reflective of a co-management funder in that it seeks to work in a consultative manner with the nonprofit. As the senior staff person of this nonprofit suggests, "we identify [services] based on the needs that [Department A] has – in other words, services to [our clients] ... and we propose how we would deliver them and they have agreed to how, and we've negotiated budgets. We don't always get the money that we want, but I would prefer to be working 100 per cent with [Department A] if I had to work with anyone." The experience of this nonprofit organization reflects the idea that how a funding instrument is employed matters as much as the nature of the instrument itself. For some departments the funding instrument, which in this case is a contract, can be used to promote either control (principal-agent) or consultation (co-management). In this example two line departments are not viewed as working conjointly, so the nonprofit organization relates separately to each department.

The next mode is investment, or grants, which involves funding that seeks to build capacity in a nonprofit organization, but does not require significant relationship building or engagement between the funder and the nonprofit. Although the recipient is subject to reporting requirements, the extensive details and resulting administrative burden are greatly reduced.

Although one senior civil servant reported that grants have seen only limited growth as a funding mechanism in Manitoba since they were reduced in the 1990s, some departments still prefer to use them. For example, another senior civil servant revealed that her department provides a substantial amount of its funding in this manner: "For the most part, it's grants for us, and basically 82 per cent of our budget goes out the door in the form of grants to external agencies – occasionally contracts, but really the vast majority of it is grants." When asked if these grants came with a significant number of conditions, the respondent noted: "I'll say [these grants] are reasonably flexible … so, for example, we give cooperating money to [nonprofit organizations], and obviously we have a reporting relationship with them and they are required to provide us with a sort of reasonable documentation … but it is not to deliver a specific program." When asked why her department relied heavily on grants, the respondent noted that grants provide more stability in an increasingly unstable funding environment: "[T]his funding is going to be here for [nonprofits] … Where we run into problems is when we are approached, enticed to cost share something with the federal government, and we often know going in that the feds are going to be here for three years and they are gone. It's still too seductive to say 'no' because you really want to get these programs up and going, and so we buy in and what we are going to do is to replace federal funding … That drives nonprofits crazy and I don't blame them."

The last mode is co-governance, which, again, supports both the formulation of public policy and the delivery of services by nonprofit organizations. This is an important distinction worth highlighting: co-governance funding recognizes the role nonprofits play in formulating public policy that is not found in co-management.

The Family Violence Prevention Program (FVPP), which is housed in Manitoba Family Services and Labour, is a well-documented example of funding that supports co-governance (see Brown and Troutt 2004). Started in the late 1970s, this program now provides funding to thirty-two family violence organizations and other related nonprofit organizations in Manitoba with the expressed goal of eliminating intimate partner and family violence. The primary funding instrument to support these nonprofits is a multiyear purchase-of-service agreement that provides per diem funding on behalf of each woman and child in care.

Brown and Troutt (2004, 15) assert that the use of this funding takes great care in its treatment of nonprofits:

> To ensure consistency across organizations, the FVPP employs a funding formula. The funding formula is a straightforward application of salary scales (including pensions) and overhead costs to particular services. Its purpose is to provide predictable, stable, and standardized funding for specific parts of an organization's budget and for specific types of workers. The use of the funding formula and cost centers allows the FVPP and organizations to have clear agreement on specific service provisions while leaving the important choices concerning how best to provide services to the organizations themselves. For example, the FVPP does not specify the number of nights women are to stay in shelters, nor does it make decisions concerning client selection. Once parameters are clearly defined by mutual agreement, these types of decisions are left to individual organizations.

In essence this type of funding is a contractual arrangement for the delivery of services. What is unique about it, however, is that the funded nonprofits are in a position not just to deliver services under these contracts, but also to have a meaningful opportunity to contribute to the formulation of policy through the development of regulatory standards. In the early 1990s shelters recognized the need for standards for better consistency of service delivery. In 1992 the executive director of the FVPP initiated a process for the development of standards that would "regulate organizations working in the area of family violence in the province" (Brown and Troutt 2004, 13), with the standards developed by family violence workers in nonprofit shelters themselves, not by government. These examples illustrate that a range of nonprofit funding regimes exists within the Manitoba government. Given this apparent variation, it is useful to now examine attempts to develop cooperation within government.

Structures for Cooperation within Government

There are few formal mediating structures in the provincial government to support the representation of the nonprofit sector. Despite no official announcement of this role, the minister of housing and community development identifies as responsible for the whole nonprofit sector,[2] yet no government officials whom we interviewed were aware of this. This minister does not deal with labour market issues facing the sector, as this role is played by another line department (Entrepreneurship,

Training and Trade). Given this lack of representation, respondents pondered what this means for the ability to speak to broader, more systemic concerns related to the sector. One senior civil servant lamented:

> I think all of us who consider the sector to be our partners are concerned about those issues [wages, pensions, and benefits] because we care about those people, but also because of the retention issues [low retention rates] ... we are working with new people quite frequently, although a lot of them stay in spite of the [low] wages and so on. There is not one of us who would not want to see that [situation] stabilize for them and see a pension system that's working well and all of that. I hesitate to say much more because I don't know what Housing and Community Development has in mind for that role ... My impression is that we all have relationships with nonprofit sector, but the lead department is where the issues related to the nonprofit sector and the policy related to it ... reside.

One nonprofit sector leader suggested that the inherent diversity of the sector itself makes it challenging for any formal government structure, whether it be a minister designated for the sector or a cabinet committee, to overcome its atomistic nature. As this respondent noted,

> it [would] be good to have somebody who would be responsible for the entire sector ... You'd like to think there would be one person you could go to, but if you think about that for a second, then you ... go back and say, "okay, now think of all the health care delivery organizations or the social services organizations or the educational organizations." Education still defines itself as part of the sector, so will the universities ... relate to this [minister of the voluntary sector]? No, they will prefer to have their own minister. So you can immediately see how it might sound appealing to jump into that, but at the end of the day it is not likely feasible.

Structures for Cooperation within the Nonprofit Sector

Do nonprofit organizations function as an organized sector, which would involve obvious advantages in advocating with government? A nascent coordinating structure for the sector that grew out of the MVSI is the Manitoba Federation of Non-Profit Organizations (MFNPO), which is a voice for the nonprofit sector as a whole, although it has a heavy emphasis on labour market issues since it is designated as an industrial sector council. A senior government official we interviewed saw the need for such a coordinating body as the MFNPO, but the respondent also recognized that the task is complicated by struggles within and between community groups. In the respondent's view, the divergent needs of nonprofit organizations make it challenging for the MFNPO to coordinate a united voice on behalf of the sector. Furthermore, since the MFNPO is not a membership-based organization, there are questions about its legitimacy in that role. Another respondent was more optimistic about the future of the MFNPO, based upon the perception of its emerging capacity. He argued that the MFNPO was in a position to hire a senior manager, and that it had been building a strategy for long enough (more than fifteen years) that it could now move forward with its organizational mission.

Interviews with nonprofit sector leaders indicated that many identified with a subsector, but not with the sector as a whole. Many did not feel that the cost, in terms of time, required for collaboration would justify the benefits. As one nonprofit sector leader said,

> There are some groups of nonprofits who get together sometimes with other nonprofits who may not be in social services like us. We don't have a lot of time, so meetings have to be relevant ... The nonprofit issues can be a little outside the box, where sometimes ... we can learn things, but ... the issues can't be so far out ... in terms of what they might be doing. For example, I have been in meetings where they are trying to look at how you collaborate with ... church groups, and I am going, "hmmm ... next." I just don't have the time. So it's got to be the right scope.

Structures for Cooperation between Government and the Nonprofit Sector

Coordination with the nonprofit sector within the provincial government is limited, as is coordination within the sector itself. How, then, can the public and nonprofit sectors cooperate in a sustained and productive manner? As alluded to above in connection with the MFNPO, the main interface for cooperation between the two involves labour market issues. The MFNPO's designation as an industrial sector council involves it in training and in collecting and analysing labour market information in collaboration with the Manitoba Bureau of Statistics. All government funding for the organization is focused on labour market issues, limiting its capacity to engage with the government on other issues of interest to the nonprofit sector.

Innovative funding relationships and regimes

In April 2011 the Selinger government committed itself to a broad two-year strategy – generally dubbed the "red-tape exercise" – to improve the relationship between the provincial government and the nonprofit sector. This strategy emphasized a multiyear funding arrangement and a single-window application process, with each nonprofit organization given to a "lead" department that would champion this process and help the organization reduce operating costs through shared services such as legal, human resources, and accounting activities. A total of thirty-five nonprofits were selected from a variety of subsectors, based on their demonstrated adherence to "best practices" criteria and whether they had a long-standing relationship with the provincial government. Our interviews with civil servants and nonprofit sector leaders, however, revealed concerns about how these organizations were selected, with some respondents suggesting they constituted an easy win for the government. One civil servant suggested that the evaluation of the two-year strategy should attempt to determine what de facto selection criteria were in place, as opposed to the stated de jure criteria:

> One piece that may be worth knowing about both within government and within the nonprofit community is that there are many questions about how the thirty-five organizations were selected. Lots of questions and a great deal of cynicism [prevailed]. [Then] there were the best practice criteria. These were circulated. We were asked to please identify agencies that met or met most of these best practice criteria.
>
> I am not aware of, or maybe I am not privy to [this] information, ... any of the agencies we are working with meeting best practice criteria ... [I]n some ways this procedure has damaged a bit of the relationship, not just within government, and increased cynicism, even outside government. There are [all] sorts of questions being asked about the organizations that were selected. They are being called the "chosen ones" or ... the favourites.

A nonprofit sector leader suggested the selection criteria might have had less to do with best practices and more to do with the number of departments involved in funding an organization: "The organizations that they chose wouldn't be organizations that I think have huge capacity, but they may have been organizations that were reporting out to [many] different departments." A central agency staff member who was directly involved in the process confirmed the use of a best practices framework as a baseline inclusion criterion, with selection also influenced by multiple diversity criteria. The issue of selection is important both in generalizing the lessons learned from the pilot exercise and in the legitimacy that nonprofit and public sector actors might invest in these lessons.

When asked about their impressions of the exercise at the time of their interview, respondents offered mixed reviews. When asked if there should be greater standardization as a response to the variation in funding practices that occur at the departmental level, two senior government officials responded that to do so might result in a loss of the history and personal relationship between the department and the nonprofit. In their estimation, the ability to build a long-term relationship between government and the nonprofit sector exists at the departmental level. Beside the loss of a personal relationship, another consequence of centralization could be the loss of departmental expertise. This, coupled with the diversity of the sector, might call attention to the idea that variation in funding regimes is beneficial, since "no one size of funding fits all" nonprofit organizations. That said, however, one respondent conceded that nineteen departments allocating funding in varying patterns created duplication and gaps in processing, so a degree of standardization could improve efficiency.

One senior government official suggested that, although the pilot exercise had encouraged greater streamlining, it had limited ability to evoke greater change since the lead department designated for each of the chosen nonprofit organizations was based on the assumption that the organization's mission would not change. Thus there was a need to incorporate more funding flexibility into the exercise to respond to changes in the operating environment. In noting that her organization had benefited from participating in the exercise, one nonprofit leader said there were "way more streamlined reporting requirements on our part ... The financial reporting requirements have gone down or have been streamlined, coordinated, and organized. We have a map of everything that has to be done by when and who's to do it and where it goes and such."

When asked what other improvements to the funding regime beyond the red tape exercise might be useful, respondents offered a series of ideas. One senior civil servant commented that the funding regime employed by the province needed to do a better job of supporting the evaluation of funded projects, and to be realistic in its expectation of evaluation results. She further noted that there was an equity issue to consider. In her estimation, smaller, newer nonprofits experience difficulty securing funding, especially when competing with larger, more established and institutionalized nonprofits that have developed a strong relationship with their funders. In her estimation,

> if you are a well-established agency who has been getting money from us [provincial government] for years, you are likely to continue getting money from us for years. You may not be the agency that's most reflective of the community, but you are credible, and you have infrastructure, and you probably also get United Way as well as Winnipeg Foundation money because you have been around for years. Then there is the little start-up agency that you know is trying to represent Somalis, or a new community of some sort, and they have a complete uphill battle. So I think we need to take a hard look at that and find out what barriers we are putting up [and] what is needed to diversify the range of organizations. But that's a tough one because, if you only have limited dollars and you know if you give [them] to a well-established organization … they are going take that money and within three weeks they are going be delivering the program that you've been hoping for. At the same time they could mobilize people so much more quickly than [taking time to] help the start-up agency that is struggling.

Another civil servant, a program manager, cited the need for more staff training to develop the quality of relationships and collaboration between the government and nonprofit sectors, since much of the funding comes down to individual relationships. Likewise, there was a need to better educate the nonprofit sector as to how government works, and to establish clear communication as to what can be realistically achieved vis-à-vis the funding regime.

A nonprofit sector leader framed the pilot as a starting point, and hoped to see openness on the government's part to even more fundamental questions:

> The multiyear funding … has brought some ideas forward about how to consider this centrally, but I think their funding model needs to be looked at very carefully because … as it currently exists … [there is also a need to] look at new models of delivery for the nonprofit sector organizations. Should they all be nonshared capital corporations? Should they be cooperatives? … Should there be more shared services or more collaborative efforts? So the notion of sharing and acting collaboratively is something that the government [should] start looking at.

In announcing the pilots, the government committed to an evaluation to determine if they should be scaled up and applied on a government-wide basis. One component of the evaluation reported on a survey of thirty of the organizations involved in the pilots (Proactive Information Services, 2013). Most organizations reported taking more time to finalize their agreements, but less time spent on financial reporting, reporting activities, cutting through red tape, and submitting applications and proposals. Most identified positive impacts, including a reduction in the number of reports, simplified reporting requirements, help getting answers to questions, clarified funding expectations, more time spent providing programming, a more coordinated approach, strengthened accountability, facilitated funding leverage, and more time for fundraising. With regard to the multiyear funding agreements, twenty-three of the thirty nonprofit organizations found that they facilitated long-term planning, sixteen indicated that they allowed longer tenures for employment contracts, but only thirteen found that multiyear contracts enhanced staff retention and training.

We should emphasize, however, that these findings relate to only one stakeholder, articulate no lessons learned, and do not enable us to draw conclusions about corporate application of the pilot exercise for funding of nonprofit organizations throughout the range of government departments. They also do not focus on the larger policy issues.

Conclusion

Developing definitive conclusions is difficult, given the significant variation we found across and within departments, even to the point of questioning the existence of a "funding regime" as such. Cross-government principles exist, but departments vary on norms and decision-making structures. If there is a regime, it is a weak one, and there might be many counterregimes. To some extent particular situational factors in each funding relationship might be determinative. Beyond this, we studied only one class of nonprofit organization, and our findings might not transfer well to arts, sport, or recreational organizations. This would have to be determined through further research.

Funding instruments and their use are centrally defined, but central control is weak, with centrifugal forces possibly dominating centripetal forces. Purchase-of-service agreements are in broad use, but their content and application result in either purchase-of-service contracting or grant making, depending on the department and situation. Government officials construct instruments differently than policy documents, focusing on the pragmatics of what metric determines the size of the payment and the specificity of deliverables.

Accountability regimes demonstrate some consistency in the subjects they address and in mechanisms. But this view is deceptive. Similarities in form might mask differences in application. Expenditure requirements might be highly detailed or unstated. Failing to meet targets might yield sanctions or negotiations. Is this flexibility justified by differences in circumstance or is it simply unfair? Again, future research should pursue detailed comparative case studies of accountability regimes.

Another conclusion is that the extent of collaboration between provincial government departments and nonprofit organizations varies considerably. Some departments deploy funding instruments so as to nurture greater involvement of nonprofits in the formulation and implementation of public policy (co-governance). Other departments deploy funding instruments that promote little collaboration, seeking instead to evoke command-and-control (principal-agent) relationships. Is there is a "norm" for collaboration across provincial departments? Since our interviews did not span all nineteen of Manitoba's departments, we cannot say if such a norm exists or what it might entail. We can conclude, however, that, despite the use of relatively few funding instruments – with purchase-of-service agreements dominating the funding toolbox – how they are used varies significantly, which has an impact on if, and how, collaboration occurs. Future research might identify some of the sources of this variation. Does it relate to departmental culture, differences in concepts of the nonprofit sector, the level of trust between civil servants administering funding and nonprofit organizational managers, or other factors?

As a last observation, we have identified some rays of sunshine as a means to build a stronger relationship between the Manitoba government and the nonprofit sector. Despite the limitations of the pilot exercise, the government has made a real attempt to improve that relationship through streamlining the application and reporting process and the use of multiyear agreements. Decisions will have to be made about adjusting the funding regime throughout the government, on the basis of a more comprehensive evaluation of the pilot exercise. Critical to the success of the evaluation and of the long-term strategy to deal with these significant funding issues will be the transparency of that process. Phase two of these pilots was announced on 15 April 2015, and will comprise thirty-five nonprofit organizations. Unlike in the first phase, where nonprofit organizations were selected solely by government, in the second phase nonprofits must apply to be considered for inclusion.

The Manitoba government's move to more stable, multiyear funding potentially constitutes a partial reversal of the neoliberal tactics of shrinking the welfare state through downloading to and then instituting contingent and flexible funding of the nonprofit sector (Shields and Evans 1998). These tactics often involve project and short-term funding (Baines 2010; Berman, Brooks, and Murphy 2006; Steedman and Rabinowicz 2006). It is difficult to draw conclusions, however, because this approach occurred only in a pilot exercise that involved just thirty-five nonprofit organizations. The real test – and the ability to draw firmer conclusions as to the degree that this streamlining strategy represents a shift away from neoliberal tactics – will come once the new strategy engages the entire nonprofit sector. If this occurs, it will be important to examine issues related to the stability of funding guaranteed in the agreements, such as limitations on the government's capacity to terminate contracts for reasons not related to malfeasance by the funded organization.

The MFNPO, like the Saskatchewan Nonprofit Network (see Garcea and DeSantis, in this volume), would be another ray of sunshine if it places itself in a better position to speak on behalf of the nonprofit sector. The organization was wise to focus on labour market issues and to demonstrate the nonprofit sector's economic role as an employer. The provincial government identified an opportunity to work with the sector by establishing the MFNPO as an industrial sector council and in making resources available to gather information about the labour market and the labour force. This is rare among provinces. Nevertheless, the MFNPO's success might rest on its ability to transcend the imposed boundaries as a sector council and speak to issues that extend beyond the labour market.

NOTES

1 Research by Wesley (2011, 224) illustrates that the NDP generally does not subscribe to the notion that its political base is reflective of Third Way principles.
2 A news release dated 6 May 2010 identified the minister of housing and community development as also the minister responsible for the voluntary sector (Manitoba 2010).

REFERENCES

Aucoin, Peter, and Mark D. Jarvis. 2005. *Modernizing Government Accountability: A Framework for Reform*. Ottawa: Canada School of Public Service.

Baines, D. 2010. "Neoliberal Restructuring, Activism/Participation, and Social Unionism in the Nonprofit Social Services." *Nonprofit and Voluntary Sector Quarterly* 39 (1): 10–28. http://dx.doi.org/10.1177/0899764008326681.

Beam, D.R., and T.J. Conlan. 2002. "Grants." In *The Tools of Government: A Guide to the New Governance*, ed. Lester Salamon, 340–80. New York: Oxford University Press.

Berman, G., R. Brooks, and J. Murphy. 2006. "Funding the Nonprofit Welfare Sector: Explaining Changing Funding Sources, 1960–1999." *Economic Papers* 25 (1): 83–99. http://dx.doi.org/10.1111/j.1759-3441.2006.tb00385.x.

Brandsen, T., and V. Pestoff. 2006. "Co-production, the Third Sector and the Delivery of Public Services." *Public Management Review* 8 (4): 493–501. http://dx.doi.org/10.1080/14719030601022874.

Broadbent, J., M. Dietrich, and R. Laughlin. 1996. "The Development of Principal-Agent, Contracting and Accountability Relationships in the Public Sector: Conceptual and Cultural Problems." *Critical Perspectives on Accounting* 7 (3): 259–84. http://dx.doi.org/10.1006/cpac.1996.0033.

Brown, L., and E. Troutt. 2004. "Funding Relations between Non-profits and Government: A Positive Example." *Nonprofit and Voluntary Sector Quarterly* 33 (1): 5–27. http://dx.doi.org/10.1177/0899764003260601.

Carter, S., and P. Speevak Sladowski. n.d. "Deliberate Relationships between Government and the Non-profit Sector: An Unfolding Picture." Toronto: Wellesley Institute.

DeHoog, R.H., and L. Salamon. 2002. "Purchase-of-Service Contracting." In *The Tools of Government: A Guide to the New Governance*, ed. Lester Salamon, 319–39. New York: Oxford University Press.

Evenson, D. 2001. "The Impact of Provincial Government Funding Arrangements on Community Based Nonprofit Organizations Providing Mental Health Services." Master's thesis, University of Manitoba.

Frankel, S. 2006. *The Non-profit and Voluntary Sector in Manitoba, Saskatchewan and the Territories*. Toronto: Imagine Canada.

Frankel, S., and J. Rodgers. 2003. *The Status of Manitoba's Voluntary Sector: An Omnibus Survey*. Winnipeg: University of Manitoba, Faculty of Social Work, Child and Family Services Research Group.

Giddens, A. 2000. *The Third Way and Its Critics*. Cambridge, UK: Polity Press.

Goodin, R. 2003. "Democratic Accountability: The Distinctiveness of the Third Sector." *European Journal of Sociology* 44 (3): 359–96. http://dx.doi.org/10.1017/S0003975603001322.

Hall, M., C. Barr, E. Easwaramoorthy, S. Wojciech Sokolowski, and L. Salamon. 2005. *The Canadian Non-Profit and Voluntary Sector in Comparative Perspective.* Toronto: Imagine Canada.

Imagine Canada. 2006. "Investing in Citizens and Communities." Submission to the Blue Ribbon Panel on Grants and Contributions under the Federal Accountability Action Plan.

Kao, W.C. 2006. "The Impact of Purchase of Service Contracting on Voluntary Community-based, Social Service Organizations." Master's thesis, University of Manitoba.

Krasner, S. 1982. "Structural Causes and Regime Consequences: Regimes as Intervening Variables." *International Organization* 36 (2): 185–205. http://dx.doi.org/10.1017/S0020818300018920.

Manitoba. 2005. *The Grant and Other Funding Accountability Guide.* Winnipeg.
———. 2010. "Manitoba's Community Services Council receives $2 million to support non-profit organizations." News release. Winnipeg, 6 May. Available online at http://news.gov.mb.ca/news/index.html?item=8401.

Miller, C. 1998. "Canadian Non-profits in Crisis: The Need for Reform." *Social Policy and Administration* 32 (4): 401–19. http://dx.doi.org/10.1111/1467-9515.00123.

Phillips, S., R. Laforest, and A. Graham. 2008. "Getting Third Sector Financing Right in Canada? Quiet Incrementalism and Subversive Innovation toward Reform." Paper presented to the Eighth International Conference of the International Society for Third Sector Research, Barcelona, 9–12 July.

Proactive Information Services. 2013. *Streamlining Access for Nonprofit Organizations, Final NPO Information Summary – Phase 1.* Winnipeg.

Roberts, D. 1993. "Manitoba taxpayers waiting for axe to fall in budget: User fees, spending cuts expected for cash-strapped province." *Globe and Mail*, 6 April, A4.

Salamon, L.M. 2002. "The New Governance and the Tools of Public Action: An Introduction." In *The Tools of Government: A Guide to the New Governance*, ed. L. Salamon, 1–47. Oxford: Oxford University Press.

Scott, K. 2003. *Funding Matters: The Impact of Canada's New Funding Regime on Non-profit and Voluntary Organizations.* Ottawa: Canadian Council on Social Development.

Shields, J., and B.M. Evans. 1998. *Shrinking the State: Globalization and Public Administration Reform.* Halifax, NS: Fernwood.

Stanton, T. 2002. "Loans and Loan Guarantees." In *The Tools of Government: A Guide to the New Governance*, ed. L. Salamon, 381–409. Oxford: Oxford University Press.

Steedman, E., and J. Rabinowicz. 2006. "Changing Dynamics in the Canadian Voluntary Sector: Challenges in Sustaining Organizational Capacity to Support Healthy Communities." *Journal of the Royal Society for the Promotion of Health* 126 (6): 275–9. http://dx.doi.org/10.1177/1466424006070489.

Stevens, H. 2010. *The Voluntary and Non-profit Health and Social Services Sectors in Manitoba: A Profile of Its Composition, Workplace Challenges and Resources for Meeting These Challenges*. Winnipeg: Manitoba Federation of Non-Profit Organizations.

Thomas, P. 2010. "The Past, Present, and Future of the Manitoba Civil Service." With C. Brown. In *Manitoba Politics and Government: Issues, Institutions, Traditions*, ed. P. Thomas and C. Brown, 227–56. Winnipeg: University of Manitoba Press.

Wesley, J. 2011. *Code Politics: Campaigns and Culture on the Canadian Prairies*. Vancouver: UBC Press.

Woolford, A., and A. Curran. 2011. "Neoliberal Restructuring, Limited Autonomy and Relational Distance in Manitoba's Non-profit Field." *Critical Social Policy* 31 (4): 583–606. http://dx.doi.org/10.1177/0261018311415571.

———. 2013. "Community Positions, Neoliberal Dispositions: Managing Nonprofit Social Services within the Bureaucratic Field." *Critical Sociology* 39 (1): 45–63. http://dx.doi.org/10.1177/0896920512439728.

10 Mainstreaming Community Economic Development in Manitoba

BRENDAN REIMER, KIRSTEN BERNAS,
AND MONICA ADELER

Introduction

Canadian communities face complex challenges including unemployment, urban and rural decline, income inequality, poverty, social exclusion, and environmental degradation. These complex challenges can be addressed effectively with comprehensive strategies that include a long-term, multifaceted, and integrated community-led approach (Canada 2009; Froy and Giguère 2010; Gorman 2007; Toye and Infanti 2004).

The community economic development (CED) model provides that approach. CED is community-led strategic action that creates economic opportunities while enhancing social and environmental conditions (Canadian CED Network 2013). The CED model enables each community to pursue comprehensive strategic actions that respond to its unique needs, priorities, and opportunities (Amyot, Downing, and Tremblay 2010; Kliewer 2010). In 2008, Canada's chief public health officer stated that "people living closest to the problem are often closest to the solution," and he added, "[i]nterventions at the community level are most successful in reaching vulnerable populations, creating local networks, and leveraging resources" (Canada 2009, 32).

Canadians have a long history of taking innovative and strategic action to respond to complex challenges in order to improve the quality of life in their communities, from Aboriginal people who thrived and survived collectively for thousands of years right up to the present context, when they and many other types of communities across the country continue to create local solutions to local challenges (Cabaj 2004). Through CED organizations, Canadians are strengthening local economies while providing access to child care services, housing, local food, capital, training, skills development opportunities, and much-needed services that enable marginalized persons and communities to thrive (Enterprising Non-Profits 2010; Markell 2004). These organizations foster local leadership, ownership of resources, labour market development, economic revitalization, poverty reduction, social inclusion, and environmental stewardship (Bernas and Reimer 2011).

The Evolution of CED in Manitoba

Policy shapes social, economic, and political outcomes, but policy itself is shaped by historical, economic, political, and social processes in a particular environment (Adeler 2013). A number of factors have contributed to a strong CED sector in Manitoba, without which the current provincial policy regime that is supportive of CED would not have emerged, and which require contemplation when considering replication in other jurisdictions.

For some, the principles of CED align with a cultural world view and way of life, the roots of which are found thousands of years ago and continue today in Aboriginal communities (Cabaj 2004). The first inhabitants of the prairies understood the importance of a holistic view of community that considered the well-being of the economy, the people, and the environment as inextricably interconnected. Cooperation was synonymous with survival, and the concepts of sharing, mutually beneficial trade, and respect for the natural environment have left an indelible mark on modern communities, economies, and environments (MacPherson 2010). Numerous Aboriginal organizations continue to affect the CED context in Manitoba.

Quarter, Mook, and Armstrong argue that "the root problem that spawns community economic development is social and economic inequality, a historic problem in capitalist economies" (2009, 82). If crisis is the mother of innovation, it is understandably those who are not benefiting from existing socio-economic and political structures who seek alternative models. However, although CED is aspirational in that it seeks better conditions for a certain group of people, divergent goals are sought through different approaches. One approach seeks the integration of people and communities into the mainstream economy, while another perspective seeks a more transformative approach through the creation of an alternative socio-economic system (Fontan 1993; Loxley 2007; Reimer 2005a). The former sees the existing socio-economic system as the answer, while the latter considers the existing system to be the root of many problems.

Cooperatives emerged in the nineteenth century, following union-ization drives and the Winnipeg Strike of 1919, as a means to reclaim control for local workers, consumers, and producers from an economic system that community actors considered exploitative. As "autono-mous association(s) of persons united voluntarily to meet their com-mon economic, social, and cultural needs and aspirations through a jointly-owned and democratically-controlled enterprise," co-ops play an important role in Manitoba's local economies and communities, serving both economic and social purposes (Manitoba Cooperative Association 2010). Co-ops create jobs, root business ownership and wealth in local communities, distribute profits equitably, and provide goods and essential services that otherwise might be unavailable to the community. Their primary function is to serve their members, not to maximize profits as in traditional business models, and the decisions they make around business operations reflect that local, community, and service orientation. Co-ops build capacity and develop community leaders through members' participation in the democratic governance of the business. Manitoba's more than 360 cooperatives serve over 500,000 members and create jobs for over 5,000 people.[1]

A major factor that shapes an economy is the nature of the finan-cial industry. As such, financial cooperatives, or credit unions, were also a key component of the historical CED context in Manitoba. They were created to provide access to credit for people and communities that mainstream financial institutions would not serve. Since the first caisse populaire (credit union) was established in 1937 in St Malo, credit unions have played an essential role in providing financial services and access to credit in support of economic opportunities for both individu-als and communities (Credit Union Central of Manitoba 2013). As of December 2012, there were 40 credit unions in Manitoba with $21.35 bil-lion in assets and 191 branches serving 585,484 members and employ-ing 3,579 people with a payroll of $150 million.[2] Demonstrating their core commitment of service to members, as opposed to the primary pursuit of profit, credit unions are the only remaining financial institu-tion in 67 of the 117 Manitoba communities (Credit Union Central of Manitoba 2013).

Community development corporations (CDCs) were created to address geographic poverty and economic disadvantage, and emerged as a CED model in rural Manitoba communities in the 1960s. Joined in 1986 by a network of sixteen Community Futures organizations in rural and northern Manitoba, and in 1996 by the Economic Develop-ment Council for Manitoba Bilingual Municipalities, these entities have played a role in supporting community-led enterprise and economic development in rural Manitoba (Loxley and Simpson 2007).

Urban CDCs emerged in Winnipeg in the late 1990s. They were more aligned with the CDCs that originated as part of the US civil rights movement in the late 1960s to overcome poverty through a focus on community empowerment, citizen engagement, and neighbourhood renewal (Quarter, Mook, and Armstrong 2009). Inner-city actors had identified the potential of this model by connecting with other CED leaders across the country through the emerging Canadian CED Network (CCEDNet). Together they worked to create the North End Community Renewal Corporation in 1999 (Colussi et al. 2003; NECRC 2013). Similar organizations also emerged in Winnipeg's inner city, including the West Broadway Development Corporation, the Spence Neighbourhood Association, and the Neeganin Development Corporation, which focused on Aboriginal CED (Loxley and Simpson 2007).

Community leaders also sought to reshape the local economy by changing existing institutions. In 1992, social activists who were part of a coalition called Cho!ces mobilized Assiniboine Credit Union (ACU) members to elect a more progressive board of directors (Loxley and Simpson 2007). This transformation led to the integration of CED principles into the operations of the credit union. ACU has since been recognized locally and nationally for its strong leadership role in CED (ACU 2013). It was a key partner in creating the Jubilee Loan Fund, an ethical investment fund launched in 2000 that works closely with ACU to finance CED initiatives through loan guarantees (Jubilee Fund 2013). Following mergers with a few other credit unions, in 2014 ACU had over $3.8 billion in assets and over 110,000 members (ACU 2014).

Seeking to combat poverty through micro and community enterprise development, CED actors established Supporting Employment and Economic Development (SEED) Winnipeg, which opened its doors in 1993 (SEED Winnipeg 2013). SEED now offers financial literacy training, asset-building programs, and business consulting for low-income individuals, workers' cooperatives, and social enterprises. In 2009 SEED Winnipeg partnered with the University of Winnipeg's Community Renewal Corporation to create Diversity Foods, a social enterprise that holds the food services contract at the University of Winnipeg (2013) and provides jobs for people with barriers to employment.

The Aboriginal community, which continues to experience the effects of oppression and exploitation through the imposition of socio-economic systems of colonialism begun hundreds of years ago, has sought to construct its own institutions to create economic opportunities while improving social conditions. For instance, Urban Circle Training Centre was created in 1991 to provide training towards meaningful employment, a need identified by Aboriginal women living in the inner city (Urban Circle 2013). Since its inception it has graduated over two thousand students, and a cost-benefit analysis of the program has calculated that savings to taxpayers by 2015 would amount to $114 million (Canadian CED Network 2011b).

Established to reclaim Aboriginal responsibility for caring for Aboriginal children and families, the Ma Mawi Chi Itata Centre (Ma Mawi) was created in 1984 as Canada's first Aboriginal family service organization. In 1997 Ma Mawi transformed its philosophy to a holistic, community-based, and capacity-building approach focused on building relationships with and between Aboriginal people (Canadian CED Network 2005). With more than fifty programs, Ma Mawi continues to support children in care and the broader community through a vision of collective responsibility and assistance (Ma Mawi 2013).

In 1990 the Aboriginal Centre of Winnipeg was incorporated to "realize the goal of providing a centre that promotes the social, educational and entrepreneurial growth of the Aboriginal community in the City of Winnipeg" (Aboriginal Centre of Winnipeg 2013). In 1992 the Centre purchased Winnipeg's former Canadian Pacific Railway station to provide a supportive home for a variety of Aboriginal-based business and nonprofit organizations.

A significant factor leading to the widespread use of the term "community economic development" in Manitoba in the early 1990s was the creation of Neechi Foods, an Aboriginal-owned workers' cooperative grocery store in Winnipeg's North End. It was established to create jobs for Aboriginal people while providing healthy food in a growing food desert. Neechi Foods articulated eleven principles to guide the co-op, which became known as the Neechi CED Principles (Canadian CED Network 2011a). These principles have been adopted by many CED organizations, and have also found their way into provincial policy (Fernandez 2005). In 2013 Neechi Foods expanded significantly, resulting in dozens of jobs in a 30,000 square foot retail hub that includes "a neighbourhood supermarket, produce courtyard, cafeteria restaurant, bakery, fish market, a specialty foods boutique, Aboriginal books, arts, crafts, music and clothing, a seasonal farmers market, and hardware" (Neechi Foods Co-op 2013).

Created in 1994 to support Neechi Foods, Local Investment Towards Employment (LITE) is an intermediary that educates the public about

CED and the value of ethical purchasing while raising funds to support CED initiatives (Duboff and Reimer 2006; Reimer 2005b). LITE has since raised over $1.4 million to purchase food from CED initiatives for "Alternative Christmas Hampers," and has provided grants for inner-city employment and training initiatives (LITE 2013). LITE also hosts the Social Purchasing Portal, another intermediary that mobilizes businesses, government, nonprofits, and public consumers to shift their purchasing to inner-city enterprises that create jobs for people with barriers to employment (Social Purchasing Portal 2013).

In 1997 the Manitoba office of the Canadian Centre for Policy Alternatives (CCPA-MB) was created to conduct research to influence public discourse and policy decisions, and in 2003 CCPA-MB was awarded a Social Sciences and Humanities Research Council (SSHRC) grant that focused on CED. In 2006 the Manitoba Research Alliance on CED in the New Economy brought together sixteen academics, fifty-five student researchers, thirty-eight community researchers, and thirty-two community partners from across the province to conduct forty-two research projects (Manitoba Research Alliance 2006). This partnership helped build the CED movement in Manitoba through the generation of knowledge, awareness built through the dissemination of that knowledge, experience and skills developed by the researchers and partners, and through the relationships developed over the multiyear project. In 2007 another SSHRC-funded collaboration, the Manitoba Research Alliance for Transforming Inner-city and Aboriginal Communities, included a research stream on CED (Manitoba Research Alliance 2013).

It is worth noting that this rich history of community organizing in Manitoba has occurred under, and survived through, various governments at all jurisdictional levels for more than a century. This is not to suggest that government support is not essential in creating an enabling environment for CED. Rather, regardless of which government is in power, CED can and will happen when communities make it a priority. In the absence of a supportive policy regime, however, community-led actions will not necessarily reach their full potential.

The CED Policy Framework and Lens

The New Democratic Party (NDP) government elected in Manitoba in 1999 brought new people into decision-making roles, some of whom had been involved in the province's CED scene. Seeking to grow CED in Manitoba, they created the Community and Economic Development

Committee of Cabinet (CEDC), the CED Policy Framework and Lens, and Neighbourhoods Alive! to support Neighbourhood Renewal Corporations and other CED initiatives in targeted urban communities (see Figure 10.1). The policy regime positively influenced other government programs, including the Winnipeg Partnership Agreement and subsequent Winnipeg Regeneration Strategy. It also increased funding for frontline organizations as well as strategic intermediaries that support them, such as the Canadian CED Network–Manitoba. Clearly the provincial government did not invent CED in Manitoba, but it did respond to community demand for a policy regime that would support CED more effectively.

In 2001 the provincial cabinet endorsed the CED Policy Framework, articulating the NDP government's commitment to integrating CED principles into its initiatives and to supporting CED initiatives in Manitoba communities (Reimer et al. 2009). This was a clear statement and policy directive signalling government support for CED as

Figure 10.1. The CED Framework and Lens

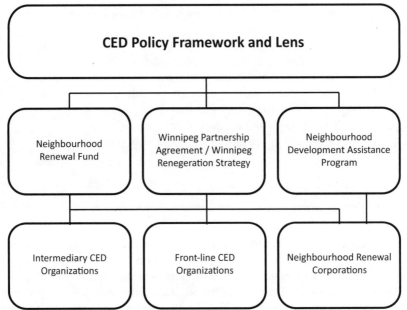

*Note: This chart does not indicate causal or chronological relationships.

an important component of Manitoba's economic strategy (Loewen 2004). The CED Policy Framework acknowledged the potential for CED to contribute to a stronger and more inclusive, equitable, and sustainable provincial economy. It also recognized the important role of community-based organizations in improving the economic, social, and environmental well-being of Manitoba communities (see Box 10.1).

BOX 10.1 COMMUNITY ECONOMIC DEVELOPMENT

The Province of Manitoba defines CED as a community-driven process that combines social, economic, and environmental goals to build healthy and economically viable communities. CED is a way of fostering economic development that is responsive to locally defined priorities. CED strategies aim to revitalize and renew local economies by developing community resources for community benefit. CED focuses on local ownership and control of resources and strives to increase community self-reliance.

Fundamental to CED is that processes and strategies must be owned and driven by communities. They must be directed towards fostering economic, social, ecological, and cultural wellbeing. Within this context, CED can have an important role in developing local economies and communities in a way that maximizes opportunities for people to work collectively in addressing community problems. CED attempts to ensure that social welfare, equity, economic development, and environmental sustainability are not left to chance but, rather, are facilitated by a flexible process guided by a strategic vision.

Source: Bernas and Reimer (2011, 4).

The CED Policy Framework has three main components: objectives, principles, and a CED lens. The CED objectives articulate what the province hopes to achieve in Manitoba's communities by integrating CED principles into government initiatives and by supporting CED community projects (see Box 10.2). The ten CED principles (see Box 10.3) articulate considerations that need to be embedded in policies, programs, and processes to ensure that the desired outcomes are achieved, and are based heavily on those created by the worker-owners of Neechi Foods (Reimer et al. 2009).

BOX 10.2 COMMUNITY ECONOMIC DEVELOPMENT OBJECTIVES

1. **Build greater community capacity.** Building community capacity involves people working together to develop programs and services that support CED. Capacity building requires education, communication, organizational development, and strategic development.

2. **Nurture individual and community pride, self-reliance, and leadership.** The ability to lead has a great deal to do with one's feelings of self-respect and confidence. The same factors affect people's ability to share and to act with a sense of community. Great care must be taken to ensure that CED policies and programs are designed to encourage and support grassroots innovation and leadership.

3. **Enhance knowledge and skills.** CED requires that community members have access to education and training opportunities. Education and training contribute to enhanced employability, greater productive capability, and social and economic innovation, making them critical to building strong economies and allowing people to live purposeful lives. Education and training enable individuals and communities to adjust to changing circumstances and thus continuously meet new needs.

4. **Encourage the development of businesses that are responsive to social, economic, and environmental needs.** When business investment is narrowly focused on commercial profit, there is no guarantee that business development will have a desirable impact on people or the environment. CED principles can be used to re-focus attention on social, environmental, and broad economic needs.

5. **Foster balanced, equitable, and sustainable economic development.** A strong economy needs diversity. Balance among different economic sectors will ensure that local and regional economies are not vulnerable to being destabilized by the inevitable ups and downs of the market. This balance implies strong linkages between industries and businesses at the community and regional level. Balance also implies reinvesting profit in the economy.

Source: Manitoba (2004).

BOX 10.3 COMMUNITY ECONOMIC DEVELOPMENT PRINCIPLES

1. Enable local employment ...
2. Encourage local ownership and decision making ...
3. Build local economic linkages ...
4. Reinvest profits in communities ...
5. Develop local knowledge and skills ...
6. Ensure a positive environmental impact ...
7. Focus on health and well-being ...
8. Foster neighbourhood stability and community cohesion ...
9. Value human dignity ...
10. Encourage interdepartmental and intergovernmental collaboration.

Source: Manitoba (2004, 3).

The CED Policy Framework was coordinated by the Community and Economic Development Committee of Cabinet (CEDC), created in 1999 to "develop policy and co-ordinate all major government initiatives related to community and economic development" (Bernas and Reimer 2011, 5). Now called the Priorities and Planning Committee of Cabinet, the CEDC was made up of ministers responsible for departments most relevant to CED. It had staff support from a CEDC Secretariat that coordinated an interdepartmental CED Working Group consisting of policy and program analysts from departments relevant to CED. The Working Group was charged with developing the CED Policy Framework through consultation with CED organizations and leaders. It was also responsible for facilitating implementation of the CED Policy Framework across government through internal education and communication strategies that included a CED video and CED lens exercise (Bernas and Reimer 2011).

The CED Working Group convened CED champions from across government to explore interdepartmental collaboration on CED initiatives and to identify what the government was doing and could be doing to implement the CED Policy Framework (Bernas and Reimer 2011; Sheldrick 2007). It also liaised with community organizations to support the CED initiatives these organizations were undertaking.

The CED principles form the basis of the CED lens, "a tool created to help government departments understand and implement the CED Policy Framework ... [and that] poses a series of questions that encourages departments to consider whether the CED principles are being integrated into new and existing initiatives, to examine the potential barriers to their integration, and to explore the actions required to overcome those barriers" (Bernas and Reimer 2011, 7). In this way, the lens helps ensure that departmental initiatives contribute to achieving the province's CED objectives (Manitoba 2001).

The CED lens can be applied to all government initiatives, including those related to employment development, business development, rural and urban revitalization, housing, homelessness, immigration, child care, food security, poverty reduction, sustainable development, and procurement. It can also be applied to legislative reform, funding, eligibility criteria, administrative procedures, client accessibility, community consultation, impact assessments, pilot programs or projects, education and awareness initiatives, research, program evaluations, staffing, and training (Manitoba 2001).

Funding for Neighbourhood-based CED Initiatives

Neighbourhoods Alive!

One initiative created to support CED was Neighbourhoods Alive!, which establishes Neighbourhood Renewal Corporations (NRCs) and funds them along with other community-based organizations that take a CED approach to renewing designated communities in Manitoba.

Neighbourhoods Alive! was launched in 2000 as a long-term, community-led, social and economic development strategy. It provides funding that enables urban communities to take a holistic, local approach to neighbourhood revitalization (Bernas and Reimer 2011). Neighbourhoods Alive! recognizes that each neighbourhood has unique needs, priorities, opportunities, and that the most effective ideas for revitalization often come directly from the community in need. Following this philosophy, Neighbourhoods Alive! offers planning assistance and flexible funding programs that enable communities to identify their needs and then to develop and implement strategies to address them (Manitoba n.d.b). By 2011 over 919 community-based projects had received more than $78 million from Neighbourhoods Alive! (Manitoba 2011a).

Although all eight Neighbourhoods Alive! funding programs contribute to neighbourhood revitalization, the Neighbourhood Development Assistance Program and the Neighbourhood Renewal Fund play particularly key roles. The former provides five-year core funding to local, democratically governed NRCs in designated communities that enables the development of long-term neighbourhood revitalization plans based on a CED approach. The latter complements the Neighbourhood Development Assistance Program by providing funding to NRCs and other organizations in their designated neighbourhoods for projects that build capacity, stability, economic development, and well-being (Bernas and Reimer 2011).

Designated neighbourhoods

Neighbourhoods Alive! initially focused on residential neighbourhoods in Brandon, Thompson, and five in Winnipeg's inner city. These designated neighbourhoods faced significant social, economic, and environmental challenges such as high rates of poverty, unemployment, and crime, as well as a lack of affordable housing, family supports, adequate recreation, and economic opportunities (Manitoba n.d.b). In 2005 Neighbourhoods Alive! expanded to seven more neighbourhoods in Winnipeg's inner city and in 2007 to neighbourhoods in Dauphin, Flin Flon, The Pas, Portage la Prairie, and Selkirk (Manitoba 2005). In 2010 a thirteenth Winnipeg neighbourhood (Elmwood) became eligible for support from the program, and in 2011 the provincial government announced the expansion of Neighbourhoods Alive! into five new Winnipeg neighbourhoods through the Localized Improvement Fund for Tomorrow with a commitment of $1.8 million (Manitoba 2011a). Each neighbourhood was to receive $90,000 in grants annually for four years, with residents and community organizations collectively identifying local priorities for the funds. Examples of projects funded by the Localized Improvement Fund for Tomorrow are

- community development and engagement projects;
- community economic development projects;
- greening projects such as community clean-ups and community gardens;
- recreation programs such as programs for youth, families, and seniors;
- art projects such as community murals;

- workshops and training, including skills development programs; and
- safety and crime prevention, including programs for at-risk youth.

Each designated neighbourhood must be represented by a locally governed and democratic NRC to receive Neighbourhoods Alive! support from the Neighbourhood Development Assistance Program or the Neighbourhood Renewal Fund. NRCs are governed by a volunteer board of directors made up of, and elected by, neighbourhood residents who represent the diverse interests of the community. Rather than duplicating the work already being done by other local organizations, NRCs fill gaps by developing, coordinating, and implementing needed neighbourhood revitalization initiatives (Silver, McCracken, and Sjoberg 2009).

To be eligible for Neighbourhoods Alive! funding, NRCs also must facilitate the creation of comprehensive, five-year neighbourhood revitalization plans through community consultation. These plans identify the needs, opportunities, priorities, and goals of the community. They also outline strategic actions to guide efforts towards achieving the collective community vision. As each neighbourhood is unique, each neighbourhood revitalization plan will also be unique. However, each community is expected to demonstrate how its plan is consistent with the provincial government's CED principles (EKOS Research Associates 2010). Each plan also must explain how it fosters neighbourhood capacity building, stability, economic development, and well-being (Bernas and Reimer 2011).[3]

The Neighbourhood Development Assistance Program

Funding from the Neighbourhood Development Assistance Program became available one year after Neighbourhoods Alive! was launched, when staff of that program and of the NRCs realized that project-based funding alone would not be sufficient to support the organizational capacity that NRCs needed to fulfil their mandates effectively (Bernas and Reimer 2011). The Neighbourhood Development Assistance Program supports each NRC with up to $25,000 in start-up funding and between $75,000 and $200,000 in core funding each year for up to five years (Manitoba 2002b), with the amount determined at the ministerial level and influenced by the size of the neighbourhood in which the NRC operates (Bernas and Reimer 2011). Neighbourhood

Development Assistance Program funding can support core organizational costs, including staff, facility, and office expenses. This enables NRCs to establish the administrative and management structures they need to develop and implement neighbourhood revitalization initiatives (Manitoba 2002a; Silver, McCracken, and Sjoberg 2009).

The Neighbourhood Renewal Fund

The Neighbourhood Renewal Fund is available for NRC projects and other organizations in designated neighbourhoods (Manitoba n.d.c). Ensuring that projects align with community priorities, proposals must demonstrate how initiatives will advance strategic priorities and goals as outlined in the NRC's neighbourhood revitalization plan, involve local resources and residents in their development and implementation, strengthen local capacity, and integrate the government's CED principles (Manitoba n.d.a). To be eligible for Neighbourhood Renewal Fund funding, projects must fit within the broad categories of neighbourhood capacity building, stability, economic development, and well-being. Although final decisions are made by the Neighbourhoods Alive! Steering Committee of Cabinet Ministers, Neighbourhood Renewal Fund proposals are reviewed by the board or board committees of local NRCs to ensure alignment with their neighbourhood revitalization plans (Bernas and Reimer 2011). Between 2000 and 2010 the Neighbourhood Renewal Fund had allocated over $20 million for community-led projects (EKOS Research Associates 2010). Examples of projects funded by the Neighbourhood Renewal Fund include

- community gardens and greenhouses;
- youth employment programs;
- safety audits;
- community murals;
- skills banks;
- composting programs;
- recreation for at-risk youth; and
- social enterprise development.

The Neighbourhood Renewal Fund also has a Small Grants Fund that provides between $25,000 and $150,000 to NRCs to allocate up to $5,000 to community-led projects (EKOS Research Associates 2010). These projects also must be consistent with the community's neighbourhood revitalization plan. Proposals are reviewed by an NRC board committee, and funding decisions are ratified by the board (Bernas and Reimer 2011). Examples of projects funded by the Small Grants Fund include

- soil and lumber for community gardens;
- uniforms for youth soccer programs;
- block parties and street festivals;
- tree-banding supplies;
- home maintenance training workshops;
- job training for newcomer women; and
- food security "Good Food Box" programs.

The Winnipeg Partnership Agreement and the Winnipeg Regeneration Strategy

The provincial government's commitment to CED also influenced the signing in 2004 of the Winnipeg Partnership Agreement, a five-year $75 million tripartite initiative to provide project funding for various programs. Previous tripartite agreements in Winnipeg had focused primarily on infrastructure projects, but two of the four Winnipeg Partnership Agreement components allocated about $25 million for "Aboriginal Participation" and "Social Economy and Community Development." In keeping with the CED principles of community leadership and decision making, each component had an advisory committee of community representatives to make recommendations on the allocation of funds (Loxley and Simpson 2007).

With federal and municipal governments unwilling to create a subsequent tripartite agreement, in 2010 the provincial government established a five-year Winnipeg Regeneration Strategy to help sustain the valuable work carried out by CED organizations and other nonprofits previously funded by the Winnipeg Partnership Agreement. The strategy had three priorities to guide fund allocation: Aboriginal capacity building, downtown renewal, and "development of inner-city resiliency to improve the physical, social, economic and environmental conditions and outcomes for the inner city through comprehensive approaches based on community economic development principles" (Manitoba 2010, 1).

Funding for Intermediaries that Support CED

Although investing directly in frontline CED organizations is essential to achieving desired neighbourhood outcomes, success also depends on having a supportive infrastructure for those frontline organizations (Turner et al. 2012). Intermediaries create an enabling ecosystem in which frontline organizations have the capacity they need to achieve their mission. Intermediaries support frontline organizations by meeting their specific needs, such as access to information, convening and coordination, access to funding and financing, policy development and government relations, public education and media engagement, research and development, and access to skills training and capacity building.

Turner and colleagues underscore the value of intermediary organizations: "Effective backbone support is a critical condition for collective impact. In fact, it is the number one reason that collective impact initiatives fail" (Turner et al. 2012, 1). However, despite their value to frontline organizations and their role in achieving desired community outcomes, intermediaries often find funding difficult to obtain. One reason is that intermediaries have difficulty proving that outcomes are attributable to their support. Instead, outcomes are generally attributed to the frontline organizations that act to achieve outcomes, even if their ability to do so was due in part to intermediaries. For example, a social enterprise might receive credit for jobs created, but its ability to create jobs might have been due to the intermediaries that provided, say, financing and skills development opportunities or worked with government to develop a tax credit to raise capital for the social enterprise. As Turner et al. find, "[a]cross organizations, the value of backbone support was commonly viewed as unmistakable; individual partners could not do the work of collective impact without it" (2012, 1).

The CED Policy Framework, however, acknowledges the value of intermediaries in supporting frontline organizations. The provincial government has invested in existing intermediaries such as Local Investment Towards Employment, the Manitoba Cooperative Association, and the Jubilee Loan Fund, as well as in the creation of new intermediaries – such as CCEDNet-Manitoba and Food Matters Manitoba – that communities identified as being essential for their ability to achieve their missions. Funding was often provided through Neighbourhoods Alive!, the Winnipeg Partnership Agreement, or the Winnipeg Regeneration Strategy. The province also has partnered with intermediaries since the introduction of the CED Policy Framework, in, for example, joining the steering committees of both Manitoba Research Alliance research projects ("CED in the New Economy" and "Transforming Aboriginal and Inner City Communities).

As the capacity of frontline organizations has grown with provincial funding, their ability to work together to identify the intermediary supports they require to do their work effectively also has increased. The provincial government has responded with investments in these intermediaries, which it recognizes as contributing to the achievement of its own CED objectives. This ad hoc responsive approach, however valuable, has meant that a comprehensive intermediary program or system has not developed, resulting in the need of some frontline organizations remaining unmet (EKOS Research Associates 2011). This responsive approach is consistent, however, with the practice of allowing communities and frontline organizations collectively to identify their own capacity gaps and intermediary needs.

For example, frontline organizations identified skills development as a strategic priority for building the CED sector's capacity to achieve its mission, which led to the creation in 2004 of the CD/CED (Community Development/Community Economic Development) Training Intermediary, hosted by a nonprofit in Winnipeg's North End and funded by the province in partnership with others. The CD/CED Training Intermediary provided a certificate program for community interns who spent three weeks per month in community organizations and the remaining week in the classroom, a one-year certificate program for existing practitioners who remained in their workplace and attended classes three days per month, a two-year diploma in "Community Development/ Community Economic Development" for full-time students through Red River Community College, and one-day skill development workshops that built capacity for community members and nonprofit practitioners (Tamarack 2004).

The CD/CED Training Intermediary no longer exists in its original form. However, Red River College continues to offer one-year certificate and two-year diploma programs in "Community Development/ Community Economic Development," and the University of Winnipeg designed a degree program in "Urban and Inner City Studies" that continues to expand the spectrum of educational opportunities for students looking to pursue careers in community development and CED. CCEDNet-Manitoba now offers capacity-building workshops in proposal writing, evaluation, strategic planning, social enterprise development, planning for financial sustainability, strengthening communications plans, calculating "Social Return on Investment," and much more. The CED sector continues to benefit from students who graduate from the education programs mentioned above and from the practitioners who participate in CCEDNet-Manitoba's capacity-building workshops.

Frontline organizations also identified the need for an intermediary to facilitate access to the technical skills required to carry out their work effectively, but that could not be developed through the CD/CED Training Intermediary. The provincial government responded with other partners by providing funding for the creation of the CED Technical Assistance Service (CEDTAS). Initially hosted by SEED Winnipeg, CEDTAS was designed to help organizations assess their capacity challenges, to refer them to relevant resources, and to match them with volunteers with specialized skills willing to do pro bono work. Now called "Spark," this intermediary continues as a service of CCEDNet-Manitoba. Nonprofits continue to benefit from this provincially funded intermediary, which provides access to volunteers with expertise in a wide variety of areas, including accounting and bookkeeping, architectural design, board governance, building renovation planning, information technology services, landscape design, human resources, legal issues pertaining to nonprofits, social enterprise development, strategic planning, web design and communications, marketing, and much more.

Another intermediary for which frontline organizations identified a need was one to convene the CED sector, facilitate communication and access to the information that nonprofits need to achieve their missions, create CED-specific learning opportunities and public education events, undertake research into innovative and effective policy and practice, and lead policy development activities for the sector. The province responded in 2003 by providing a local CCEDNet chapter the resources to support such activities. In keeping with the practice of having community leaders set priorities, the key activities outlined in funding agreements were established by the CCEDNet-Manitoba membership through various forums. This has empowered the CED community to direct the network to focus on strategic activities that most effectively address those priorities. This approach, along with consistent funding from the province, has allowed CCEDNet-Manitoba to become an effective intermediary contributing to numerous policy changes that support CED, establishing a robust communications strategy, holding many public education and capacity-building events each year, including the annual Manitoba CD/CED Gathering attended by over six hundred practitioners, and raising the profile of CED activities through publications and media engagement.

An evaluation by EKOS Research in 2011, funded as part of the implementation of the CED Policy Framework, concluded that the CED sector as a whole and the capacity of frontline organizations had grown as a result of investments in intermediaries (EKOS Research Associates 2011).

Lessons from Manitoba

The role of community strength and leadership in shaping the policy regime

Various socio-economic, cultural, and political factors have played a key role in shaping the CED environment in Manitoba. Without strong community leadership, it is unlikely that the current policy regime for CED would exist, since policy does not emerge in a vacuum. Particularly in the 1990s, community actors created many CED initiatives in response to local socio-economic challenges. For example, one leader helped create SEED Winnipeg, the North End Community Renewal Corporation, Opportunities for Employment, and the Jubilee Loan Fund, and was the first permanent executive director of CCEDNet. Another social justice activist with CHO!CES was hired by the new NDP government and became the champion and catalyst for the creation of the CED Policy Framework before transitioning to a leadership role with CCPA-MB.

Many others also played key roles, but the key point is that both innovative individuals and a critical mass of collective leadership already were in place before 1999. They knew their priorities, and once the government changed, they were ready to act. Some community leaders found themselves in decision-making roles in the new government, which gave other community leaders a more direct avenue to influence policy because of the relationships built over years of community organizing.

Leaders, both those in government and in nonprofit organizations, were integrally involved in shaping the government's creation of a supportive policy regime for CED. Members of the emerging Canadian CED Network also played a key role in building up CCEDNet-Manitoba as an effective intermediary supporting and advocating for the sector.

Their political and policy development skills, courage to be innovative, and value orientation towards CED were critical factors leading to those policy developments. The staff and members of CCEDNet-Manitoba have also played a critical role in maintaining pressure on the government to implement the CED Policy Framework, identifying opportunities for government action as well as current policy barriers to CED, and often being the conduit intermediary for communication between the government and frontline CED organizations.

The impact of public policy on strengthening CED

CED was alive and well in Manitoba before 1999, but a supportive policy regime since then has elevated CED activity in the province. Strong and effective leadership by key individuals in the provincial government was critical in both the creation of the CED Policy Framework and its implementation. Without the social worker and community activist hired by the Community and Economic Development Committee of Cabinet who facilitated the creation of the framework, it is unlikely this policy shift would have happened. The extent to which the framework was championed internally was also determined by the leadership staff responsible for its implementation. This, in turn, depended significantly on ministerial leadership, meaning that departmental commitment to CED varied as individuals leading these departments changed. Even with policies in place, impact can be limited without well-positioned, knowledgeable, and effective champions to ensure implementation.

Policy matters, however, and the creation of the CED Policy Framework increased government understanding of, and support for, CED. The framework offers a rationale for, and a clearly articulated description of, the province's approach to supporting communities, thus providing a strong basis upon which thinking and discourse around CED could emerge. By articulating CED objectives and the strategies to achieve them, the framework itself has become a tool for increasing the understanding and value of CED within government. The participation of departmental representatives in the process of developing the framework itself was educational, as it deepened their understanding of CED and the provincial government's role in achieving CED objectives. As a result, there are individuals across government who now value CED and actively explore ways to support it by integrating its principles into government activities using the CED lens. The lens provides a template that facilitates a methodical means of ensuring that government initiatives support CED. This tool has strengthened the province's capacity to develop and implement programs that promote strong, fair, sustainable, and resilient local economies and communities across Manitoba.

The CED Policy Framework has influenced many provincial initiatives in addition to those already described, including the following:

- the Manitoba Hydro Northern Training and Employment Initiative, which expects to provide up to twenty years of employment for northern Aboriginal Manitobans, and education and training opportunities for more than one thousand Aboriginal residents;
- the Aboriginal Procurement Initiative, which directs all departments to increase the number of Aboriginal businesses providing goods and services to government;
- the Community Enterprise Tax Credit, which encourages Manitobans to invest in local, collectively owned businesses;
- the Cooperative Community Vision and Strategy, which was developed with the co-op community as an action plan for strengthening and growing cooperatives in Manitoba;
- provincial government support for the creation and growth of social enterprises – particularly Building Urban Industries for Local Development and the Brandon Energy Efficiency Program – that provide training and employment opportunities for low-income people while improving energy efficiency in low-income homes and Manitoba Housing units. This culminated in the creation of the Manitoba Social Enterprise Strategy co-created with the sector (see Canadian CED Network and Manitoba 2015); and
- the Neighbourhoods Alive! Tax Credit, which provides an incentive for corporations to donate funds and business consulting services to new social enterprises that create jobs for people facing barriers to employment.

Although these results are significant, they are less than those in government and the community who contributed the creation of the CED Policy Framework had hoped. The framework was never legislated, so that its enforcement mechanism is less than it could have been. Limited resources have been dedicated to internal education, meaning that many government employees are unaware of the policy and even more are unsure of how to implement it in their departments and programs. Accountability for implementation, despite early attempts to have departments report annually on results, has been weak. Policy implementation has been strong when ministerial leadership has demanded it, and neglected when it has not.

Notwithstanding these limitations, the longevity of a favourable policy regime, in place since 1999, has made the growth of the CED approach possible in Manitoba. This consistency has created a stable and supportive policy environment that has enabled the sector to grow in a manner that would have been impossible with multiple changes in government. With this in mind, in 2012 the provincial government passed the Community Renewal Act to further institutionalize the CED model in legislation (Manitoba 2013).

The contract culture

Government funding is essential for CED, but the nature of funding and of the government-nonprofit relationship is also important. Neighbourhood renewal requires a consistent, long-term approach, and appropriate funding is crucial for both core and project costs. The Neighbourhood Development Assistance Program component of Neighbourhoods Alive! is an exemplary model with five-year core funding agreements that enable long-term organizational stability. This has allowed Neighbourhood Renewal Corporations to engage and mobilize communities to develop and implement initiatives that create effective solutions to community challenges through a long-term approach, rather than through a series of short-term projects. Unfortunately, other than a 1 per cent increase in 2010, there has not been any increase in the Neighbourhood Development Assistance Program funding amounts since 2000, despite inflationary cost increases and the significant growth of NRCs. The core funding they receive, in our view, is no longer adequate.

The Neighbourhood Renewal Fund, the Winnipeg Partnership Agreement, and the Winnipeg Regeneration Strategy (the latter two now expired) also represent effective models of multiyear, project-based funding to NRCs and other CED organizations, including intermediaries. Such funding mechanisms provide essential resources to implement projects that address the priorities set by residents. However, funding is insufficient for resourcing long-term community renewal projects, as NRCs and other CED organizations still need to reapply, often annually, for project funding even when projects are well established (EKOS Research Associates 2010). Also, the length of project funding agreements has been decreasing, creating greater instability for programs (EKOS Research Associates 2011).

To address the administrative burden nonprofits experience with multiple provincial funding sources for various programs and activities, in 2010 the province launched a two-year initiative to improve the contract culture for CED organizations and other nonprofits (see also Frankel and Levasseur, in this volume). The initiative continues to provide multiyear, multiprogram funding for a group of nonprofits with proven track records of success, and eliminates reporting duplication for organizations dealing with multiple provincial programs (Manitoba 2011b). The initiative stabilizes organizations while reducing their administrative workloads so that they can focus on achieving their missions.

The contract culture in Manitoba is unusual in placing decision-making power regarding program activities with residents and CED organizations. Although the province has identified the desired objectives and principles of CED through the CED Policy Framework and selected the neighbourhoods to be aided by the Neighbourhoods Alive! program, decisions on activities are determined at the community level. Neighbourhood Development Assistance Program funding is contingent on completion of a community-designed neighbourhood revitalization plan based on strategic priorities set by local residents. Money from the Neighbourhood Renewal Fund and the Small Grants Funds is available only for projects that fit within those strategic priorities. Funding for intermediaries is also directed at initiatives that address community-identified priorities. The provincial government has thus created a contract culture that reflects its commitment to CED by empowering communities to set their own priorities and then ensuring they have the resources to address those priorities and achieve their missions.

This practice is not without challenges. CED organizations sometimes still feel that provincial contracts do not allow them sufficient flexibility to address their priorities. There are also concerns that the provincial government does not always accept the recommendations of NRCs regarding Neighbourhood Renewal Fund allocations (EKOS Research Associates 2010).

Advocacy and voice

Given the Manitoba government's strong support of CED organizations and intermediaries, it is worth considering their ability to advocate for themselves and their communities regarding the policy changes they would like to see to enable them to do their work and pursue their mission.

Community residents have been empowered, through NRCs, to become engaged in creating neighbourhood revitalization plans. Ensuring that NRCs have long-term core and project funding gives them the capacity to grow the scope and scale of their work, and to increase their ability to speak with their communities regarding local priorities, resulting in these neighbourhoods having a much stronger voice.

The funding model has also enabled CED organizations to identify and create the intermediaries they need to achieve their missions. The NRCs, for example, have formed an association to exchange knowledge and build a collective voice to represent their interests to government. Their capacity to organize is partially due to the provincial government's ongoing funding for regular teleconference calls and in-person meetings. CCEDNet-Manitoba has been building the capacity of NRCs and other CED organizations to understand policy and develop strategies for advancement.

Provincial funding for sector-created intermediaries such as Food Matters Manitoba, the Manitoba Cooperative Association, and CCED-Net-Manitoba also strengthens the voice of frontline organizations, and improves their capacity to develop and advance policy priorities on behalf of their members. In October 2012 Premier Selinger announced a local and sustainable food procurement initiative advocated by Food Matters Manitoba. Two successive five-year Co-op Community Vision and Strategies, amendments to the Co-op Act to allow for the creation of multistakeholder cooperatives, and the introduction of a Co-op Development Tax Credit were all policy changes advanced by the Manitoba Co-op Association. Research by the Manitoba office of the Canadian Centre for Policy Alternatives and advocacy by the Right to Housing Coalition have influenced the provincial government's commitment to create social and affordable housing units. CCEDNet-Manitoba has worked with its members to advance all of these policy priorities, and has also been involved in successfully advancing others, including the Poverty Reduction Strategy Act, the Energy Savings Act, the Community Renewal Act, the Neighbourhoods Alive! Tax Credit for social enterprise development, and the Winnipeg Partnership Agreement renewal that led to the creation of the Winnipeg Regeneration Strategy. In 2007 CCEDNet-Manitoba met with the provincial CED Working Group to present twelve policy priorities that were then explored by six working groups, one of which involved strengthening support for intermediaries that build the capacity of CED organizations to achieve their missions. CCEDNet-Manitoba also worked together with the province to co-create the Manitoba Social Enterprise Strategy together with government and social enterprise stakeholders.

The provincial government considers CED organizations and intermediaries to be partners in implementing the CED Policy Framework, and recognizes the sector's knowledge of what is required to achieve CED objectives, inclusive of policy implications. This is not to say that all CED organizations and intermediaries are equally comfortable advocating for policy change; some do not want to rock the boat or bite the hand that feeds them. Yet, although a strong funding relationship dampens the advocacy appetite of some organizations, the strong voice that the funding relationship has built has resulted in the sector's successful advancement of numerous policy changes.

Looking Forward

The CED sector in Manitoba has been strong for a long time, and the policy regime in place since 1999 has contributed to its exponential growth. In a reciprocating manner, frontline organizations have created and strengthened intermediaries that, in turn, have strengthened the capacity of frontline organizations to achieve their missions – and both frontline organizations and intermediaries have had the support of the CED Policy Framework. This mutually reinforcing relationship between frontline and intermediary organizations will continue to be important for identifying and advancing priorities for policy change and for providing the support the sector needs to achieve CED objectives and community mandates.

The strength of the CED sector in Manitoba would be tested by a change in provincial government, as a new administration might not share the same commitment to the CED Policy Framework and Neighbourhoods Alive!. The sector thus should not take the current favourable policy regime for granted, but ensure that its work is able to continue in the future for the well-being of Manitoba communities. CED organizations thus should work to secure continued support by developing rigorous evaluation methods that clearly demonstrate the impact of their approach and activities in the communities they serve. It will be particularly important for intermediaries to strengthen their evaluation and impact analysis systems (EKOS Research Associates

2011). A new government might not continue this supportive policy regime under any circumstances, but it would certainly be more difficult to reduce or terminate support for organizations and initiatives that clearly demonstrate significant benefit to neighbourhood residents and a significant return on their investment.

CED organizations should continue strengthening their financial positions by diversifying their revenue streams and building reserves to ensure financial and organizational sustainability. This is effective practice for nonprofits in any policy regime, but will be essential for survival should the nature of current support change. Even now, as the provincial government limits investments in CED due to budget deficits while other funders, such the federal government, are also significantly reducing funding of nonprofits, organizations are being forced to become more innovative, entrepreneurial, and financially astute in order to continue their work.

NOTES

1 Authors' personal communication with V. Goussaert, 14 March 2013.
2 Ibid.
3 For an example of a plan, see the website of the North End Community Renewal Corporation at http://necrc.org/.

REFERENCES

Aboriginal Centre of Winnipeg. 2013. "About Us." Available online at http://www.abcentre.org/; accessed 8 March 2013.
ACU (Assiniboine Credit Union). 2014. Annual Report 2014. [Winnipeg]. Available online at http://annualreport.assiniboine.mb.ca/Financial%20Results.html; accessed 12 July 2015.
——. 2013. "ACU wins national CED award." Press release. Winnipeg. Available online at http://www.assiniboine.mb.ca/My-Assiniboine/Awards-and-Accolades/National-CED-Award.aspx; accessed 3 March 2013.
Adeler, M. 2013. "Enabling Policy Environments for Co-operative Development: A Comparative Experience." PhD diss., University of Saskatchewan.
Amyot, S., R. Downing, and C. Tremblay. 2010. "Public Policy for the Social Economy: Building a People-centred Economy in Canada." Public Policy Paper Series 3. Victoria, BC: Canadian Social Economy Research Partnership.

Available online at http://socialeconomyhub.ca/sites/socialeconomyhub.
ca/files/PublicPolicyPaper3_0.pdf; accessed 15 March 2013.

Bernas, K., and B. Reimer. 2011. "Building a Policy Framework and Program
in Support of Community Economic Development." Report prepared
for the Winnipeg Inner City Research Alliance, University of Winnipeg.
Available online at https://ccednet-rcdec.ca/en/document/building-
federal-framework-and-program-support-ced; accessed 12 July 2015.

Cabaj, M. 2004. "CED & Social Economy in Canada: A People's History."
Making Waves 15 (1): 13–20.

Canada. 2009. Parliament. Senate. Standing Senate Committee on Social
Affairs, Science and Technology. Subcommittee on Population Health.
A Healthy, Productive Canada: A Determinant of Health Approach. Ottawa.
Available online at http://www.parl.gc.ca/Content/SEN/Committee/402/
popu/rep/rephealthjun09-e.pdf; accessed 7 March 2013.

Canadian CED Network. 2005. "Ma Mawi Wi Chi Itata Centre." Victoria, BC.
Available online at http://ccednet-rcdec.ca/sites/ccednet-rcdec.ca/files/
mamawi-e.pdf; accessed 8 March 2013.

——. 2011a. "CED Profile: Neechi Foods Co-op Ltd. (Operates Neechi
Foods Community Store)." Available online at https://ccednet-rcdec.ca/
en/toolbox/ced-profile-neechi-foods-co-op-ltd-operates-neechi-foods;
accessed 19 May 2015.

——. 2011b. "Urban Circle Training Centre." Available online at http://
ccednet-rcdec.ca/sites/ccednet-rcdec.ca/files/ccednet/Profile_-_Urban_
Circle_Training_Centre_Incx_2.pdf; accessed 8 March 2013.

——. 2013. "What Is CED?" Available online at http://ccednet-rcdec.ca/
en/what_is_ced; accessed 31 March 2013.

Canadian CED Network and Manitoba. 2015. "Manitoba Social Enterprise
Strategy: A Strategy for Creating Jobs through Social Enterprise." Winnipeg.
Available online at http://www.gov.mb.ca/housing/pubs/mb_social_
enterprise_strategy_2015.pdf.

Colussi, M., S. Perry, M. Lewis, and G. Loewen. 2003. "From This Earth:
NECRC & the Evolution of a Development System in Winnipeg's North
End." *Making Waves* 13 (1): 20–37.

Credit Union Central of Manitoba. 2013. "About Credit Unions." Available online
at http://www.creditunion.mb.ca/about/history.htm; accessed 1 March 1 2013.

Duboff, C., and B. Reimer. 2006. "Traveling LITE: A Winnipeg NonProfit Helps
Bridge the Gap from Charity to CED." *Making Waves* 16 (4): 23–7. Available
online at http://lite.mb.ca/wp-content/uploads/2012/05/making_waves_
lite_jan2006.pdf.

EKOS Research Associates. 2010. *Neighbourhoods Alive! Community Outcomes.* Final
report. Winnipeg: Department of Housing and Community Development.

———. 2011. *Manitoba Community Economic Development (CED) Project: Program Evaluation*. Final report. Winnipeg: Department of Municipal Government, Planning Policy and Programs Branch, Community Planning and Development Division.

Enterprising Non-Profits. 2010. "What Social Enterprise Can Do in Your Community." Available online at http://www.socialenterprisecanada.ca/webconcepteurcontent63/000024540000/upload/Resources/What_SE_Can_Do(LR).pdf; accessed 19 May 2015.

Fernandez, L. 2005. "Government Policy towards Community Economic Development in Manitoba." Master's thesis, University of Manitoba. Available online at http://mspace.lib.umanitoba.ca/handle/1993/3824; accessed 19 May 2015.

Fontan, J. 1993. "A Critical Review of Canadian, American, & European Community Economic Development Literature." Vernon, BC: Westcoast Development Group. Available online at http://www.communityrenewal.ca/sites/all/files/resource/P073.pdf; accessed 11 March 2013.

Froy, F., and S. Giguère. 2010. *Breaking Out of Policy Silos: Doing More with Less*. Local Economic and Employment Development (LEED). Paris: Organisation for Economic Co-operation and Development. http://dx.doi.org/10.1787/9789264094987-en.

Gorman, C. 2007. "Final Reflections from the Action for Neighbourhood Change Research Project." Ottawa: Caledon Institute of Social Policy. Available online at http://www.caledoninst.org/Publications/PDF/641ENG.pdf; accessed 19 May 2015.

Jubilee Fund. 2013. "About Us." Available online at http://www.jubileefund.ca/about.php; accessed 7 March 2013.

Kliewer, K. 2010. *Community-Based Planning, Engagement, Collaboration, and Meaningful Participation in the Creation of Neighbourhood Plans*. Saskatoon: University of Saskatchewan, Centre for the Study of Co-operatives; Winnipeg: University of Winnipeg, Institute of Urban Studies.

LITE (Local Investment Toward Employment). 2013. "About Us." Available online at http://lite.mb.ca/who-we-are/mission-and-action; accessed 10 March 2013.

Loewen, G. 2004. "The Good News from Manitoba." *Making Waves* 15 (2): 26–9.

Loxley, J. 2007. *Transforming or Reforming Capitalism: Towards a Theory of Community Economic Development*. Halifax, NS: Fernwood Publishing.

Loxley, J., and D. Simpson. 2007. *Government Policies towards Community Economic Development and the Social Economy in Quebec and Manitoba*.

Saskatoon: University of Saskatchewan, Centre for the Study of Co-operatives; Victoria, BC: Canadian CED Network. Available online at http://usaskstudies.coop/documents/social-economy-reports-and-newsltrs/Government%20Policies%20towards%20CED.pdf; accessed 20 May 2015.

Ma Mawi (Ma Mawi Wi Chi Itata Centre). 2013. "Ma Mawi Wi Chi Itata Centre." Available online at http://www.mamawi.com/; accessed 8 March 2013.

MacPherson, I. 2010. "Cultivating Co-operation: Roots Run Deep." Speech presented at the 2010 Manitoba Community Development/Community Economic Development Gathering, Winnipeg, 22 October.

Manitoba. 2001. *The Community Economic Development (CED) Lens: Applying the CED Policy Framework.* Winnipeg.

———. 2002a. "Neighbourhoods Alive! Invests in Community Economic Development." Available online at http://www.gov.mb.ca/chc/press/top/2002/02/2002-02-22-01.html; accessed 12 March 2013.

———. 2002b. Department of Housing and Community Development. "Neighbourhoods Alive! Report to the Community," vol. 1. Winnipeg. Available online at http://www.gov.mb.ca/housing/neighbourhoods/na_bg/pdf/comm_report1.pdf; accessed 20 May 2015.

———. 2004. "Community Contact: Manitoba Aboriginal and Northern Affairs."

———. 2005. "Province celebrates and expands successful Neighbourhoods Alive! initiative." *News Release,* 8 June. Available online at http://www.gov.mb.ca/chc/press/top/2005/06/2005-06-08-02.html; accessed 12 March 2013.

———. 2010. "New Winnipeg Regeneration Strategy designed to support inner-city revitalization. Initiative would renew infrastructure, stimulate economy, preserve heritage, improve lives of Aboriginal residents: Lemieux." *News Release,* 9 June. Available online at http://news.gov.mb.ca/news/?archive=2010-06-01&item=8801; accessed 13 March 2013.

———. 2011a. "Five Winnipeg communities to be revitalized with $1.8 million from Neighbourhoods Alive!: Irvin-Ross." News Release, 13 May. Available online at http://news.gov.mb.ca/news/index.html?archive=2011-05-01&item=11484; accessed 12 March 2013.

———. 2011b. "Two-year plan cuts red tape, offers non-profit groups stable funding: Selinger." *News Release,* 8 April. Available online at http://news.gov.mb.ca/news/index.html?item=11205; accessed 12 March 2013.

———. 2013. *The Community Renewal Act.* Available online at http://web2.gov.mb.ca/bills/40-1/b007e.php; accessed 12 March 2013.

———. n.d.a. Department of Housing and Community Development. "Community Economic Development." Available online at http://www.gov.mb.ca/housing/neighbourhoods/neighbourhoods/nda.html; accessed 17 November 2015.

———. n.d.b. Department of Housing and Community Development. "Neighbourhoods Alive!" Available online at http://www.gov.mb.ca/housing/neighbourhoods/; accessed 17 November 2015.

———. n.d.c. Department of Housing and Community Development. "Neighbourhood Renewal Fund." Available online at http://www.gov.mb.ca/housing/neighbourhoods/progs/nrf.html; accessed 17 November 2015.

Manitoba Cooperative Association. 2010. "About Co-ops." Available online at http://www.manitoba.coop/about-co-ops/; accessed 1 March 2013.

Manitoba Research Alliance. 2006. "Manitoba Research Alliance on CED in the New Economy: Final Report." Winnipeg: Manitoba Research Alliance.

———. 2013. "Transforming Inner-city and Aboriginal Communities." Available online at http://mra-mb.ca/about/; accessed 20 May 2015.

Markell, L. 2004. "Building Assets in Low-income Communities through Co-operatives: A Policy Framework." [Ottawa]: Canadian Co-operative Association.

Neechi Foods Co-op. 2013. "Neechi Commons." Available online at http://neechi.ca/neechi-commons/; accessed 8 March 2013.

NNECRC (North End Community Renewal Corporation). 2013. "About NECRC." Available online at http://necrc.org/?page_id=87; accessed 26 November 2013.

Quarter, J., L. Mook, and A. Armstrong. 2009. *Understanding the Social Economy: A Canadian Perspective.* Toronto: University of Toronto Press.

Reimer, B. 2005a. *CED-oriented Business Development Strategies for Winnipeg's North End.* Winnipeg: Manitoba Research Alliance. Available online at https://mbresearchalliance.files.wordpress.com/2012/11/7cedbusinessmodels1.pdf; accessed 20 May 2015.

———. 2005b. "The Christmas Hamper that Gives Twice." *Fast Facts* (Canadian Centre for Policy Alternatives-Manitoba), 15 December. Available online at http://www.policyalternatives.ca/sites/default/files/uploads/publications/Manitoba_Pubs/2005/FastFacts_Dec15_05.pdf; accessed 9 March 2013.

Reimer, B., D. Simpson, J. Hajer, and J. Loxley. 2009. *The Importance of Policy for Community Economic Development: A Case Study of the Manitoba Context.* Saskatoon: University of Saskatchewan, Centre for the Study of Co-operatives. Available online at http://www.ccednet-rcdec.ca/files/ccednet/Manitoba_Policy_Paper1.pdf; accessed 2 March 2013.

SEED Winnipeg. 2013. "About Us." Available online at http://seedwinnipeg.
ca/about; accessed 13 March 2013.

Sheldrick, B.M. 2007. "The Manitoba Community Economic Development
Lens: Local Participation and Democratic State Restructuring." Department
of Political Science, University of Guelph. Available online at http://
ccednet-rcdec.ca/sites/ccednet-rcdec.ca/files/ccednet/pdfs/the_
manitoba_community_economic_development_lens_local_participation_
and_democratic_state_restructuring.pdf.

Silver, J., M. McCracken, and K. Sjoberg. 2009. "Neighbourhood Renewal
Corporations in Winnipeg's Inner City: Practical Activism in a Complex
Environment." Winnipeg: Canadian Centre for Policy Alternatives-
Manitoba. Available online at https://www.policyalternatives.ca/
sites/default/files/uploads/publications/Manitoba_Pubs/2009/
InsideNCRsSilver.pdf; accessed 12 March 2013.

Social Purchasing Portal. 2013. "Social Purchasing Portal." Available online at
http://www.sppwinnipeg.org; accessed 9 March 2013.

Tamarack. 2004. "Community Development/Community Economic
Development: Highlights from the March 18, 2004, Report Session."
[Winnipeg]. Available online at http://tamarackcommunity.ca/downloads/
vc/win_ced_mar04.pdf.

Toye, M., and J. Infanti. 2004. *Social Inclusion and Community Economic
Development: Literature Review*. Victoria, BC: Canadian CED Network.
Available online at http://ccednet-rcdec.ca/sites/ccednet-rcdec.ca/files/
PCCDLN_20040803_LitReview-H.pdf; accessed 20 May 2015.

Turner, S., K. Merchant, J. Kania, and E. Martin. 2012. "Understanding the
Value of Backbone Organizations in Collective Impact, Part 1." *Stanford
Social Innovation Review*, 17 July.

University of Winnipeg. 2013. Food Services. "About Diversity Food
Services." Available online at http://www.uwinnipeg.ca/food-services/;
accessed 20 May 2015.

Urban Circle. 2013. "About Us." Available online at http://
urbancircletraining.com/contact/about-us/who-we-are/; accessed 20 May
2015.

11 Funding Policies and the Nonprofit Sector in Western Canada

PETER R. ELSON

Concepts, Contexts, and Comparisons

Case studies provide an opportunity to explore a particular event or a pattern of circumstances at a depth that other research methods are unable to emulate (George and Bennett 2005). As this book exemplifies, case studies often explore historical events or developments with the goal of identifying trends, lessons, and, in some cases, generalizable explanations. This book has attempted to accomplish all three purposes. Each chapter has provided a historical context for current funding regime dynamics; patterns are delineated, and lessons learned. In this chapter I attempt to draw out some overall themes and threads, and draw some general conclusions. A hidden value of the case study approach is that the same information can be analysed from a variety of perspectives. I invite you to draw your own themes, threads, conclusions, and then, to paraphrase Sid Frankel and Karine Levasseur (Chapter 9), decide whether you are working with a patchwork quilt or a wool blanket.

Organizational case studies, as found in that of the BC Non-Profit Housing Association (Atkey and Stone, Chapter 3) reveal the time, effort, talent, and opportunity required to build and sustain a leading voice in the context of a dominant provincial funding regime. In the Alberta Mentoring Partnership (O'Neill et al., Chapter 6), the provincial lottery in Saskatchewan (Gidluck, Chapter 8), and the Community Economic Development movement in Manitoba (Reimer, Bernas, and Adeler, Chapter 10), we see the critical role of intermediary organizations that embrace both system and agency governance and build strong ties to both community-focused organizations and provincial funding regimes.

Nonprofit policy governance

In British Columbia the Government Non-Profit Initiative (GNPI) was dominated by engagement at the deputy ministerial or equivalent level (Lindquist and Vakil, Chapter 2). In Alberta an affiliated minister and dedicated deputy minister have been assigned the voluntary sector-government portfolio. The term "affiliated minister" is used here because all ministers to date simultaneously have held other portfolios, of which voluntary sector-government relations is often a minor part. Nevertheless it does signal a clear intention by these governments that nonprofit sector-government relations are valued and have a voice at the cabinet table.

British Columbia and Alberta have each established a nonprofit governance secretariat within their provincial government. In all other cases where a dedicated secretariat has been established, a deputy minister is either associated with or dedicated to the task of overseeing the secretariat. The actual structure of the secretariat and associated nonprofit sector advisory committees varies considerably, ranging from "separate-but-equal," as is the case in British Columbia and Manitoba, to advisory and by provincial appointment only, as was the case with the Alberta Nonprofit Voluntary Sector Initiative (Elson 2012).

Government representation in these initiatives is generally more organized, resourced, and institutionalized than in the more nonformal nonprofit sector.[1] Existing structures within government are used as a conduit for internal policy dialogue – for example, issues concerning voluntary sector-government relations are raised at standing committee meetings of deputy ministers. Government representatives in an intersectoral representational forum seldom meet independently, although informal discussions with secretariat staff are common. There is also variation in the level of representation from each department. Because designated government representatives have reporting and representational responsibilities for their home department, together with formal reporting structures, a more formal institutional structure governs the representation from government.

The intersectoral policy forums vary considerably in size, and are generally informal in nature (see Table 11.1). In British Columbia, for example, the GNPI was seen as a policy "think tank," rather than as a formal forum for policy formulation. That is not to say that policy issues do not find their way to and from government decision makers; it is just that the connection is nonformal. Participation in these intersectoral representational forums also varies considerably. Where

Table 11.1. Provincial Government-Nonprofit Sector Policy Forums

Province	Nonprofit Sector Policy Forum	Type and Focus
British Columbia	Government Non-Profit Initiative (2009–12) 2013 (currently under review)	Joint policy "think tank"; partnership focused on human services
Alberta	Alberta Nonprofit/Voluntary Sector Initiative (2007–12) 2012 (currently under review)	Joint partnership focused on liaison with cross-section of representative government and nonprofit leaders
Saskatchewan	Premier's Voluntary Sector Initiative (2002–07) Saskatchewan Nonprofit Partnership (2012–)	Partnership focused on sector-wide issues and liaison with representative leaders Common voice and collaborative mechanism for sector
Manitoba	Alliance of Manitoba Sector Councils (2010–) Manitoba Federation of Non-Profit Organizations (2003–)	Memorandum of Understanding on labour market issues

there are representative umbrella organizations, representatives are internally designated. In the case of joint committees, voluntary sector members are nominated by leaders in the field or appointed by a governing steering committee or government minister. Having a policy forum of one dimension or another is one part of the policy picture; the other dimension is the policies that are addressed within these forums, and the consequences of these deliberations.

Government's internal management of the nonprofit sector file is rarely as formal as its external representation to the sector. The very scope and complexity of the nonprofit sector begs for a degree of formal internal coordination, yet even when this designation is explicit, as in the case of Manitoba's Department of Housing and Community Development (Frankel and Levasseur, Chapter 9), the reality is more informal. What is more frequently the case is that a ministry slowly builds a degree of nonformal internal and external institutional credibility concerning its knowledge and experience with the nonprofit sector. Over time this knowledge and experience manifest themselves in a reputation as a repository of institutional memory and the "go to" status for many matters nonprofit. This is certainly appears to be the case with the Ministry of Culture in Alberta and the Ministry of Social Development and Social Innovation in British Columbia.

British Columbia

The decision in British Columbia to configure the GNPI around community human services (Lindquist and Vakil, Chapter 2) was deliberate. Beyond education and health funding, human services represents a substantive and complex funding regime for provincial governments. It is also one where there was a declared self-interest on the part of the government and the nonprofit sector to increase the latter's capacity to deliver these services. The GNPI was coordinated by a seventeen-member Leadership Council comprised primarily of senior sectoral representatives and government deputy ministers. In addition, ninety-seven government and voluntary sector representatives sat on four advisory groups (Business and Finance, Human Resource Capacity, Aboriginal Engagement, and Inclusion and Inclusion). These four groups in turn developed five advisory committees to address specific substrategies, providing a substantive venue for nonprofit and public sector engagement. The joint and equal participation by both sectors was evident throughout the GNPI structure. This, as Lindquist and Vakil explore, was augmented by annual sector-wide summits to report progress and receive sector feedback.

Alberta

The Alberta Nonprofit Voluntary Sector Initiative was coordinated by a twenty-two-person committee with equal representation from government ministries and the voluntary sector. The government co-chair was the deputy minister for culture and community spirit (now culture and tourism); the nonprofit sector co-chair was nominated by a subcommittee of nonprofit sector representatives for consideration by the minister. Nonprofit representation was confirmed by ministerial appointment and was not always assured.[2] Over the course of the ANVSI a wide range of mutual issues was introduced and discussed. Beyond this centralized structure, however, only sporadic and limited external engagement within either the public or nonprofit sector occurred. As with the GNPI, the ANVSI could be considered a "think tank"–like policy forum where developments, ideas, and implications were discussed, but generally isolated from internal government decision-making processes.

Saskatchewan

In Saskatchewan the Premier's Voluntary Sector Initiative (VSI), like the GNPI in British Columbia and the ANVSI in Alberta, was populated with nonprofit sector and government co-chairs and approximately ten representatives from each sector (Hamilton and Mann 2006). The objectives of the Premier's VSI were high on consultative processes and low on policy outcomes, with attention focused on relationship building, capacity building, and awareness building. What was accomplished was a clearer understanding of the funding, human resources, and volunteer issues facing nonprofit organizations – or community-based organizations, as they are known in Saskatchewan (Garcea and DeSantis, Chapter 7). What is less clear was the capacity of the Premier's VSI to move beyond issue identification and consultation to concrete action. Independent from line ministry reporting responsibility, and yet circumstantially positioned in the Premier's Office, the structure lacked the authority to give direction. Unfortunately the very structure that gave rise to the political status of the Premier's VSI when the New Democratic Party (NDP) government was in power led to its demise when the Saskatchewan Party was elected.

Manitoba

The Manitoba Voluntary Sector Initiative, initiated in 2000 for a three-year period (Frankel and Levasseur, Chapter 9), was a significant departure from similar initiatives before or since in the other three western provinces. First, it was led by the nonprofit sector, not the provincial government. Second, it went beyond the identification of sectoral issues and addressed the issue of voice. In its own words: "The primary focus was to identify ways to sustain the sector's infrastructure, which uses volunteers for direct service, administration and the overall governance of organizations and groups. It also became apparent that the voluntary sector needs cohesive voices to represent the interests of the sector to government, business, labour and the public-at large" (Itzkow, Krelewetz, and White 2002, 6).

The issue of voice came to manifest itself in the formulation of a joint government-nonprofit sector declaration of support for the nonprofit sector and the formation of the Manitoba Federation of Non-Profit Organizations (MFNPO) (Manitoba Voluntary Sector Initiative 2003). Although the MFNPO has evolved slower than some would like, it has sustained a sector voice with nominal funding, and is now an active member of the Sector Councils of Manitoba and starting to address key labour force issues (Stevens 2010). As Frankel and Levasseur point out, and as is echoed throughout the developments in the other three western provinces, having a signed declaration of intentional collaboration is no substitute for sustained government support, concrete policy action, and a well-organized and representative provincial voice. One characteristic of note is that, as the MFNPO has evolved, there is rarely one report or project that has not involved multiple levels of government, multiple departments, and multiple sources of funding from collaborating community agencies (Itzkow, Krelewetz, and White. 2002; Manitoba Voluntary Sector Initiative 2003; Stevens 2010). As Frankel and Levasseur present and as echoed by Reimer, Bernas, and Adeler (Chapter 10), multiple funding and collaborating partners permeate the nonprofit funding culture in Manitoba.

Thematic Analysis

Evolving relationships in a changing environment is an overarching theme each author addresses. To their credit they have captured important examples, themes, and lessons for teachers, students, policymakers, and practitioners. As Susan Phillips points out in her guest introduction, there are four major components to an emerging (economic) framework for government-nonprofit funding regimes: (1) reinvented, more integrated service delivery; (2) pressures to demonstrate impact in programming and in funding; (3) interest in social innovation and venture philanthropy that encourage new business models, risk taking, and scaling up; and (4) new forms of community mobilization and responsibility taking. With some blurring at the edges, and no attempt at mutual exclusivity, these four themes reflect changes, to varying degrees across all four Western provinces. Table 11.2 summarizes the following dominant policy, funding, and nonprofit relations themes that emerge across the four Western provinces.

Of all four western provinces, British Columbia has embraced, more than the others, social innovation and venture philanthropy, encouraging new business models, risk taking, and scaling up. If scale is indeed an outcome of the Community Contribution Company Act, time will tell (British Columbia 2013). Meanwhile the dominant policy frame overriding the government's policy agenda is to build an effective contract and funding regime in a climate of fiscal constraint. Certainly

Table 11.2. Government, Funding, and Nonprofit Policy Frames

Province	Dominant Policy Frame	Dominant Funding Frame	Dominant Nonprofit Frame
British Columbia	Fiscal constraint and an effective contract and funding regime	Social innovation and venture philanthropy that encourage new business models, risk taking, and scaling up	Adapting and aligning sector interests and capacities to government policy priorities
Alberta	Fiscal retrenchment and service value	Demonstrate impact in programming and funding	Program outcome focus in an institutionalized neoliberal climate
Saskatchewan	Fiscal and advocacy constraint	Emerging forms of community mobilization and responsibility taking	Fragmented advocacy and financial instability
Manitoba	Fiscal efficiencies and community impact	Reinvented, more integrated contracting model	Balancing fiscal constraint and community impact

the GNPI operated in a climate of mutuality and the creation of more effective procurement, contract, and labour market policies. Meanwhile the nonprofit policy frame reflected in the work of Lindquist and Vakil (Chapter 2), as well as that of Atkey and Stone (Chapter 3), is a sector that adapts and aligns its interests and capacities to changing government policy priorities. This is good. Failure to adapt to a changing external environment is a recipe for obsolescence. Given the politicized and generally engaged environment (pun intended) in British Columbia, the modular characteristic of representation in the province might be the nonprofit sector's particular way of simultaneously covering multiple policy fronts and tacking as close to the wind as possible.

The frontier spirit of independence and self-reliance is alive and well in Alberta, where fiscal constraint is the barometer that measures policy outcomes. The ongoing policy of fiscal retrenchment to either counter or override the resource cycle economy is no stranger to Albertans. The Ralph Klein legacy entrenched fiscal conservatism; the review of the Persons with Developmental Disabilities Community Governance Act taught fiscal conservatism and popularism; and the Alberta Mentoring Partnership blends fiscal conservatism with compassion for community. Fiscal retrenchment is blended with service value to such a degree in Alberta that the term "public enterprise" would not go amiss. The extent to which this balance will be modified by Alberta's first NDP government, elected in 2015, is an open question.

There is no doubt that the Saskatchewan Lotteries Trust Fund for Sport, Culture and Recreation is the crown jewel of funding regimes for community-based organizations in that province. And while the Community Initiatives Fund spreads this wealth a little broader, this regime is also in stark contrast to the "contract culture" that dominates the provincial government's relationship with service-based community organizations. The sense of solidarity and community connectedness that permeated Saskatchewan Lotteries from its inception is only now starting to manifest itself in the emergent and sector-wide Saskatchewan Nonprofit Partnership. This emerging form of community mobilization could be the consequence of too many previous government-led consultation processes – such as the 2008 Summits and Regional Intersectoral Committees – that resulted in promissory notes going untendered. Fiscal and advocacy constraint appears to be the watchword in Saskatchewan, independent of the state of the economy. The very rationale that the provincial government uses to justify its short-term funding policy – as Garcea and DeSantis put it, to "ensure the services system is responsive to changes in clients' needs by being able to adjust the precise services it funds and the level at which it funds them" – is the very type of funding regime that perpetuates financial vulnerability, unnecessary competition, and fragmented advocacy among CBOs. In this context both larger CBOs and better organized groups, such as Aboriginal organizations, have a significant strategic advantage in terms of both services delivery capacity and representative voice.

Pragmatism and moderation went out the window as the Filmon government in Manitoba reeled from the economic downturn of the early 1990s, exacerbated by the substantial loss of transfer payments from the federal government. The NDP government that followed in 1999 moved the policy gauge to the centre, attempting to balance social justice and economic gain *à la* Tony Blair's Third Way. When the fiscal crisis of 2008 made its presence felt on the provincial balance sheet, the nonprofit sector again caught pneumonia from the provincial government's cold. Nevertheless the capacity and willingness of the Manitoba government to hold this creative social-economic tension is remarkable and insightful. In other words, fiscal efficiencies and community impact is not an oxymoron in Manitoba – the "red tape" pilot project involving thirty-five nonprofit organizations is a case in point (see Frankel and Levasseur, Chapter 9). In short, this government is prepared to attempt to reinvent itself from within and work towards a more integrated contracting model.

Does this type of initiative mitigate all the trials and tribulations of multiple bureaucratic relationships inherent in government-nonprofit funding regimes? Absolutely not. What it does do, in my view, is create a more collaborative and supportive environment in which these issues can be identified and struggled with. It is this sense of balancing fiscal constraint with community impact that is a common purpose to be shared by bureaucrat and nonprofit alike. This creative tension is also manifested in the mainstreaming of support for Community Economic Development (CED), as outlined in detail by Reimer, Bernas, and Adeler (Chapter 10). The CED policy framework in Manitoba provides a platform for both government departments and community economic development intermediaries to engage in system governance, building bridges between community and politics that keep both parties clearly focused on the ultimate endgame: social and economic inclusion.

Conclusion

Funding policies and the nonprofit sector in Western Canada is an apt and timely subject for in-depth analysis. It is timely because fiscal pressures, a classic structural weakness of nonprofit organizations (Salamon 1987), are no longer counterbalanced by government largess, if they ever were. Current fiscal challenges foster creativity, and social innovation more broadly – and specifically social enterprise – is but one manifestation of a blended value return. Another, more sinister consequence is felt in communities as nonprofits become agents for a hollowed-out state and contract compliance, rather than social inclusion; and community development becomes the raison-d'être of nonprofit organizations.

Funding policies and the nonprofit sector in Western Canada is also an apt subject because, as Western Canada comes of age, both economically and politically, economic growth – particularly growth that is resource dependent – must go hand-in-hand with social, environmental, and cultural stewardship. And how better to steward the balance between economic and social inclusion than to invest in a meaningful, respectful, and interdependent relationship between the nonprofit and public sectors? In the end funding regimes are a means to an end, not an end in themselves. In the end the true measure of a society is no less than how it treats those that are most vulnerable.

NOTES

1 By nonformal, I specifically mean transitory representational and reporting protocols that are nontransferable across time. For example, coalitions that collaboratively make a deputation on one issue, but tend not to transfer this experience or expertise to another issue.
2 The author was an appointed member of the ANVSI from 2010 to 2012.

REFERENCES

British Columbia. 2013. Ministry of Finance. "Community Contribution Companies." Available online at http://www.fin.gov.bc.ca/prs/ccc/; accessed 2 December 2013.

Elson, P. 2012. "Canada's Voluntary Sector Initiative and Sub-national Voluntary Sector-Government Relations: A Third Wave." *Nonprofit Policy Forum* 3 (2): article 4.

George, A.L., and A. Bennett. 2005. *Case Studies and Theory Development in the Social Sciences*. Cambridge, MA: MIT Press.

Hamilton, D., and T. Mann. 2006. *The Premier's Voluntary Sector Initiative: 2006 Update*. Regina: Saskatchewan Culture, Youth and Recreation.

Itzkow, M., C. Krelewetz, and E. White. 2002. *Sustaining Manitoba's Voluntary Sector: Qualitative Research on Manitoba's Voluntary Sector Challenges*. Winnipeg: Manitoba Voluntary Sector Initiative, Volunteer Centre of Winnipeg.

Manitoba Voluntary Sector Initiative. 2003. *Supporting Voices: Sustaining Manitoba's Voluntary and Non-profit Sector in the 21st Century*. Winnipeg: Social Development Canada.

Salamon, L.M. 1987. "Of Market Failure, Voluntary Failure, and Third-Party Government: Toward a Theory of Government-Nonprofit Relations in the Modern Welfare State." *Journal of Voluntary Action Research* 16 (1): 29–49.

Stevens, H. 2010. *The Voluntary and Non-Profit Health and Social Services Sectors in Manitoba: A Profile of Its Composition, Workplace Challenges and Resources for Meeting Those Challenges*. Winnipeg: Manitoba Federation of Non-Profit Organizations.

Contributors

Monica Adeler (PhD, University of Saskatchewan, Centre for the Study of Co-operatives) is enrolled in the Robson School, Faculty of Law, University of Manitoba.

Jill Atkey (MA, University of British Columbia, School of Community and Regional Planning) is Director, Research and Education, for the BC Non-Profit Housing Association.

Kirsten Bernas (MA, Carleton University, Norman Paterson School of International Affairs) is on staff with the Canadian Community Economic Development Network (CCEDNet) as a researcher and policy manager.

Gloria DeSantis (PhD, University of Regina, Interdisciplinary Studies) is an Assistant Professor in the Department of Justice Studies, University of Regina, and the founding director of the Voluntary Sector Studies Network at Luther College, University of Regina.

Ken Dropko (MA, University of Alberta, Curriculum and leadership) is Executive Director of Community Partnerships with Alberta Human Services and Co-Chair of the Alberta Mentoring Partnership.

Peter R. Elson (PhD, University of Toronto, Adult Education and Community Development) is Senior Research Fellow, Institute for Community Prosperity, Mount Royal University, and Adjunct Assistant Professor, School of Public Administration, University of Victoria.

Sid Frankel (PhD, University of California, Berkeley, Social Welfare) is Associate Professor, Faculty of Social Work, University of Manitoba, and founding board member, Manitoba Federation of Non-Profit Organizations.

Joseph Garcea (PhD, Carleton University, Political Science) is Head and Associate Professor, Department of Political Studies, University of Saskatchewan.

Lynn Gidluck (PhD, University of Regina, Interdisciplinary Studies, Johnson-Shoyama Graduate School of Public Policy) is a partner in a Regina-based public relations firm.

W.H. (Wilma) Haas (MBA, University of Alberta) is a recent retiree from the Alberta Public Service. She was a co-chair of the Alberta Mentoring Partnership between 2009 and 2011.

Karine Levasseur (PhD, Carleton University, Public Policy) is Associate Professor, Department of Political Studies, University of Manitoba, and Director of the Joint Master of Public Administration Co-op.

Evert Lindquist (PhD, University of California, Berkeley, Public Policy) is Professor, School of Public Administration, University of Victoria, and Editor of *Canadian Public Administration*.

Liz O'Neill is Executive Director, Boys and Girls Clubs Big Brothers Big Sisters of Edmonton and Area, and Co-Chair of the Alberta Mentoring Partnership.

Marni Pearce (PhD, University of Alberta, Education) is Director, School and Community Supports for Children and Youth, Alberta Education and Co-Chair of the Alberta Mentoring Partnership.

Susan D. Phillips (PhD, Carleton University, Political Science) is Professor, School of Public Policy and Administration, Carleton University, and Research Fellow with the Carleton Centre for Community Innovation (3CI).

Brendan Reimer (University of Winnipeg, Sociology and International Development Studies) is Strategic Partner, Values-Based Banking, Assiniboine Credit Union, Winnipeg.

Keith Seel (PhD, University of Calgary, Graduate Division of Educational Research) is Dean, Centre for Excellence in Foundation Learning, Bow Valley College, Calgary.

Lori Sigurdson (MSW, RSW, University of Calgary) at the time of writing was Manager, Professional Affairs, Alberta College of Social Workers, and Vice President of Public Interest Alberta. She was subsequently elected to the Alberta Legislature and appointed Minister of Innovation and Advanced Education and Minister of Jobs, Skills, Training and Labour.

Nilima Sonpal-Valias (PhD Candidate [ABD]) is in the Department of Sociology, University of Calgary, and is a private consultant to the nonprofit sector.

Karen Stone (BA, LLB, LLM, University of KwaZulu-Natal) is former executive director of the BC Non-Profit Housing Association and the Alberta Interagency Council on Homelessness.

Thea Vakil (PhD, University of Victoria, Public Administration) is Associate Professor and Associate Director, School of Public Administration, University of Victoria, and responsible for the Centre of Public Sector Studies at the School of Public Administration.

Index

The Institute of Public Administration of Canada Series in Public
Management and Governance